Voice over IP Fundamentals

Voice over IP Fundamentals

Jonathan Davidson

James Peters

with contributions from Brian Gracely

Cisco Press
201 West 103rd Street
Indianapolis, IN 46290 USA

Voice over IP Fundamentals

Jonathan Davidson

James Peters

with contributions from Brian Gracely

Copyright© 2000 Cisco Press

Cisco Press logo is a trademark of Cisco Systems, Inc.

Published by:
Cisco Press
201 West 103rd Street
Indianapolis, IN 46290 USA

Printed in the United States of America 3 4 5 6 7 8 9 0

Library of Congress Cataloging-in-Publication Number: 99-61716

ISBN: 1-57870-168-6

Warning and Disclaimer

This book is designed to provide information about **Voice over IP**. Every effort has been made to make this book as complete and as accurate as possible, but no warranty or fitness is implied.

The information is provided on an "as is" basis. The authors, Cisco Press, and Cisco Systems, Inc., shall have neither liability nor responsibility to any person or entity with respect to any loss or damages arising from the information contained in this book or from the use of the discs or programs that may accompany it.

The opinions expressed in this book belong to the authors and are not necessarily those of Cisco Systems, Inc.

Trademark Acknowledgments

All terms mentioned in this book that are known to be trademarks or service marks have been appropriately capitalized. Cisco Press or Cisco Systems, Inc., cannot attest to the accuracy of this information. Use of a term in this book should not be regarded as affecting the validity of any trademark or service mark.

Feedback Information

At Cisco Press, our goal is to create in-depth technical books of the highest quality and value. Each book is crafted with care and precision, undergoing rigorous development that involves the unique expertise of members from the professional technical community.

Reader feedback is a natural continuation of this process. If you have any comments regarding how we could improve the quality of this book, or otherwise alter it to better suit your needs, you can contact us through e-mail at ciscopress@mcp.com. Please make sure to include the book title and ISBN in your message.

We greatly appreciate your assistance.

Publisher	John Wait
Executive Editor	John Kane
Cisco Systems Program Manager	Jim LeValley
Managing Editor	Patrick Kanouse
Development Editor	Kezia Endsley
Project Editor	Sheri Replin
Copy Editor	Audrey Doyle
Technical Editors	Conrad Price
	Massimo Lucchina
	Ida Leung
	Alan Sawyer
	Joel Ekis
	Mark Monday
	Cary Fitzgerald
Team Coordinator	Amy Lewis
Book Designer	Regina Rexrode
Cover Designer	Louisa Klucznik
Indexer	Tim Wright
Compositor	Steve Balle-Gifford

CISCO SYSTEMS

CISCO PRESS

Corporate Headquarters
Cisco Systems, Inc.
170 West Tasman Drive
San Jose, CA 95134-1706
USA
http://www.cisco.com
Tel: 408 526-4000
    800 553-NETS (6387)
Fax: 408 526-4100

European Headquarters
Cisco Systems Europe s.a.r.l.
Parc Evolic, Batiment L1/L2
16 Avenue du Quebec
Villebon, BP 706
91961 Courtaboeuf Cedex
France
http://www-europe.cisco.com
Tel: 33 1 69 18 61 00
Fax: 33 1 69 28 83 26

Americas
Headquarters
Cisco Systems, Inc.
170 West Tasman Drive
San Jose, CA 95134-1706
USA
http://www.cisco.com
Tel: 408 526-7660
Fax: 408 527-0883

Asia Headquarters
Nihon Cisco Systems K.K.
Fuji Building, 9th Floor
3-2-3 Marunouchi
Chiyoda-ku, Tokyo 100
Japan
http://www.cisco.com
Tel: 81 3 5219 6250
Fax: 81 3 5219 6001

Cisco Systems has more than 200 offices in the following countries. Addresses, phone numbers, and fax numbers are listed on the Cisco Connection Online Web site at http://www.cisco.com/offices.

Argentina • Australia • Austria • Belgium • Brazil • Canada • Chile • China • Colombia • Costa Rica • Croatia • Czech Republic • Denmark • Dubai, UAE Finland • France • Germany • Greece • Hong Kong • Hungary • India • Indonesia • Ireland • Israel • Italy • Japan • Korea • Luxembourg • Malaysia Mexico • The Netherlands • New Zealand • Norway • Peru • Philippines • Poland • Portugal • Puerto Rico • Romania • Russia • Saudi Arabia • Singapore Slovakia • Slovenia • South Africa • Spain • Sweden • Switzerland • Taiwan • Thailand • Turkey • Ukraine • United Kingdom • United States • Venezuela

About the Authors

Jonathan Davidson (CCIE #2560) is the Manager of Service Provider Technical Marketing for Packet Voice at Cisco Systems. He focuses on working with service provider and enterprise customers to develop solutions that are deployable in the new infrastructure of data and voice convergence. This includes designing customer networks and assisting with product direction.

Jonathan has been working on packet voice technologies for three years. During his seven years in the data networking industry, he worked in various capacities, including network design, configuring, troubleshooting, and deploying data and voice networks.

James Peters has 15 years experience in designing and implementing networks for Internet service providers and telephone companies. He is currently the Manager of Engineering at Cisco Systems, responsible for solution and network design within the service provider line of business. He focuses on the end-to-end design of voice and data network solutions that encompass Cisco products, physical and logical specifications, and third-party applications. James spent 10 years at Bell Canada, where he was responsible for the architecture and design of many packet networks, including the first Canadian IP-based Intranet network in 1993, a consumer dial-up Internet service in 1995, and a transaction-based health network in 1996.

Brian Gracely (CCIE #3077) is a Technical Marketing Engineer for Cisco Systems Inc., working on VoIP, VoATM, and VoFR initiatives. His current projects involve H.323 and SIP, as well as IP telephony, unified messaging, and VoIP QoS for both enterprise and service provider customers.

Previously, Brian worked with Cisco customers on LAN and ATM switching networks.

About the Technical Reviewers

Conrad Price, Cisco Systems, Inc., Escalation Engineer

Massimo Lucchina, Cisco Systems, Inc., Europe, Consulting Engineer Manager

Ida Leung, UUNET, MCI WorldCom Company, Network Developer

Alan Sawyer, VICNET, Network Operations/Engineering Manager

Joel Ekis, Systems Engineer

Dedications

Jonathan Davidson:

Wife, Daughter, Son

To my beautiful wife Shelly for putting up with me during the nights and weekends spent working on this book. A better wife, mother, and friend could not be asked for.

To my daughter Megan, who will probably be learning data and voice networking in high school by the time she gets there. Also, my son Ethan, who will probably think that video and audio conferencing is as common as videogames and VCRs were to my generation.

James Peters:

To my son Justin, for his curiousity, friendship, and the bond that we share.

To my son Zachary, who has taught me to laugh and to not take life so seriously.

To my daughter Breanna, whose smile makes me realize how beautiful life is.

Acknowledgments

Jonathan Davidson:

To Brian Gracely, Gene Arantowicz, and James Peters—for without their help, this book would not be what it is today.

Many other people helped in answering questions and providing guidance as to the proper path both for this book and my knowledge of VoIP: Mark Monday, Cary Fitzgerald, Binh Ha, Jas Jain, Herb Wildfeur, Gavin Jin, Mark Rumer, Mike Knappe, Tony Gallagher, Art Howarth, Rommel Bajamundi, Vikas Butaney, Alistair Woodman, Sanjay Kalra, Stephen Liu, Jim Murphy, Nour Elouali, Massimo Lucchina.

Thanks to you all for your help and assistance.

A special thanks to Art Howarth, Mark Monday, and Alistair Woodman for their always available professional advice and willingness to help.

Also, a thank you to Cisco Systems for allowing individuals to pursue limitless knowledge and personal growth opportunities.

And a thank you goes to the following people at Cisco Press:

Alicia Buckley—For getting the project going and for her help and persuasion for keeping us "on the bike!"

Kezia Endsley—This book truly would not be what it is today without all of the time, effort, and blood put into this book on Kezia's part.

Kathy Trace, Sheri Replin, and Lynette Quinn.

James Peters:

To Andrew Adamian, Mark Bakies, Jonathan Davidson, Cary Fitzgerald, Douglas Frosst, and Charlie Giancarlo, for which, without their guidance and support, this book would not be possible.

To Kathy Trace, for taking the time and having the patience to help me become a better writer.

I would also like to thank my family, Connie, Justin, Zachary, and Breanna, for putting up with the years of long hours and travel I spent learning and working in the Internet community.

Finally, I thank Cisco Systems for providing an environment where employees are able to contribute and accomplish tasks equal to their passion and interests.

Contents at a Glance

Contents

Introduction

Many of my friends rant about the simplicity and elegance of the Apple Macintosh computer. But, as with many technologies, the simpler the user's experience is, the more complex the underlying infrastructure must be. This is true of the telephone network.

Currently more than 4,000 telephony service providers—inter-exchange carriers (IXCs), Competitive Local Exchange Carriers (CLECs), and so on—exist in the United States alone. Global deregulation of telephone markets is forcing government-owned incumbent telephone carriers to begin competing with new, often innovative carriers. These new carriers frequently use new infrastructures so that they can compete at a lower price point than the incumbent carriers. They also are using these new infrastructures to deploy new applications to their customers faster than they can on legacy equipment.

Many of these new carriers use Voice over IP (VoIP) to lower their cost of operations and give them the flexibility they need to enter the global marketplace.

A key part of this flexibility is the ubiquity of the Internet Protocol (IP). Because of the prevalence of the Internet, and because IP is the de facto protocol connecting almost all devices, application developers can use IP to write an application only once for use in many different network types. This makes VoIP a powerful service platform for next-generation applications.

Purpose of This Book

What is VoIP and in what ways does it apply to you? VoIP provides the capability to break up your voice into small pieces (known as samples) and place them in an IP packet. Voice and data networking are complex technologies. This book explains how telephony infrastructure is built and works today, major concepts concerning voice and data networking, transmission of voice over data, and IP signaling protocols used to interwork with current telephony systems. It also answers the following key questions:

- What is IP?
- How is voice signaled in telephone networks today?
- What are the various IP signaling protocols, and which one is best for which types of networks?
- What is quality of service (QoS), and how does one ensure good voice quality in a network?

In addition to covering these concepts, this book also explains the basics of VoIP so that a network administrator, software engineer, or someone simply interested in the technology has the foundation of information needed to understand VoIP networks.

This book is meant to accomplish the following goals:

- Provide an introduction to the basics of enterprise and public telephony networking
- Introduce IP networking concepts
- Provide a solid explanation of how voice is transported over IP networks
- Cover the various caveats of converging voice and data networks
- Provide detailed reference information on various Public Switched Telephone Network (PSTN) and IP signaling protocols

Although this book contains plenty of technical information and suggestions for ways you can build a VoIP network, it is not a design and implementation guide in that it doesn't really give you comparisons between actual voice gateways throughout the industry.

Audience

Even though this book is written for anyone seeking to understand how to use IP to transport voice, its target audience comprises voice and networking experts. In the past, voice and data gurus did not have to know each other's jobs. In this world of time-division multiplexing (TDM) and packet convergence, however, it is important to understand how these technologies work. This book explains the details so that voice experts can begin to understand data networking, and vice versa.

This writing style generates yet another audience: Those who have limited data and voice networking knowledge but are technically savvy will be able to understand the basics of both voice and data networking along with how the two converge.

Despite its discussions of voice and data networking, this book is really about VoIP, and the protocols that affect VoIP are explained in great detail. This makes this book a reference guide for those designing, building, deploying, or even writing software for VoIP networks.

Readers familiar with IP networking might want to skip Chapter 7, "IP Tutorial." Similarly, voice-networking experts might want to skip Chapter 3, "Basic Telephony Signaling."

Chapter Organization

Chapter 1, "Overview of the PSTN and Comparisons to Voice over IP," contrasts the similarities and differences between traditional TDM networks and networks running packetized voice.

Chapter 2, "Enterprise Telephony Today," Chapter 3, "Basic Telephony Signaling," Chapter 4, "Signaling System 7," and Chapter 5, "PSTN Services," cover enterprise telephony, the basics of PSTN signaling, Signaling System 7 (SS7), and other PSTN services. These chapters provide the background information needed by data networking professionals who are just stepping into the voice realm. They also act as a good primer for those in specific voice areas that want to brush up on various other voice-networking protocols.

Chapter 6, "Voice over IP Benefits and Applications," contrasts and compares in detail how packet voice can run the same applications as the current telephony system but in a more cost-effective and scalable manner.

Chapter 7 is an introduction into the world of IP. Basic subnetting and the Open Systems Interconnection (OSI) reference model are covered, and comparisons between Transmission Control Protocol (TCP) and User Datagram Protocol (UDP) are provided.

Chapter 8, "VoIP: An In-Depth Analysis," and Chapter 9, "Quality of Service," go into great detail on VoIP and how all the functional components fit together to form a solution. They include discussions of jitter, latency, packet loss, codecs, QoS tools, mean opinion scores (MOSes), and the caveats to consider when implementing packet voice networks.

Chapter 10, "H.323," Chapter 11, "Session Initiation Protocol," Chapter 12, "Gateway Control Protocols," and Chapter 13, "Virtual Switch Controller," cover the various signaling protocols and how they are wrapped together using Cisco's Virtual Switch Controller (VSC). These chapters enable implementers to understand how all the various VoIP components set up calls, tear down calls, and offer services.

Chapter 14, "Voice over IP Configuration Issues," and Chapter 15, "Voice over IP Applications and Services," cover the functional components of using Cisco gateways to deploy a VoIP network. These chapters include configuration details and sample case studies.

Features and Text Conventions

Text design and content features used in this book are intended to make the complexities of VoIP clearer and more accessible.

Key terms are italicized the first time they are used and defined. In addition, key terms are spelled out and followed with their acronym in parentheses, where applicable. Cisco configuration commands appear in **bold** in regular text and `monospace` in listings.

Note boxes point out areas of special concern or interest that might not fit precisely into the discussion at hand but are worth considering. Sometimes, these boxes contain extraneous information in the form of tips, and sometimes they appear in the form of warnings to help you avoid certain pitfalls.

Chapter summaries provide a chance for readers to review and reflect upon the information discussed in each chapter. A reader might also use these summaries to determine whether a particular chapter is appropriate to him or her.

References to further information, including many Requests For Comments (RFCs), are included at the end of many chapters. Although not all the references are cited directly in each chapter, all were useful to us as we prepared this book.

Timeliness

As of the writing of this book, many new protocols concerning VoIP were still being designed and worked out by the standards bodies. Also, legal aspects of VoIP constantly arise in different parts of the world. Therefore, this book is meant as a guide, in that it provides necessary foundational information. The next step is to read new signaling drafts from the Internet Engineering Task Force (IETF; http://www.ietf.org) and the International Telecommunication Union (ITU; http://www.itu.int/). The International Telecommunication Union Telecommunication Standardization Sector (ITU-T) documents require a login password.

The Road Ahead...

VoIP is changing the way telecommunications is been deployed globally. This change is synonymous with how the Internet changed our lives to date. VoIP technology is a big step toward a world where information and communication are the most important tools for success. We hope you enjoy reading this book as much as we enjoyed writing it.

PSTN

CHAPTER 1

Overview of the PSTN and Comparisons to Voice over IP

The Public Switched Telephone Network (PSTN) has been evolving ever since Alexander Graham Bell made the first voice transmission over wire in 1876. But, before explaining the present state of the PSTN and what's in store for the future, it is important that you understand PSTN history and it's basics. As such, this chapter discusses the beginnings of the PSTN and explains why the PSTN exists in its current state.

This chapter also covers PSTN basics, components, and services to give you a good introduction to how the PSTN operates today. Finally, it discusses where the PSTN could be improved and ways in which it and other voice networks are evolving to the point at which they combine data, video, and voice.

The Beginning of the PSTN

The first voice transmission, sent by Alexander Graham Bell, was accomplished in 1876 through what is called a *ring-down* circuit. A ring-down circuit means that there was no dialing of numbers, Instead, a physical wire connected two devices. Basically, one person picked up the phone and another person was on the other end (no ringing was involved).

Over time, this simple design evolved from a one-way voice transmission, by which only one user could speak, to a bi-directional voice transmission, whereby both users could speak. Moving the voices across the wire required a carbon microphone, a battery, an electromagnet, and an iron diaphragm.

It also required a physical cable between each location that the user wanted to call. The concept of dialing a number to reach a destination, however, did not exist at this time.

To further illustrate the beginnings of the PSTN, see the basic four-telephone network shown in Figure 1-1. As you can see, a physical cable exists between each location.

Figure 1-1   *Basic Four-Phone Network*

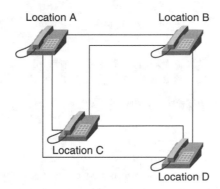

Place a physical cable between every household requiring access to a telephone, however, and you'll see that such a setup is neither cost-effective nor feasible (see Figure 1-2). To determine how many lines you need to your house, think about everyone you call as a value of N and use the following equation: $N \times (N-1)/2$. As such, if you want to call 10 people, you need 45 pairs of lines running into your house.

Figure 1-2   *Physical Cable Between All Telephone Users*

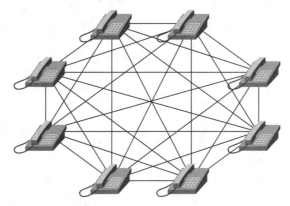

Due to the cost concerns and the impossibility of running a physical cable between everyone on Earth who wanted access to a telephone, another mechanism was developed that could map any phone to another phone. With this device, called a *switch*, the telephone users needed only one cable to the centralized switch office, instead of seven.

At first, a telephone operator acted as the switch. This operator asked callers where they wanted to dial and then manually connected the two voice paths. Figure 1-3 shows how the four-phone network example would look today with a centralized operator to switch the calls.

Figure 1-3   *Centralized Operator: The Human Switch*

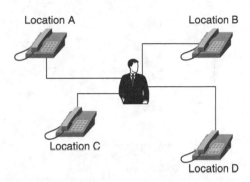

Now, skip ahead 100 years or so—the human switch is replaced by electronic switches. At this point, you can learn how the modern PSTN network is built.

Understanding PSTN Basics

Although it is difficult to explain every component of the PSTN, this section explains the most important pieces that make the PSTN work. The following sections discuss how your voice is transmitted across a digital network, basic circuit-switching concepts, and why your phone number is 10 digits long.

Analog and Digital Signaling

Everything you hear, including human speech, is in analog form. Until several decades ago, the telephony network was based on an analog infrastructure as well.

Although analog communication is ideal for human interaction, it is neither robust nor efficient at recovering from line noise. (*Line noise* is normally caused by the introduction of static into a voice network.) In the early telephony network, analog transmission was passed through amplifiers to boost the signal. But, this practice amplified not just the voice, but the line noise as well. This line noise resulted in an often unusable connection.

Analog communication is a mix of time and amplitude. Figure 1-4, which takes a high-level view of an analog waveform, shows what your voice looks like through an oscilloscope.

Figure 1-4   *Analog Waveform*

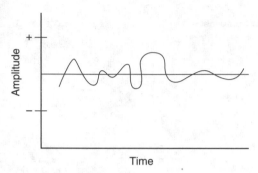

If you were far away from the *end office switch* (which provides the physical cable to your home), an amplifier might be required to boost the analog transmission (your voice). Analog signals that receive line noise can distort the analog waveform and cause garbled reception. This is more obvious to the listener if many amplifiers are located between your home and the end office switch. Figure 1-5 shows that an amplifier does not clean the signal as it amplifies, but simply amplifies the distorted signal. This process of going through several amplifiers with one voice signal is called *accumulated noise*.

Figure 1-5   *Analog Line Distortion*

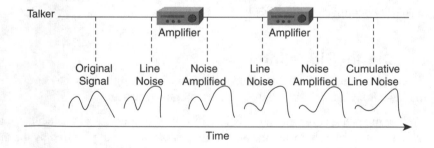

In digital networks, line noise is less of an issue because repeaters not only amplify the signal, but clean it to its original condition. This is possible with digital communication because such communication is based on 1s and 0s. So, as shown in Figure 1-6, the *repeater* (a digital amplifier) only has to decide whether to regenerate a 1 or a 0.

Figure 1-6   *Digital Line Distortion*

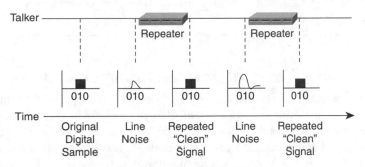

Therefore, when signals are repeated, a clean sound is maintained. When the benefits of this digital representation became evident, the telephony network migrated to *pulse code modulation* (PCM).

Digital Voice Signals

PCM is the most common method of encoding an analog voice signal into a digital stream of 1s and 0s. All sampling techniques use the *Nyquist theorem*, which basically states that if you sample at twice the highest frequency on a voice line, you achieve good-quality voice transmission.

The PCM process is as follows:

- Analog waveforms are put through a voice frequency filter to filter out anything greater than 4000 Hz. These frequencies are filtered to 4000 Hz to limit the amount of crosstalk in the voice network. Using the Nyquist theorem, you need to sample at 8000 samples per second to achieve good-quality voice transmission.

- The filtered analog signal is then sampled at a rate of 8000 times per second.

- After the waveform is sampled, it is converted into a discrete digital form. This sample is represented by a code that indicates the amplitude of the waveform at the instant the sample was taken. The telephony form of PCM uses eight bits for the code and a logarithm compression method that assigns more bits to lower-amplitude signals.

If you multiply the eight-bit words by 8000 times per second, you get 64,000 bits per second (bps). The basis for the telephone infrastructure is 64,000 bps (or 64 kbps).

Two basic variations of 64 kbps PCM are commonly used: μ-law, the standard used in North America; and a-law, the standard used in Europe. The methods are similar in that both use logarithmic compression to achieve from 12 to 13 bits of linear PCM quality in only eight-bit words, but they differ in relatively minor details. The μ-law method has a slight advantage over the a-law method in terms of low-level signal-to-noise ratio performance, for instance.

Local Loops, Trunks, and Interswitch Communication

The telephone infrastructure starts with a simple pair of copper wires running to your home.
This physical cabling is known as a *local loop*. The local loop physically connects your
home telephone to the central office switch (also known as a *Class 5 switch* or *end office
switch*). The communication path between the central office switch and your home is
known as the *phone line,* and it normally runs over the local loop.

The communication path between several central office switches is known as a *trunk*. Just
as it is not cost-effective to place a physical wire between your house and every other house
you want to call, it is also not cost-effective to place a physical wire between every central
office switch. You can see in Figure 1-7 that a meshed telephone network is not as
scalable as one with a hierarchy of switches.

Figure 1-7   *Meshed Network Versus Hierarchical Network*

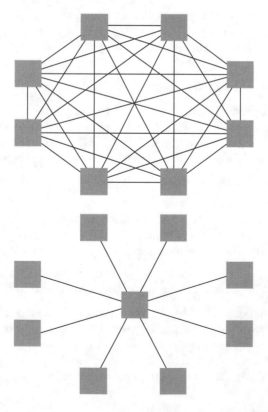

Switches are currently deployed in hierarchies. End office switches (or central office switches) interconnect through trunks to *tandem switches* (also referred to as Class 4 switches). Higher-layer tandem switches connect local tandem switches. Figure 1-8 shows a typical model of switching hierarchy.

Figure 1-8   *Circuit-Switching Hierarchy*

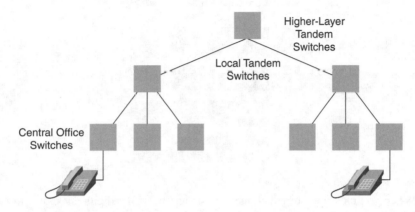

Central office switches often directly connect to each other. Where the direct connections occur between central office switches depends to a great extent on call patterns. If enough traffic occurs between two central office switches, a dedicated circuit is placed between the two switches to offload those calls from the local tandem switches. Some portions of the PSTN use as many as five levels of switching hierarchy.

Now that you know how and why the PSTN is broken into a hierarchy of switches, you need to understand how they are physically connected, and how the network communicates.

PSTN Signaling

Generally, two types of signaling methods run over various transmission media. The signaling methods are broken into the following groups:

- *User-to-network signaling*—This is how an end user communicates with the PSTN.
- *Network-to-network signaling*—This is generally how the switches in the PSTN intercommunicate.

User-to-Network Signaling

Generally, when using *twisted copper pair* as the transport, a user connects to the PSTN through analog, Integrated Services Digital Network (ISDN), or through a T1 carrier.

The most common signaling method for user-to-network analog communication is *Dual Tone Multi-Frequency (DTMF)*. DTMF is known as in-band signaling because the tones are carried through the voice path. Figure 1-9 shows how DTMF tones are derived.

Figure 1-9   *Dual Tone Multi-Frequency*

Dual Tone Multi-Frequency

	1209	1336	1477	1633
697	1	2	3	A
770	4	5	6	B
852	7	8	9	C
941	*	0	#	D

When you pick up your telephone handset and press the digits (as shown in Figure 1-9), the tone that passes from your phone to the central office switch to which you are connected tells the switch what number you want to call.

ISDN uses another method of signaling known as *out-of-band*. With this method, the signaling is transported on a channel separate from the voice. The channel on which the voice is carried is called a *bearer* (or B channel) and is 64 kbps. The channel on which the signal is carried is called a data channel (D channel) and is 16 kbps. Figure 1-10 shows a Basic Rate Interface (BRI) that consists of two B channels and one D channel.

Figure 1-10   *Basic Rate Interface*

Out-of-band signaling offers many benefits, including the following:

- Signaling is multiplexed (consolidated) into a common channel.
- Glare is reduced (glare occurs when two people on the same circuit seize opposite ends of that circuit at the same time).
- A lower post dialing delay.
- Additional features, such as higher bandwidth, are realized.

- Because setup messages are not subject to the same line noise as DTMF tones, call completion is greatly increased.

In-band signaling suffers from a few problems, the largest of which is the possibility for *lost tones*. This occurs when signaling is carried across the voice path and it is a common reason why you can sometimes experience problems remotely accessing your voice mail.

Network-to-Network Signaling

Network-to-network communication is normally carried across the following transmission media:

- T1/E1 carrier over twisted pair

  T1 is a 1.544-Mbps digital transmission link normally used in North America and Japan.

  E1 is a 2.048-Mbps digital transmission link normally used in Europe.

- T3/E3, T4 carrier over coaxial cable

  T3 carries 28 T1s or 672 64-kbps connections and is 44.736 Mbps.

  E3 carries 16 E1s or 512 64-kbps connections and is 34.368 Mbps.

  T4 handles 168 T1 circuits or 4032 4-kbps connections and is 274.176 Mbps.

- T3, T4 carrier over a microwave link

- Synchronous Optical Network (SONET) across fiber media

  SONET is normally deployed in OC-3, OC-12, and OC-48 rates, which are 155.52 Mbps, 622.08 Mbps, and 2.488 Gbps, respectively.

Network-to-network signaling types include in-band signaling methods such as Multi-Frequency (MF) and Robbed Bit Signaling (RBS). These signaling types can also be used to network signaling methods.

Digital carrier systems (T1, T3) use A and B bits to indicate on/off hook supervision. The A/B bits are set to emulate Single Frequency (SF) tones (SF typically uses the presence or absence of a signal to signal A/B bit transitions). These bits might be *robbed* from the information channel or multiplexed in a common channel (the latter occurs mainly in Europe). More information on these signaling types is found in Chapter 3, "Basic Telephony Signaling."

MF is similar to DTMF, but it utilizes a different set of frequencies. As with DTMF, MF tones are sent in-band. But, instead of signaling from a home to an end office switch, MF signals from switch to switch.

Network-to-network signaling also uses an out-of-band signaling method known as *Signaling System 7* (SS7) (or C7 in European countries). This section covers some of the benefits of SS7, however SS7 is covered in depth in Chapter 4, "Signaling System 7."

NOTE   SS7 is beneficial because it is an out-of-band signaling method and it interconnects to the Intelligent Network (IN). Connection to the IN enables the PSTN to offer Custom Local Area Signaling Services (CLASS) services.

SS7 is a method of sending messages between switches for basic call control and for CLASS. These CLASS services still rely on the end-office switches and the SS7 network. SS7 is also used to connect switches and databases for network-based services (for example, 800-number services and Local Number Portability [LNP]).

Some of the benefits of moving to an SS7 network are as follows:

- Reduced post-dialing delay

  There is no need to transmit DTMF tones on each hop of the PSTN. The SS7 network transmits all the digits in an initial setup message that includes the entire calling and called number. When using in-band signaling, each MF tone normally takes 50 ms to transmit. This means you have at least a .5-second post-dialing delay per PSTN hop. This number is based on 11-digit dialing (11 MF tones × 50 ms = 550 ms).

- Increased call completion

  SS7 is a packet-based, out-of-band signaling protocol, compared to the DTMF or MF in-band signaling types. Single packets containing all the necessary information (phone numbers, services, and so on) are transmitted faster than tones generated one at a time across an in-band network.

- Connection to the IN

  This connection provides new applications and services transparently across multiple vendors' switching equipment as well as the capability to create new services and applications more quickly.

To further explain the PSTN, visualize a call from my house to my Grandma's house 10 miles away. This call traverses an end office switch, the SS7 network (signaling only), and a second end office switch. Figure 1-11 displays the call flow from my house to Grandma's.

Figure 1-11 *PSTN Call Flow to Grandma's House*

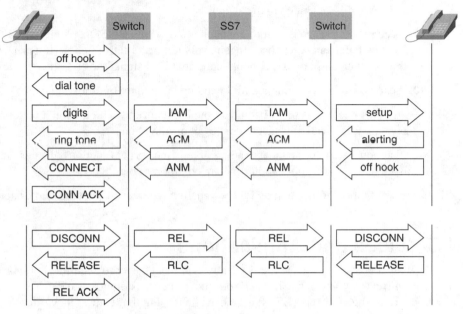

To better explain the diagram in Figure 1-11, let's walk through the flow of the call:

1 I pick up the phone and send an off-hook indication to the end office switch.

2 The switch sends back a dial tone.

3 I dial the digits to call Grandma's house (they are sent in-band through DTMF).

4 The switch interprets the digits and sends an Initial Address Message (IAM, or setup message) to the SS7 network.

5 The SS7 network reads the incoming IAM and sends a new IAM to Grandma's switch.

6 Grandma's switch sends a setup message to Grandma's phone (it rings her phone).

7 An alerting message (alerting is the same as the phone ringing) is sent from Grandma's switch (not from her phone) back to the SS7 network through an Address Complete Message (ACM).

8 The SS7 network reads the incoming ACM and generates an ACM to my switch.

9 I can hear a ringing sound and know that Grandma's phone is ringing. (The ringing is not synchronized; your local switch normally generates the ringing when the ACM is received from the SS7 network.)

10 Grandma picks up her phone, sending an off-hook indication to her switch.

11 Grandma's switch sends an ANswer Message (ANM) that is read by the SS7, and a new ANM is generated to my switch.

12 A connect message is sent to my phone (only if it's an ISDN phone) and a connect acknowledgment is sent back (again, only if it's an ISDN phone). (If it is not an ISDN phone, then on-hook or off-hook representations signal the end office switch.)

13 I can now talk to Grandma until I hang up the phone (on-hook indication).

If Grandma's phone was busy, I could use an IN feature by which I could park on her line and have the PSTN call me back after she got off the phone.

Now that you have a basic understanding of how the PSTN functions, the next section discusses services and applications that are common in the PSTN.

If you want more information on PSTN signaling types, see Chapter 3 and Chapter 4.

PSTN Services and Applications

As with almost every industry, it is usually better and easier to acquire additional business from current customers than it is to go out and get new customers. The PSTN is no different. Local Exchange Carriers (LECs) have been increasing the features they offer to create a higher revenue stream per consumer.

Numerous services are now available, for example, which were not available just a few years ago. These services come in two common flavors: *custom calling* features and CLASS features.

Custom calling features rely upon the end office switch, not the entire PSTN, to carry information from circuit-switch to circuit-switch. CLASS features, however, require SS7 connectivity to carry these features from end to end in the PSTN.

The following list includes a few of the popular custom calling features commonly found in the PSTN today:

- Call waiting—Notifies customers who already placed a call that they are receiving an incoming call.
- Call forwarding—Enables a subscriber to forward incoming calls to a different destination.
- Three-way calling—Enables conference calling.

With the deployment of the SS7 network, advanced features can now be carried end to end. A few of the CLASS features are mentioned in the following list:

- Display—Displays the calling party's directory number, or Automatic Number Identification (ANI).

- Call blocking—Blocks specific incoming numbers so that callers are greeted with a message saying the call is not accepted.
- Calling line ID blocking—Blocks the outgoing directory number from being shown on someone else's display. (This does not work when calling 800-numbers or certain other numbers.)
- Automatic callback—Enables you to put a hold on the last number dialed if a busy signal is received, and then place the call after the line is free.
- Call return (*69)—Enables users to quickly reply to missed calls.

A majority of these features are possible due to the use of SS7 and the IN. Many inter-exchange carriers (IXCs) also offer business features, such as the following:

- Circuit-switched long distance—Basic long-distance services (normally at a steeply discounted rate).
- Calling cards—Pre-paid and post-paid calling cards. You dial a number, enter a password, and then call your destination.
- 800/888/877 numbers—The calling party is not charged for the call; Rather, the party called is charged (normally at a premium rate).
- Virtual Private Networks (VPNs)—The telephone company manages a private dialing plan. This can greatly reduce the number of internal Information Service (IS) telecommunications personnel.
- Private leased lines—Private leased lines from 56 kbps to OC-48s enable both data and voice to traverse different networks. The most popular speed by far in North America is T1.
- Virtual circuits (Frame Relay or Asynchronous Transfer Mode [ATM])—The telephone carrier (IXC or LEC) switches your packets. It does this packet by packet (or cell by cell in ATM), not based upon a dedicated circuit.

This list of IXC business features is merely a sampling of the more popular features and applications available in the PSTN. Although the PSTN is evolving and consumers are using more of its features, the basic user experience has remained somewhat consistent since the inception of digital networking for telephony communications.

PSTN Numbering Plans

One feature that slowly changed over time is the dial plan. The addition of second lines for Internet access, cell phones, and fax machines has created a relative shortage of phone numbers. The next section delves into how the PSTN dial plan is put together and what you can expect over the next few years.

In some places in the United States, it is necessary to dial 1+10 digits for even a local call. This will become more and more prevalent as more devices require telephone numbers. The need to dial 1+10 digits for a local number is normally due to an *overlay*. An overlay can result in next-door neighbors having different area codes. An overlay is when a region with an existing area code has another area code "overlayed." This offers the existing customers the benefits of not having to switch area codes, but forces everyone in that region to dial 10 digits to call anywhere.

Essentially, two numbering plans are used with the PSTN: the North American Numbering Plan (NANP) and the International Telecommunication Union Telecommunication Standardization Sector (ITU-T; formerly CCITT) International Numbering Plan. They are discussed in the following sections.

NANP

NANP is an 11-digit dialing plan that contains three parts: the Numbering Plan Area (NPA, also referring to as area code), Central Office Code (NXX), and Station Number. This plan is often referred to as NPA-NXX-XXXX.

NPA codes use the following format:

NXX, where N is a value between 2–9 and X is a value between 0–9.

NANP is also referred to as 1+10. This means that when a 1 is the first number dialed, it will be proceeded by a 10-digit NPA-NXX-XXXX number. This enables the end office switch to determine whether it should expect a 7- or 10-digit telephone number.

Your LEC keeps track of what long-distance provider you use in a static table on the end office switch. Each long-distance carrier has a code. This long-distance code is assigned by the North American Numbering Plan Association (NANPA) and is added to the number you call so that it is routed to the proper long-distance network carrier (or IXC).

NOTE
Popular today, carrier-selection numbers are used to have a "secondary" long-distance carrier. Dial-around numbers allow you to choose a long-distance carrier call by call by adding 7 digits to each outgoing call. Much advertising has been done to have telephony users specify 10+XX+XXX to not use their primary carrier.

The reason for carrier selection is simple. You don't have to switch and can use different LD carriers based upon the time of day, week, location called, type of call, or personal preference.

ITU-T International Numbering Plan

ITU-T Recommendation E.164 specifies that a Country Code (CC), National Destination Code (NDC), and Subscriber Number (SN) be used to route a call to a specific subscriber.

The CC consists of one, two, or three digits. The first digit (1–9) defines world numbering zones. A list of all the defined CCs is found in ITU-T Recommendation E.164 Annex A.

NDC and SN vary in length based on the needs of the country. Neither one has more than 15 digits.

Many other recommendations and specifications for international number plans are found in the E. recommendations from the ITU-T.

Although dial plans might not seem extremely important at the moment, they are crucial to the successful deployment and implementation of Voice over IP (VoIP) or traditional circuit-switched networks.

Regardless of which dialing plan is used in your country, you can expect to see changes in the ways you can dial as well as whom you dial.

Drivers Behind the Convergence Between Voice and Data Networking

Understanding PSTN basics includes knowing why the existing PSTN does not fit all the needs of its builders or users. After you understand where today's PSTN is lacking, you will know where to look to find a solution. This section sets the stage for why the voice and data networks are merging into a signal network.

Drawbacks to the PSTN

Although the PSTN is effective and does a good job at what it was built to do (that is, switch voice calls), many business drivers are striving to change it to a new network, whereby voice is an application on top of a data network. This is happening for several reasons:

- Data has overtaken voice as the primary traffic on many networks built for voice.

  Data is now running on top of networks that were built to carry voice efficiently. Data has different characteristics, however, such as a variable use of bandwidth and a need for higher bandwidth.

  Soon, voice networks will run on top of networks built with a data-centric approach. Traffic will then be differentiated based upon application instead of physical circuits. New technologies (such as Fast Ethernet, Gigabit Ethernet, and Optical Networking) will be used to deploy the high-speed networks that needed to carry all this additional data.

- The PSTN cannot create and deploy features quickly enough.

With increased competition due to deregulation in many telecommunications markets, LECs are looking for ways to keep their existing clientele. The primary method of keeping customers is by enticing them through new services and applications.

The PSTN is built on an infrastructure whereby only the vendors of the equipment develop the applications for that equipment. This means you have one-stop shopping for all your needs. It is very difficult for one company to meet all the needs of a customer. A more open infrastructure, by which many vendors can provide applications, enables more creative solutions and applications to be developed. It is also not possible with the current architecture to enable many vendors to write new applications for the PSTN. Imagine where the world would be today if vendors, such as Microsoft, did not want other vendors to write applications for its software.

- Data/Voice/Video (D/V/V) cannot converge on the PSTN as currently built.

With only an analog line to most homes, you cannot have data access (Internet access), phone access, and video access across one 56-kbps modem. High-speed broadband access, such as digital subscriber line (DSL), cable, or wireless, is needed to enable this convergence. After the last bandwidth issues are resolved, the convergence can happen to the home. In the backbone of the PSTN, the convergence has already started.

- The architecture built for voice is not flexible enough to carry data.

Because the bearer channels (B channels and T1 circuits), call-control (SS7 and Q.931), and service logic (applications) are tightly bound in one closed platform, it is not possible to make minor changes that might improve audio quality.

It is also important to note that circuit-switched calls require a permanent 64-kbps dedicated circuit between the two telephones. Whether the caller or the person called is talking, the 64-kbps connection cannot be used by any other party. This means that the telephone company cannot use this bandwidth for any other purpose and must bill the parties for consuming its resources.

Data networking, on the other hand, has the capability to use bandwidth only when it is required. This difference, although seemingly small, is a major benefit of packet-based voice networking.

Telecommunications Deregulation

So far, you have looked at the technical issues of how the PSTN operates, the basic hierarchy, and why you might need to converge voice and data networks. One important reason for this convergence is more political than technical.

Various countries throughout Europe, Asia, and the Americas are opening up their telecommunications markets to competition. In addition, in some cases, they are selling off the existing government-run telephone carriers to a private company (or many companies).

In the United States, a publicly owned utility ran the PSTN from its inception until its divestiture in the early 1980s. In many other countries, however, the government ran the PSTN. This is changing as governments realize that communication is important to survival in the next century. These governments also realize that with communication comes knowledge, and with knowledge comes strength and prosperity.

Many new voice carriers are rushing to join these new deregulated markets. With the influx of fresh competition, pricing models are changing, and new, as well as old, carriers are considering deploying the latest technology to lower the cost of doing business.

The additional advantage of deploying new technology is the ability to offer value-added services and deploy these new services in a short amount of time. Services include bundled voice and Internet access, unified communications, Internet call waiting, and others.

Let's use the United States as an example of how competition affects the telecommunications marketplace by taking a look at the breakup of the utility in the early 1980s. American Telephone and Telegraph (AT&T) signed a divestiture agreement that stated it would divest itself of its 22 telephone operating companies. These 22 telephone companies were placed into 7 holding companies, which came to be known as the LECs.

AT&T was broken into a long-distance carrier or an IXC, which kept the AT&T name, and many regional Bell operating companies (RBOCs). These RBOCs actually provided the local loop and line to everyone in their local regions.

The U.S. RBOCs (Pacific Telesis, Southwestern Bell, Nynex, Bell Atlantic, Southern Bell, US West, and NYNEX) all had areas known as Local Area and Transport Areas (LATAs), which are local calling areas. These RBOCs were also known as LECs. If these LECs wanted to pass traffic between LATAs, they had to use an IXC.

As a result, many IXCs (AT&T, MCI, Sprint, and others) could offer long-distance domestic service and develop agreements with international carriers to provide inter-national services. The local LECs, however, were not allowed to provide long-distance service, and pricing was highly regulated to avoid monopolies.

When competition arose in the LEC market, the existing LECs were then called Incumbent LECs (ILECs) and the newcomers were called Competitive LECs (CLECs).

Many of the ILECs have started to consolidate. They are currently attempting to meet certain requirements to be able to enter the long-distance marketplace. This will enable them to bypass such IXCs as AT&T and MCI and keep the money they normally pay them for long-distance service.

More recently, new competitors to LECs, CLECs, and IXCs have emerged. These competitors come in the form of Internet telephony service providers (ITSPs) and Greenfield carriers. ITSPs are Internet service providers (ISPs) that add voice functionality to their portfolio and carry voice traffic across data networks, which frequently span traditional ILEC boundaries.

Greenfield carriers are carriers that build networks from scratch (for instance, a data network built specifically to carry packet voice) instead of using circuit-switching networks normally used by the LECs and IXCs.

NOTE   Although deregulation and competition have existed in the U.S. since 1982, their emergence in other countries is more recent. China and Germany, for example, have opened up their respective telephone markets only within the last few years.

In different countries' respective markets, these competitors can exploit different PSTN market niches. A Greenfield carrier in any country might attempt to offer business customers both voice and data over a high-speed data infrastructure. Meanwhile, a traditional CLEC might attempt to offer high-speed access to both residential customers and businesses over traditional access, such as T1 circuits, as well as new high-bandwidth services, such as DSL.

Packet Telephony Network Drivers

The previous section discussed political drivers for competition in the PSTN. This section explains why a carrier might choose to develop a packet telephony network in lieu of a traditional circuit-switching network.

The integration of D/V/V is more than just a change in infrastructure. D/V/V integration also enables new features to be developed more quickly and opens up application development to thousands of Independent Software Vendors (ISVs). You can compare this integration of D/V/V to the change from mainframe computers, for which very few vendors developed applications, to client/servers, for which multiple vendors developed applications for distributed systems.

Figure 1-12 shows how the circuit-switching model is breaking into a new model by which open standards exist between all three layers. A packet infrastructure will carry the actual voice (media), the call-control layer will be separate from the media layer, and open APIs (Application Programming Interfaces) will enable new services to be created by ISVs.

Figure 1-12 *Circuit Switching Versus Packet Switching*

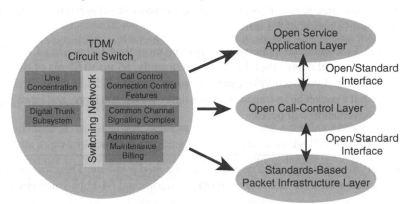

Figure 1-12 is an over-simplification of the changes that are actually happening. To further discuss these changes, you need to take a closer look at each of the three layers.

Standards-Based Packet Infrastructure Layer

The packet infrastructure replaces the circuit-switching infrastructure in this new model. This infrastructure most likely will be IP, although this model also works if ATM is the underlying transport and IP rides across the top. IP is so attractive as the packet infrastructure because of its ubiquitous nature and the fact that it is the de facto application interface. This means that software applications running over IP do not have to be known. IP simply transports the data end to end, with no real interest in the payload.

NOTE   To provide the proper prioritization on a *congested* IP network, the IP network must have some knowledge of the applications.

Real-time Transport Protocol (RTP) is utilized in addition to a User Datagram Protocol (UDP)/IP header to provide *timestamping*. RTP runs atop UDP and IP and is commonly noted as RTP/UDP/IP. RTP is currently the cornerstone for carrying real-time traffic across IP networks. (Microsoft Netmeeting, for instance, utilizes RTP to carry audio and video communications.) To date, all VoIP signaling protocols utilize RTP/UDP/IP as their transport mechanism for voice traffic. Often, RTP packet flows are known as *RTP streams*. This nomenclature is used to describe the audio path.

In IP networks, it is common and normal for packet loss to occur. In fact, Transmission Control Protocol/Internet Protocol (TCP/IP) was built to utilize packet loss as a means of

VoIP Call-Control Protocols

As of this writing, the main VoIP call-control protocols are H.323, Simple Gateway Control Protocol (SGCP), Internet Protocol Device Control (IPDC), MGCP, and SIP. They are defined as follows:

- H.323 is the ITU-T recommendation with the largest installed base, simply because it has been around the longest and no other protocol choices existed before H.323. Chapter 10, "H.323," discusses this protocol in detail.

- SGCP was developed starting in 1998 to reduce the cost of endpoints (gateways) by having the intelligent call-control occur in a centralized platform (or gateway controller). Chapter 12, "Gateway Control Protocols," covers this in more detail.

- IPDC is very similar to SGCP, but it has many other mechanisms for operations, administration, management, and provisioning (OAM&P) than SGCP. OAM&P is crucial to carrier networks because it covers how they are maintained and deployed.

- In late 1998, the IETF put IPDC and SGCP in a room and out popped MGCP. MGCP is basically SGCP with a few additions for OAM&P. MGCP is covered in more detail in Chapter 12.

- SIP is being developed as a media-based protocol that will enable end devices (endpoints or gateways) to be more intelligent, and enable enhanced services down at the call-control layer. Chapter 11, "Session Initiation Protocol," covers SIP in detail.

To briefly explain the various differences between these call-control protocols, let's take a look at how they signal endpoints.

H.323

H.323 is an ITU-T recommendation that specifies how multimedia traffic is carried over packet networks. H.323 utilizes existing standards (Q.931, for example) to accomplish its goals. H.323 is a rather complex protocol that was not created for simple development of applications. Rather, it was created to enable multimedia applications to run over "unreliable" data networks. Voice traffic is only one of the applications for H.323. Most of the initial work in this area focused on multimedia applications, with video and data-sharing a major part of the protocol.

Applications require significant work if they are to be scalable with H.323; for example, to accomplish a call transfer requires a separate specification (H.450.2). SGCP and MGCP, on the other hand, can accomplish a call transfer with a simple command, known as a modify connection (MDCX), to the gateway or endpoint. This simple example represents the different approaches built into the protocol design itself—one tailored to large deployment for simple applications (MGCP), and the other tailored to more complicated applications but showing limitations in its scalability (H.323).

To further demonstrate the complexity of H.323, Figure 1-13 shows a call-flow between two H.323 endpoints.

Figure 1-13 *H.323 Call-Flow*

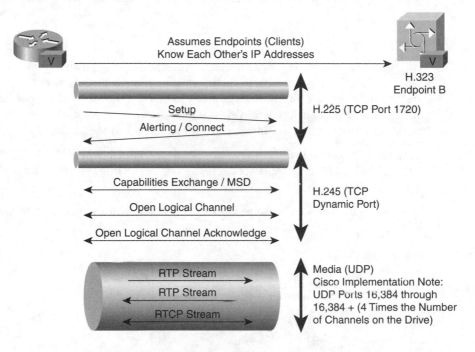

Figure 1-13 illustrates the most basic H.323 call-flow. In most cases, more steps are needed because gatekeepers are involved.

To better explain Figure 1-13, let's step through the call-flow:

1 Endpoint A sends a setup message to Endpoint B on TCP Port 1720.

2 Endpoint B replies to the setup message with an alerting message and a port number to start H.245 negotiation.

3 H.245 negotiation includes codec types (G.729 and G.723.1), port numbers for the RTP streams, and notification of other capabilities the endpoints have.

4 Logical channels for the UDP stream are then negotiated, opened, and acknowledged.

5 Voice is then carried over RTP streams.

6 Real Time Transport Control Protocol is used to transmit information about the RTP stream to both endpoints.

This call-flow is based on H.323 v1. H.323 v2, however, enables H.245 negotiation to be tunneled in the H.225 setup message. This is known as *fast-start*, and it cuts down on the number of roundtrips required to set up an H.323 call. It does not, however, make the protocol any less complex. More detailed analysis of H.323 is found in Chapter 10.

SGCP and MGCP

SGCP and MGCP were developed to enable a central device, known as a Media Gateway Controller (MGC) or *soft-switch,* to control endpoints or Media Gateways (MGs). Both of those protocols are referenced simultaneously as *xGCP.* You can develop applications through the use of standard-based APIs that interface with the MGCs and offer additional functionality (such as call waiting and CLASS features) and applications.

The Cisco version of this technology is known as the Virtual Switch Controller (VSC). In this scenario, the entire IP network acts like one large virtual switch, with the VSC controlling all the MGs.

Figure 1-14 shows how a typical network design works with a virtual switch running MGCP.

Figure 1-14 *Virtual Switch Controller*

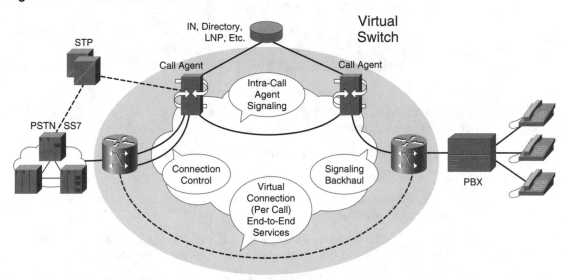

Figure 1-14 also shows how the legacy PSTN and enterprise networks are connected to gateways or endpoints that enable access into the new packet network. This packet gateway receives direction from the Call Agent (VSC), which can communicate with the SS7 network and the IN and can tell the gateways or endpoints how and when to set up the call.

To understand Figure 1-14 in greater detail, all the various components must be described. The existing PSTN/SS7 network is connected to the Switching Transfer Point (STP), which also is connected to the MGC or Call Agent. This connection is where the signaling (SS7) takes place.

The PSTN/SS7 network is also connected to an MG, which is a signal-less trunk that is often known as an *Inter-Machine Trunk* or IMT. The MG is where the 64-kbps voice trunks are converted into packets and placed onto the IP network.

The MGCs or Call Agents also intercommunicate. This protocol is currently undefined in the standards bodies. Based on the current state of the industry, however, it appears that a variant of SIP or ISDN User Part (ISUP) over IP—a portion of SS7 running on top of IP—will be the primary protocol. The MGCs have a connection to the IN (described earlier in this chapter) to provide CLASS services. The MGCs receive signals from the SS7 network and tell the MGs when to set up IP connections and with which other MGs they should set them up.

The MG on the right side of Figure 1-14 does not have a connection to the SS7 network. Therefore, a mechanism known as *signaling backhaul* must be used to tell the VSC when and how a call is arriving. Signaling backhaul is normally done with ISDN. The MG or some other device separates the D channel from the B channels and forwards the D channel to the MGC through IP. Signaling backhaul is currently undefined in the standards bodies. By the time this book is printed, however, there should be a specification for signaling backhaul.

For a more detailed explanation of how all these components work together, see Chapter 12, "Gateway Control Protocols" and Chapter 13, "Virtual Switch Controller."

SIP

SIP is best described by RFC 2543, which states that it is an application-layer control (signaling) protocol for creating, modifying, and terminating sessions with one or more participants.

These multimedia sessions include audio, video, and data and can include multiple partners. SIP enables participants to be invited into an impromptu conference. These multimedia sessions can communicate through multicast, unicast, or a combination of both delivery mechanisms.

Very few implementations of SIP are currently running, although many vendors and customers are interested in using SIP to deploy enhanced services.

See Chapter 11 for more detailed information on SIP.

Open Service Application Layer

By far the most interesting layer of any networking protocol is the application layer. Without good applications, the network infrastructure is built for naught. When moving to a new infrastructure, it is not necessary to carry over all the features that are on the old infrastructure. Only the features or applications that customers need are required.

When building a network that has open interfaces from the packet layer to the call-control layer and from the call-control layer to the application layer, vendors no longer have to develop applications. Now, they can simply write to these standard APIs and have access to a whole new infrastructure. When a new packet infrastructure is built, opportunities for new applications become widely available.

Legacy applications such as call-centers for enterprise networks, and standard PSTN applications such as call waiting and call forwarding, must be ported onto a new infrastructure without the end user realizing that the change occurred. After these legacy applications are ported, literally thousands of new enhanced applications can be specifically developed for packet infrastructures. These include (but are not limited to) Internet call waiting, push to talk, find me-follow me, and unified messaging. These applications are discussed in Chapter 6, "Voice over IP Benefits and Applications."

New PSTN Network Infrastructure Model

As discussed in the previous sections, the new infrastructure will focus on the ability to separate the old stagnant infrastructure into a model by which multiple vendors can develop applications and features quickly for the consumer. Figure 1-15 shows how Cisco Systems wants to carry this model forward.

Figure 1-15 clearly shows the relationship between all three layers as well as the relationship between these layers and the components that would be used in a live network. Carriers will enjoy this method, as it means they won't be locked into a single solution for any of their layers. They will be able to mix and match all three layers to offer the services, functionality, and time-to-market that they need.

Figure 1-15 *Elements of Packet Telephony*

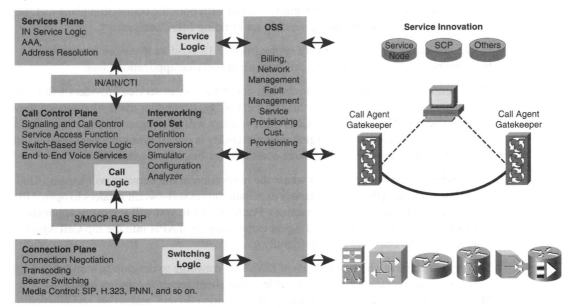

Some carriers might be hesitant to utilize more than one equipment vendor to cut down on their integration timeframe, but many service providers will partner with a minimum of two vendors to ensure competition.

The reality of Figure 1-15 is that the bearers, connection plane, or media transport will be either IP gateways or ATM gateways, or a combination of both. Multiple vendors will be in this space initially, but most likely, they will consolidate to three to five major players.

NOTE   A common trend in the manufacturing and carrier arena is *consolidation*. The consolidation of manufacturers is one reason for the dramatic reduction in the number of players in this space.

CHAPTER 2

Enterprise Telephony Today

Enterprise Telephony (ET) is a business telephone system because it provides basic business features, such as hold, three-way calling, call transfer, and call forwarding. ET shares many similarities with it's big brother, the Public Switched Telephone Network (PSTN), but it also has many differences. This chapter details both the similarities and differences between these two networks, the ways in which they interoperate, and typical ET network designs.

Similarities Between PSTN and ET

PSTN and ET are similar in the following ways:

- Circuit Switching—Both networks are based on the switching of 64-kbps circuits.

- Common Infrastructure Model—Bearers, call-control, and service planes are contained in one platform. These features are described in Chapter 1, "Overview of the PSTN and Comparisons to Voice over IP."

- Local Loop—Phones can plug directly into the switch and receive a dial tone, place and receive phone calls, and so on.

- Services Offered—Both networks can provide basic services such as call hold, three-way calling, call transfer, and call forwarding.

Both networks also switch 64-kbps circuits, however, the scale at which each does so is much different. The PSTN uses a Class 5 switch that can support hundreds of thousands of local loops. The ET equivalent to a Class 5 switch, the Private Branch eXchange (PBX), supports from five to several thousand local loops.

The primary task of a Class 5 switch is to provide residential telephony, but it also offers a few basic business features, such as call waiting and call return. A PBX, however, usually offers more features, including call hold, three-way calling, call transfer, voice mail, and many others.

Differences Between PSTN and ET

PSTN and ET are different from each other in the way they treat signaling and in the types of features they offer.

Signaling Treatment

Although the PSTN uses signaling interfaces developed by industry bodies, PBX manufacturers often create proprietary protocols to enable their PBXs to intercommunicate and carry additional features transparently throughout their voice network.

Chapter 1 discusses how the PSTN uses Signaling System 7 (SS7), ISDN, and in-band signaling as its primary signaling links. These are well-documented standards that have been evolving for many years. Although these signaling protocols cannot solve all signaling problems today, anyone can develop software to interface into the PSTN network.

Many PBXs in ET use CAS and PRI for signaling. In many cases, computer telephony integration (CTI) links also are used to enable a third-party computer application to control some of the PBX's operations. Most PBX vendors, however, implement a proprietary signaling mechanism. This forces enterprise networks to consolidate on one brand of PBX. Although this can be good for the manufacturer, the enterprise business customer is now locked into one vendor.

NOTE   Many vendors are starting to implement standards-based signaling protocols that enable interoperability between different vendors' PBXs. A list of these protocols is as follows:

- Q Signaling (QSIG)—This is an open standard designed to enable multiple vendors to agree on supplementary services, dial plans, and much more. (The "Q" comes from the International Telecommunication Union Telecommunication Standardization Sector [ITU-T] Q.xxx set of standards.)

- Digital Private Network Signaling System (DPNSS)—This is a British standard designed to enable cross-vendor, inter-PBX communication. This standard was rolled into QSIG.

Advanced Features

Providing advanced features is also an important differentiation between ET and PSTN. Business requirements for telephone networks are much greater than the average home user. Enterprise customers have the need for high-use, feature-rich systems that enable applications such as the following:

- Inbound and outbound call centers—ET networks with this feature usually contain a CTI link that enables new applications—for instance, a screen pops up on the representative's computer screen that gives the representative the caller-ID information, as well as other information about that caller (buying habits, shipping address, and so on).

- Financial Enterprise Telephony—ET networks with this feature often include a network known as *hoot-n-holler*, in which one person speaks and many people listen. This is common in stock brokerage.

ET customers can use the PSTN to service basic PBX needs, but the PSTN does not have advanced applications such as call centers. Also, using PSTN is usually more costly than using ET, and the PSTN might not have all the necessary functionality that the enterprise customer needs.

Common ET Designs

ET designs generally consist of an inter-working between PSTN and the enterprise network. This inter-working can be as simple as an analog line from the PSTN or a leased line between two PBXs. Or, it can be as complex as an Asynchronous Transfer Mode (ATM) connection using an inter-exchange carrier's (IXC's) public ATM network. This section covers the various methods and network designs commonly used in most ET networks.

There are five methods that businesses can choose, each of which uses slightly different components. These methods include the following:

- Simple business line—This method involves using a line directly from the PSTN as a business line. This line is similar to a residential line, however the business customer is normally charged a higher monthly rate. This simple business line is usually used for very small businesses that do not need many telephony features. This service is provided and managed by the Local Exchange Carrier (LEC) or Competitive LEC (CLEC).

- PBX—A PBX provides many features (such as hold, transfer, park, and so on)that business customers require. This switch often connects to the PSTN through a T1 or E1 circuit. These systems often integrate voice mail, local lines, and PSTN trunks.

- Key-system—This is a smaller version of a PBX and is generally used in offices of fewer than 50 people.

- Centrex line—Provided and managed by the LEC or CLEC, this line offers additional services similar to a PBX, but an additional monthly charge is involved. These services include transfer, three-way calling, and a closed user-dialing plan.

- Virtual Private Networks (VPNs)—With a VPN, the PSTN contains a private dial plan for the enterprise customer. LECs, CLECs, and IXCs can provide VPNs. A local PBX can provide additional features, however.

These methods are broken into two groups: those that the PSTN provides and manages, and those that are privately owned and merely need to interconnect with the PSTN. Each category is discussed in the following sections.

ET Networks Provided by PSTN

If a business has little capital resources for an internal department to manage the telephone network, it often looks to PSTN to provide telephony services. A business might also use PSTN because it is too large for an internal Information Services (IS) department to efficiently manage the entire network, so the telephony network is outsourced through a VPN to the PSTN carrier. The three PSTN-provided telephony networks include the following:

- A simple business line
- A Centrex line
- A VPN

Simple Business Line

The most basic of these methods is a simple business line. This service is usually used by small businesses of one or two people who do not need additional phone services.

A landscaping company with one owner and one employee, for example, does not need more than one telephone line with an answering machine attached. Such a company does not need features such as call hold or call transfer. A simple business line is similar to a residential line, but it usually has a higher monthly fee than a residential line. The local carrier charges this additional cost because it assumes the business line is used more often than a residential line.

Centrex Line

As a business begins to grow, it starts to require additional services, such as call transfer, call hold, and call waiting. The business can purchase a key-system or PBX, which starts at around U.S. $2000, or it can simply pay a few extra dollars every month (U.S. $20–$30) to the PSTN for additional services.

These services enable the PSTN to offer features in a Closed User Group (CUG). A *CUG* describes a situation where all the phones within the business become a virtual switch and can dial one another with only four or five digits, transfer calls, and put callers on hold. This service offers more functionality than a simple business line, but it usually becomes cost-prohibitive to implement as the company grows.

VPN

Another option available to business users is VPN. VPNs offer enterprise customers the benefits of a private network (CUG) without the administration or equipment hassles of a large *tie-line* network (a tie-line is simply a permanent circuit between two points).

A VPN enables an enterprise customer to dial a specific number, which then directs the PSTN to treat the customer as a CUG. Say, for example, that a large retail corporation with offices throughout the U.S. does not want to have key-systems or PBXs in each of its 3000 stores. That would be a large network to manage and administer.

This retail corporation decides to contract with a long-distance (IXC) company to provide a VPN for all 3000 of its retail stores. Each store has its own four-digit store ID, assigned by the company, which is used for inter-company business. Therefore, the store ID is a good way to uniquely identify each branch of the retail operation. Figure 2-1 shows a graphical representation of the potential network and call-flow.

Figure 2-1   *Virtual Private Network*

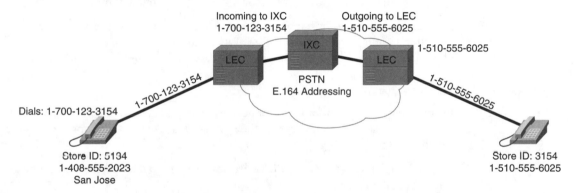

The IXC gives the retail store a phone number to dial—1-700-123-3154. The IXC informs the LEC to hand off the call to the IXC so that the IXC knows which dial plan applies to the incoming number. (The last four digits of the dialed number correspond to the store ID.)

The store ID for the store in San Jose, California, for example, is 5134. Store 5134 is running low on toasters and needs to call the nearby store in Fremont (Store 3154). The old method was to look at a lengthy table and place a long-distance call from the 1-408 (San Jose) area code to the 1-510 (Fremont) area code. Today, Store 5134 only needs to know the ID of the Fremont store and can dial 1-700-123-3154 to reach that store.

The IXC translates the 1-700-123-3154 number to the "real" telephone number assigned by the local LEC, but this is completely transparent to the retail store clerks. (As a side note, the Fremont store had the toasters and sent them over right away.)

By referring to Figure 2-1, you can step through the call in more detail:

1 The user in San Jose dials 1-700-123-3154.

2 The LEC receives the dialed digits.

3 The LEC switch sends those digits to the IXC.

4 The IXC receives the digits 1-700-123-3154, knows this is a VPN, and translates the digits to 1-510-555-6025, which is the true phone number for the Fremont retail store.

5 The IXC sends the call to the local LEC as 1-510-555-6025 because that is what the LEC can understand. If the IXC had sent 1-700, the LEC would route the call back to the IXC.

6 The LEC receives the call from the IXC.

7 The LEC looks up the particular local line for 555-6025 and routes the call to that local loop.

8 The retail store receives the call, not knowing that it was routed through the VPN.

VPN enables the enterprise to save money on internal IS costs as well as provides the enterprise with a simpler network for all 3000 of its remote offices to use.

Private ET Networks

By far, the most popular option for ET is for businesses to purchase their own key-system or PBX to provide local telephone access to their employees. This method provides many benefits, including the following:

- No recurring charges—Owning a PBX costs less per month than purchasing Centrex services from the PSTN.

- Control over adds, moves, and changes—There is no need to contact the PSTN carrier to add new lines, move a phone, or change subscriber information.

PBX Networks

Figure 2-2 shows the relationship between having individual lines from the PSTN, or using a PBX to lower the number of lines (trunks) from the PSTN. Because most users of the telephone system are not calling externally at the same time (depending upon the business type), cost savings on PSTN trunks are realized.

Figure 2-2   *PSTN Compared to a PBX or Key-System*

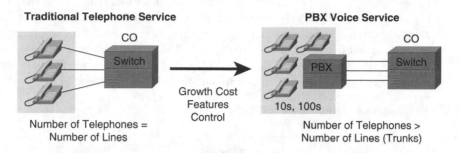

Another advantage to enterprise customers who have their own circuit-switch (PBX) is the control such a setup offers. If you need to add a new user, change a feature, or move a user to a different location, there is no need to contact the PSTN carrier.

The PBX adds another level of complexity, however. The enterprise customer must now deal with the additional burden of configuring and maintaining call routing on the PBX. Figure 2-3 shows a sample block diagram of a user now dialing outside the PBX to the PSTN.

Figure 2-3   *PSTN Call Through a PBX*

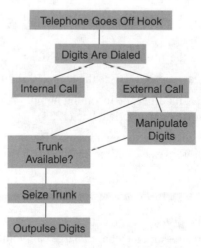

Figure 2-3 details how a PBX makes a basic call-routing decision regarding when to route the call to the PSTN or to an internal phone extension. This process can be hidden from the user (all calls starting with a "1" use an outbound trunk, for example), or the user can be "trained" (forcing the user to dial "9" for an outbound trunk, for instance) to assist the PBX to choose the proper path.

In many cases, the user decides to route the call to the PSTN based on an "escape" digit (this is usually "9" in the U.S. and "0" in Europe). Other times, the user is unaware that the call is routed over the PSTN. As an example, consider a five-digit dialing plan for a company that has locations over a large geographical area. Each PBX can be programmed to translate that five-digit number to a 1+10 (ITU-T Recommendation E.164) number and route the call over the PSTN, as shown in Figure 2-4. This 1+10 number also can be referenced as an E.164 number, as it follows that ITU-T recommendation.

Figure 2-4   *Number Translation Through a PBX*

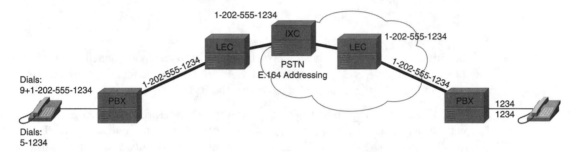

In Figure 2-4, the following occurs:

- A user dials 5-1234, which the local PBX translates to 1-202-555-1234 and sends to the LEC switch.
- The LEC passes the 1+10 number to the IXC, which passes it to another LEC.
- The LEC in area code 202 passes the entire 10-digit number to the remote PBX.
- The remote PBX modifies the incoming number from 202-555-1234 to a four-digit number and rings the appropriate line (1234).

This process of digit manipulation enables the PBX user to dial the least amount of digits possible. This not only saves users time, but it also makes it easier for users to remember frequently used extensions.

Tie-Lines for PBX Interconnection

If a business has two sites and they have a large call volume between them, the business usually purchases a tie-line. Recall that a *tie-line* is simply a permanent circuit between two points (T1, E1, fractional T1/E1, or some other transport). For this scenario to be cost-effective, it must cost less to run a call between site A and site B over the PSTN than it does to send a call over a permanent circuit.

Figure 2-5 shows two sites (one in San Jose, California, and one in Dallas, Texas), with a T1 circuit between them.

Figure 2-5   *Tie-Line Between San Jose and Dallas*

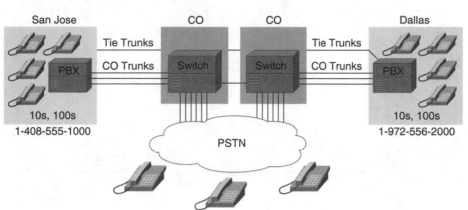

This tie-line still uses the PSTN, but the business pays a flat rate for the dedicated use of the circuit between San Jose and Dallas.

The PBX uses a preprogrammed Automatic Route Selection (ARS) table to determine which trunk should be used. Referring back to Figure 2-5, the PBX is configured to use the tie-line between San Jose and Dallas. If that tie-line becomes full, the PBX uses the Central Office (CO) trunks as overflow to the PSTN.

To determine whether having a tie-line is cost-effective, a careful analysis of the call volume and cost between San Jose and Dallas as compared to the cost of the T1 circuit must be performed. Figure 2-6 shows that the break-even point for a tie line is reached when there are 30–35 hours worth of calls between San Jose and Dallas each month. (This is sample data, and your experience might differ.) Anything over the 30–35 hours of calls between these two sites becomes additional savings, as long as the traffic is balanced so that it might all traverse the dedicated T1 circuit.

Tie-lines are another way in which ET network designers can route their traffic. The routing of call traffic is a very complex issue that requires a myriad of experience and knowledge. Entire books cover the subject of call-traffic modeling. Chapter 15, "Voice over IP Applications and Services," covers traffic analysis in more detail.

Figure 2-6   *Tie-Line Costs Compared to PSTN Costs*

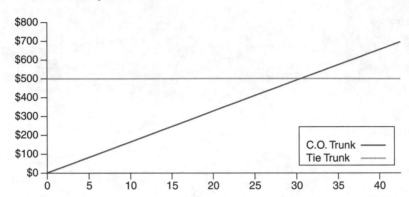

Summary

ET users have requirements that are different from those of the average user on the PSTN. Therefore, ET users have equipment and networks built specifically for those needs. As telecommunications moves to open standards, the alternatives to enterprise customers will grow exponentially.

These alternatives—including packet-based networks for voice and data, integrated access, and much more—will change the way least-cost routing and trunking/busy hour calculations are accomplished.

CHAPTER 3

Basic Telephony Signaling

Many corporations find it advantageous to operate their own voice networks, and they do so by connecting dedicated links between Private Branch eXchanges (PBXs) for inter-office communication, or by using Virtual Private Networks (VPNs) for voice. Originally, PBXs were connected to the Public Switched Telephone Network (PSTN) for voice services, or they were interconnected using analog tie-lines to transfer voice. When the need for more voice trunks and the technology matured, analog tie-lines were replaced with higher-speed digital facilities capable of accessing sophisticated and feature-rich networks. This chapter analyzes the signaling techniques that traverse analog and digital facilities in corporate and interexchange networks.

This chapter also discusses channel-associated signaling (CAS) systems, such as Bell System MF, Consultative Committee for International Telegraph and Telephone (CCITT) No. 5, R1, and R2, and it reviews how these CAS systems operate.

It also describes access protocols, such as Integrated Services Digital Network (ISDN), Q Signaling (QSIG), and Digital Private Network Signaling System (DPNSS). These protocols deliver PBX signaling through a network to distant PBXs. Private ISDN networks use the PSTN for connectivity and services. QSIG is an inter-PBX signaling system similar to ISDN that enables corporate PBXs to connect, thus creating a private voice network. DPNSS is an ISDN-type protocol that enables PBX connectivity; however, it is not as widely used as ISDN and QSIG.

Signaling Overview

Before covering signaling methods and standards, it's important to discuss some basic concepts. These basic concepts are applied in the individual signaling methods further along in the chapter.

Analog and Digital Signaling

Originally, PBXs were connected by simple analog lines that enabled the transmission of voice-band information. Analog systems are not as common today as they used to be, however, and in many cases, they have been replaced by higher-speed digital facilities that cost less than their analog counterparts.

Digital signaling is the most common type of telephony signaling used in today's corporate and service provider networks. In digital networks, many forms of signaling techniques are used.

One form is robbed-bit signaling. With this method, a bit is "robbed" from designated frames to use for signaling purposes. Robbed-bit signaling inserts the signaling information into the digital voice stream without affecting voice quality. This signaling technique is discussed in more detail in the "CAS" section later in this chapter. In addition to CAS, other digital protocols include R1, R2, ISDN, QSIG, and DPNSS.

Direct Current Signaling

This form of signaling relies on direct current (DC) to signal the end switch or office. DC signaling indicates transition state changes by toggling on or off the flow of DC. These end office switches use current detectors to identify changes in state. DC signaling is used in the following two signaling arrangements:

- Subscriber Loop—This is a simple form of DC signaling between the subscriber and the local end office. When a subscriber goes off-hook, DC (-48V) flows across the line or loop between the telephone and the local end office switch. Line cards in the local office are equipped with current detectors to determine when a connection is being requested. When a subscriber goes on-hook, the capacitor in the telephone blocks the flow of current.

  Similarly to off-hook, the change in DC signals to the end office switch that the call was terminated. In this case, the same pair of wires is used to provide the voice and signaling path.

- recEive and transMit (E&M)—This trunking arrangement uses a form of DC signaling to indicate state changes on trunks or tie-lines. With E&M, two leads—one called "E" and the other called "M"—are dedicated to signaling. You can detect the toggling of E&M leads by applying either ground (earth) or a voltage potential (magneto). This form of signaling is covered in the "E&M Signaling" section later in this chapter.

DC signaling has some limitations. Signaling is limited to the number of states you can represent by DC, for instance. Also, when you use the same pair of wires for voice and signaling, the lines or trunks are kept busy even when the two subscribers are not connected.

In-Band and Out-of-Band Signaling

In-band signaling uses tones in place of DC. These tones are transmitted over the same facility as voice and, therefore, are within the 0–4kHz voice band. The tones include Single Frequency, Multi-Frequency (MF), and Dual-Tone Multi-Frequency (DTMF), described here:

- Single Frequency—This tone is used for interoffice trunks and has two possible states: on-hook or idle, and off-hook or busy. The Single Frequency tone is based on a single frequency of 2600 Hz and is used to identify a change in state. Therefore, no tone is present when a connection or circuit is up. When either party hangs up, however, a 2600 Hz tone is sent over the circuit, notifying all interoffice exchanges of the disconnect.

  At one time, the Single Frequency tone was used to gain fraudulent long-distance services from service providers. The perpetrator attached a "blue box" to the subscriber line and used it to fool interoffice exchanges into interpreting the 2600 Hz tone as a clear-forward signal. The interoffice switch then accepted the called party number and believed that the local switch would charge for the call. Access to the interoffice switch was accomplished by dialing 0 and fooling the interoffice switch before the operator answered. Service providers eventually curbed this activity by implementing certain protective measures.

- MF—This tone is used by interoffice trunks to indicate events, such as seizure, release, answer, and acknowledge, and to transmit information, such as the calling party number. MF signaling uses a combination of pulses specified by frequencies to signal across a network. These frequencies are system-specified and are covered in more detail in the "CAS," "R1," and "R2" sections later in this chapter. MF signaling uses the same facilities as the voice path and, therefore, is less efficient than common channel signaling (CCS) systems, such as Signaling System 7 (SS7).

- DTMF—This form of addressing is used to transmit telephone number digits from the subscriber to the local office. With the development of DTMF came the replacement of transistor oscillators in telephones with keypads and dual-tone oscillators. DTMF tones identify the numbers 0 through to 9 and the "*" and "#" symbols. When a subscriber presses one of these keys, the oscillator sends two simultaneous tones. Digits are represented by a particular combination of frequencies: one from the low group (697, 770, 852, and 941 Hz) and one from the high group (1290, 1336, 1447, and 1633 Hz). Sixteen possible combinations exist; however, only 12 are implemented on the keypad.

Loop-Start and Ground-Start Signaling

The two most common methods for end-loop signaling are loop-start and ground-start signaling.

- Loop-Start Signaling—This is the simplest and least intelligent of the two signaling protocols. It also is the most common form of subscriber loop signaling. This protocol basically works in the same way as the telephone and the local end office, whereby the creation of a loop initiates a call and the closure of a loop terminates a call. Loop-start signaling is not common for PBX signaling and has one significant drawback, in that glare can occur. *Glare* occurs when two endpoints try to seize the line at the same time, and it often results in two people being connected unknowingly. The person picking up the phone thinks he has a dial tone, but unbeknownst to him he is connected to someone who called him.

- Ground-Start Signaling—This signaling protocol differs from loop-start signaling, in that it provides positive recognition of connects and disconnects. Current-detection mechanisms are used at each end of the trunk, enabling end office switches to agree on which end is seizing the trunk before it is seized. This form of signaling minimizes the effect of glare and costs the same as loop-start signaling. As such, it is the preferred signaling method for PBXs.

CAS and CCS

CAS exists in many networks today. CAS systems carry signaling information from the trunk in the trunk itself. CAS systems were originally developed by different equipment vendors and, therefore, exist in many versions or variants. Today's telecommunication networks require more efficient means for signaling, however, so they are moving to common channel-type systems, such as CCS.

CCS uses a common link to carry signaling information for a number of trunks. This form of signaling is cheaper, has faster connect times, and is more flexible than CAS. The first generation of CCS is known as SS6; the second generation, SS7, is the basis of Chapter 4, "Signaling System 7."

E&M Signaling

E&M is a common trunk-signaling technique used on telephony switches and PBXs. The signaling and voice trunks in E&M are separated. In E&M, voice is transmitted over either two or four-wire circuits, with six methods for signaling. E&M signaling methods are referred to as Types I, II, III, IV, and V; they also are known by the British Telecom (BT) standard, SSDC5.

The remainder of this section focuses on four-wire E&M Types I through V. E&M lead conditions for off-hook and on-hook for Types I through V are summarized in Table 3-1.

Table 3-1   *E&M Signaling*

Type	M Lead		E Lead	
	Off-Hook	**On-Hook**	**Off-Hook**	**On-Hook**
I	Battery	Ground	Ground	Open
II	Battery	Open	Ground	Open
III	Loop current	Ground	Ground	Open
IV	Ground	Open	Ground	Open
V	Ground	Open	Ground	Open

Type I

With the Type I interface, the trunk equipment generates the E signal to the PBX by grounding the E lead (shown in Figure 3-1). The PBX detects the E signal by sensing the increase in current through a resistive load. Similarly, the PBX generates the M signal by sourcing a current to the trunk equipment, which detects it through a resistive load. The numbers 7, 2, 6, and 3 are the pinouts used on an RJ-48c connector.

Figure 3-1   *E&M Type I*

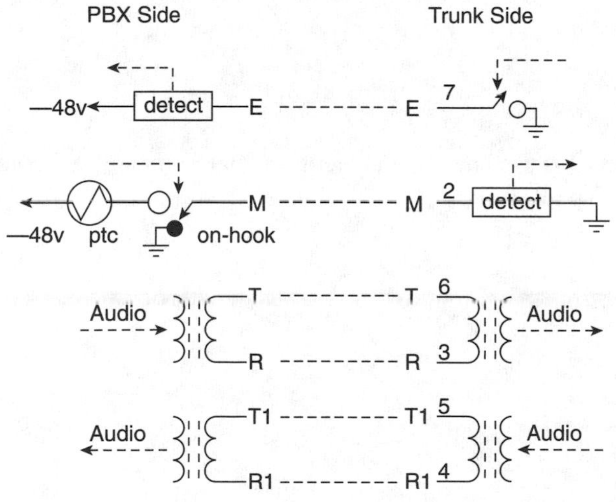

Type II

E&M Type II has two additional leads over Type I: signal battery (SB) and signal ground (SG). In this method, the E lead is paired up with the SG lead, and the M lead is paired up with the SB lead. An on-hook at the PBX end is indicated when the E and M leads are open. Alternatively, an off-hook is indicated when the E lead is grounded and the M lead is providing battery (see Figure 3-2).

Figure 3-2   *E&M Type II*

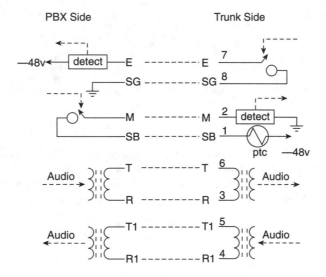

Type III

E&M Type III is used mostly in older telephone company switching centers. Figure 3-3 shows the Type III setup.

Figure 3-3   *E&M Type III*

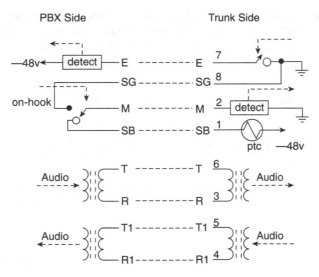

Type IV

E&M Type IV is similar to E&M Type II; however, from the PBX side, an on-hook occurs when the E and M leads are open, and an off-hook occurs when both leads are at ground (see Figure 3-4).

Figure 3-4   *E&M Type IV*

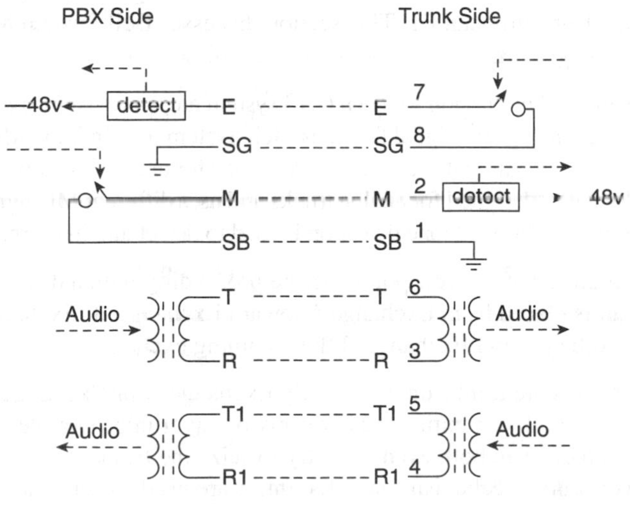

PBX Side   Trunk Side

Supervision signals operate slightly differently for analog and digital trunks.

Analog Trunks

A Single Frequency 2600 Hz tone is used to indicate trunk state between exchanges over analog facilities. This tone is applied in-band over the trunk and is turned off when a call is in progress or established. Therefore, the state is on-hook or idle when the tone is present and off-hook or in use when the tone is absent. The supervision signals for the Single Frequency method are illustrated in Figure 3-6.

Figure 3-6   *Forward and Backward Supervision Signals for a Call*

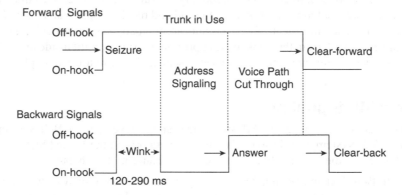

In Figure 3-6, assume that Switch A sends the forward signals and Switch B sends the backward signals. Switch A sends a forward seizure or off-hook signal to Switch B on a chosen trunk. Then, Switch B sends a backward wink or proceed-to-send to Switch A and waits for address signaling or dialed digits. After the digits are sent and the call is answered, Switch B sends a backward answer or off-hook to Switch A, enabling an end-to-end voice path.

In this case, the calling party hangs up first and a clear-forward is sent from Switch A to Switch B. When the called party hangs up, a clear-back signal is sent by Switch B.

Two important aspects of this signaling method need to be discussed:

- First, Bell System MF does not have backward signaling for connections that fail during setup. Therefore, the exchange where the call failed must connect an announcement server indicating to the calling party that a problem occurred.

   The signaling system then relies on the calling party to release or drop the call so that clear-forward procedures can be initiated.

- Second, no release guard-type signal exists, and timers are used after trunks are released. Therefore, after an exchange releases a trunk, it initiates a timer for approximately 1 second. After this timer expires, the exchange assumes that the trunk was released at the other end and is available for use.

Digital Trunks

The digital trunks most commonly used today are either T1 or E1 facilities (as described in the "Physical Layer—MTP L1" section of Chapter 4). With digital trunks, bits are robbed from specific frames and are used for signaling purposes. This discussion focuses on T1 digital trunks.

T1 has two types of framing formats: Super Frame (SF) and Extended Superframe (ESF). The least significant bits are robbed from frames 6 and 12 for SF and frames 6, 12, 18, and 24 for ESF. These bits are referred to as the Sa and Sb bits for SF, and the Sa, Sb, Sc, and Sd bits for ESF. Robbing these bits has a negligible effect on voice quality.

The SF signaling bits—Sa and Sb—are equal to each other and provide two-state, continuous supervision signaling. Bit values of zero are used to indicate on-hook, and bit values of 1 are used to indicate off-hook.

Address Signaling

Address signaling is used to indicate the called and calling number as well as to identify the start and end of the address information. In the Bell System MF method, address signals are a combination of two voice-band frequencies chosen from six different frequencies, as illustrated in Table 3-3.

Table 3-3   *Bell System MF Address Signals*

Signal	Frequencies in Hz
Digit 1	700 and 900
Digit 2	700 and 1100
Digit 3	900 and 1100
Digit 4	700 and 1300
Digit 5	900 and 1300
Digit 6	1100 and 1300
Digit 7	700 and 1500
Digit 8	900 and 1500
Digit 9	1100 and 1500
Digit 0	1300 and 1500
KP (start)	1100 and 1700
ST (end)	1500 and 1700

The address signaling sequence is initiated with a KP or start-of-pulsing signal and terminated with an ST or end-of-pulsing signal. Two important timing intervals exist:

The KP signal's duration is from 90 to 110 ms, and the ST signal's duration is from 61 to 75 ms. The silent interval between signals also is from 61 to 75 ms. Figure 3-7 demonstrates supervision and address signaling sequences.

Figure 3-7 *Supervision and Address Signaling Sequences*

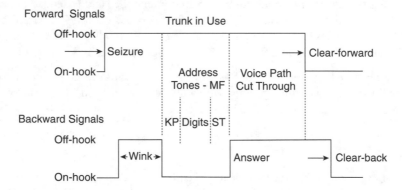

Address signaling uses two other key information digits. The codes in this information (or I bits) indicate the calling number or Automatic Number ID (ANI), as well as operator services (see Table 3-4).

Table 3-4 *Address Signaling Codes*

I-Codes	Information
I = 00	Calling number is available.
I = 02	Calling number is not available.
I = 06	Hotel room identification required.
I = 10	Test call.

The information codes are sent after the KP signal and before the called party number. I codes 02 and 06 identify that operator assistance is required to proceed with these calls.

CCITT No. 5 Signaling

The CCITT adopted the CCITT No. 5 signaling system in the 1960s for use in international networks. This signaling system is still used today, usually on long international trunks and, in some cases, over transoceanic and satellite links. This signaling system was designed to operate over analog trunks equipped with Time Assignment Speech Interpolation (TASI). TASI is similar to voice activity detection (VAD), in that it enables unused bandwidth (silences or pauses in speech) to be used for other phone conversations. Link-by-link and in-band signaling are used for both supervision and address signaling.

Supervision Signaling

Supervision signaling is accomplished by two frequencies, sent either individually or in combination. CCITT No. 5 uses compelled supervision signaling, whereby the signaling tone is left on until an acknowledgment is received.

The two in-band frequencies are f1, which equals 2400 Hz, and f2, which equals 2600 Hz. The combination of f1 and f2 produces a composite signal; these signals and frequencies are listed in Table 3-5.

Table 3-5   *CCITT No. 5 Supervision Signals*

Direction	Signal Type	Frequency
Forward	Seizure	f1
Backward	Proceed-to-send	f2
Backward	Answer	f1
Forward	Acknowledgment	f1
Backward	Clear-back	f2
Forward	Acknowledgment	f1
Forward	Clear-forward	f1 and f2
Backward	Release-guard	f1 and f2
Backward	Busy-flash	f2
Forward	Acknowledgment	f1
Forward	Forward-transfer	f2

Three new signals are introduced in Table 3-5: Release-guard, Busy-flash, and Forward-transfer.

- Release-guard—This signal is used by the incoming exchange to acknowledge a clear-forward from the outgoing exchange. It also indicates to the outgoing exchange that the trunk is now available for an incoming call.

- Busy-flash—This signal is used by the incoming exchange to indicate to the outgoing exchange that call setup cannot be extended toward the destination.

- Forward-transfer—This signal is used on calls for operator services.

Address Signaling

In CCITT No. 5, address signaling is based on the combination of two frequencies, as illustrated in Table 3-6. The address signaling sequence starts with KP1 for national numbers and KP2 for international numbers. Codes 11 and 12 are used to connect international operator services.

Table 3-6   *CCITT No. 5 Address Signals*

Signal	Frequencies in Hz
Digit 1	700 and 900
Digit 2	700 and 1100
Digit 3	900 and 1100
Digit 4	700 and 1300
Digit 5	900 and 1300
Digit 6	1100 and 1300
Digit 7	700 and 1500
Digit 8	900 and 1500
Digit 9	1100 and 1500
Digit 0	1300 and 1500
Code 11	700 and 1700
Code 12	900 and 1700
KP1	1100 and 1700
KP2	1300 and 1700
ST	1500 and 1700

R1

The CAS system known as R1 is available in the International Telecommunication Union Telecommunication Standardization Sector (ITU-T) Q.310 to Q.332 specifications. This signaling system is almost identical to Bell System MF signaling and, therefore, is not further discussed.

R2

R2 signaling is a CAS system developed in the 1960s that is still in use today in Europe, Latin America, Australia, and Asia. Originally known as multi-frequency code (MFC) signaling, R2 signaling exists in several country versions or variants and in an international version called CCITT-R2.

R2 signaling operates over two- or four-wire analog and digital trunks and does not operate over TASI-equipped trunks or satellite links. R2 signaling is more suitable for relatively short international trunks. One of the differentiating aspects of this system compared to R1 is its register or inter-register signaling.

This section focuses on supervision and inter-register signaling for CCITT-R2 and National R2 signaling systems.

Supervision Signaling on Analog Trunks

For the purposes of supervision signaling on analog trunks, this section covers operation over four-wire trunks. The transmission path is divided into two parts: a 300- to 3400 Hz voice-band and a 3825Hz narrow-band for signaling. In this method, filters separate the signaling tone from the voice path. This is considered out-of-band signaling, even though signaling is over the same facility.

CCITT-R2 uses the tone-on-idle signaling supervision method; National R2 uses pulse signaling.

CCITT-R2

This method is commonly used on one-way trunks, is tone-on-idle, and provides two-state signaling. The forward and backward signals and transition states are similar to Bell System MF signaling and are illustrated in Table 3-7.

Table 3-7   *CCITT-R2 Supervision Signals*

Direction	Signal Type	Transition
Forward	Seizure	Tone-on to tone-off
Forward	Clear-forward	Tone-off to tone-on
Backward	Answer	Tone-on to tone-off
Backward	Clear-back	Tone-off to tone-on
Backward	Release-guard	Tone-off to tone-on
Backward	Blocking	Tone-on to tone-off

National R2

National R2 signaling has many country variants. Most versions of National R2 use pulse out-of-band supervision signals, however. Examples of National R2 supervision signals are illustrated in Table 3-8.

Table 3-8 *Examples of National R2 Supervision Signals*

Direction	Signal Type	Pulse Duration in ms
Forward	Seizure	150
Forward	Clear-forward	600
Backward	Answer	150
Backward	Clear-back	600
Backward	Release-guard	600
Backward	Blocking	Continuous

Supervision Signaling on Digital Trunks

R2 signaling operates over E1 digital facilities (described in the "Physical Layer—MTP L1" section of Chapter 4). E1 has 32 time-slots, numbered TS0 to TS31, whereby TS1–TS15 and TS17–TS31 are used to carry voice encoded with pulse code modulation (PCM), or to carry 64 kbps data.

Sixteen consecutive frames are in the SF format, and they are numbered 0 to 15. TS16 in frame 0 is used for SF alignment, and TS16 in the remaining frames (1–15) is used for trunk signaling. Four status bits are used from TS16 for signaling. They are called a, b, c, and d.

In the case of CCITT-R2 signaling, only the a and b bits are used. The c and d bits are set to 0 and 1, respectively. An idle state is denoted when a and b are equal to 1 and 0. Signaling is continuous. For two-way trunks, the supervision roles for forward and backward signaling vary on a call-by-call basis. Table 3-9 illustrates the R2 supervision signal, transition, and direction used on digital trunks.

Table 3-9 *R2 Supervision Signaling on Digital Trunks*

Direction	Signal Type	Transition
Forward	Seizure	a,b: 1,0 to 0,0
Forward	Clear-forward	a,b: 0,0 to 1,0
Backward	Seizure acknowledgment	a,b: 1,0 to 1,1
Backward	Answer	a,b: 1,1 to 0,1

continues

Table 3-9   *R2 Supervision Signaling on Digital Trunks (Continued)*

Direction	Signal Type	Transition
Backward	Clear-back	a,b: 0,1 to 1,1
Backward	Release-guard	a,b: 0,1 to 1,0

Inter-Register Signaling

The concept of address signaling in R2 is slightly different from that used in the other CAS systems previously discussed. In the case of R2, the exchanges are considered registers, and the signaling between these exchanges is called inter-register signaling. *Inter-register signaling* uses forward and backward in-band MF signals to transfer called and calling party numbers as well as the calling party category.

In this case, signaling is compelled because the registers in the outgoing and incoming exchanges hold the signal until an acknowledgment is received. The signals consist of two voice-band frequencies and are listed in Table 3-10.

Table 3-10   *CCITT-R2 and National R2 Inter-Register Signal Frequencies*

Signal	Forward Frequency in Hz	Backward Frequency in Hz
Digit 1	1380 and 1500	1140 and 1020
Digit 2	1380 and 1620	1140 and 900
Digit 3	1500 and 1620	1020 and 900
Digit 4	1380 and 1740	1140 and 780
Digit 5	1500 and 1740	1020 and 780
Digit 6	1620 and 1740	900 and 780
Digit 7	1380 and 1860	1140 and 660
Digit 8	1500 and 1860	1020 and 660
Digit 9	1620 and 1860	900 and 660
Digit 0	1740 and 1860	780 and 660
Not used	1380 and 1980	1140 and 540
Not used	1500 and 1980	1020 and 540
Not used	1620 and 1980	900 and 540
Not used	1740 and 1980	780 and 540
End of #	1860 and 1980	660 and 540

Groups for Inter-Register Signaling

In R2 signaling, the forward and backward signals can have different meanings depending on which group is used. Three groups of forward signals and two groups of backward signals exist. The forward groups are I, II, and III, and the backward groups are A and B.

- Group I—These forward signals represent the called party number or dialed digits.
- Group II—These forward signals identify the calling party category.
- Group III—These forward signals represent the digits of the calling party number.
- Group A—These backward signals indicate if the signaling ended or if a particular forward signal is required.
- Group B—These backward signals are sent by the terminating switch to acknowledge a forward signal, or to provide call charging and called party information.

The following inter-register group sequence rules are used to identify the signal's group:

- The initial signal received by the incoming exchange is a Group I signal.
- Outgoing exchanges consider backward signals as Group A signals.
- Group A signals received by outgoing exchanges are used to identify whether the next signal is a Group B signal.
- Group B signals always indicate an end-of-signaling sequence.

Feature Support

The end-to-end information and status that National R2 signaling provides enable support for several features. These features include free calls, called party hold, malicious call tracing, and release on failed connections.

ISDN

ISDN has been available to the public since the 1980s. International Telecommunication Union (ITU; formerly CCITT) I series recommendations define the international standards for ISDN. This subscriber or user-based interface protocol provides single access to multiple services.

ISDN signaling is compatible with SS7 and inter-works with the ISDN User Part (ISUP) protocol. This inter-working enables ISDN subscribers to access the same services and intelligence as they can on the SS7 network. ISDN also enables PBXs to connect over the PSTN and create VPNs. This is accomplished by delivering PBX signaling over the network to distant PBXs.

The ISDN suite defines the specifications for access to the network. The following list outlines some ISDN functions and capabilities:

- ISDN provides circuit-based (voice and data) communications and packet-based communications to its users.
- Many new services can be extended to users.
- ISDN includes two access methods: Basic Rate Interface (BRI) and Primary Rate Interface (PRI).
- ISDN includes single access for PSTN, Direct-Inward-Dial (DID), Direct-Outward-Dial (DOD), 800, Foreign Exchange (FX), tie-lines, packet-switched data, circuit-switched data, and dedicated data.
- ISDN is capable of adding additional channels for high-speed data communications.
- ISDN is capable of transmitting voice and data on the same facility.
- ISDN uses separate channels for signaling.
- ISDN signaling is compatible with SS7.
- ISDN enables the creation of VPNs.

ISDN Services

The following communication services are available in circuit-switched ISDN networks:

- Bearer Services—Three types of bearer services are available for a call. They include speech, 3.1 kHz audio (for modem data), and 64 kbps digital data.

  Bearer services are specified by the calling user in the call setup message and are transferred over the network to the called user. The exchanges within the network also use this information when selecting the appropriate outgoing trunk. In the case of speech, exchanges can use analog or digital trunks for interconnection, whereas 64 kbps digital data requires digital trunks.

- Teleservice—This service enables the calling user to specify the type of data service for 3.1 kHz audio and 64 kbps digital data. The teleservice information (fax, telex, and so on) is transmitted transparently across the network to the called user. The called user processes the information to select the appropriate terminal equipment (TE) function to terminate the incoming call.

- Supplementary Services—The ISDN service offering also provides many supplementary services. These services also are typically found on PBXs and virtual private voice networks. The following are examples of supplementary services: calling line identification (caller ID), closed users groups, call waiting, user-to-user signaling, advice of charge, call forward, and call hold. When a user requests these services, supplementary service messages are sent to the network to invoke the requested processes. In the case of user-to-user signaling, the two ISDN users send signaling information transparently during the call setup and teardown parts of the call.

ISDN Access Interfaces

Before discussing ISDN access methods, it is important to cover the concept of B and D channels:

- B Channel—The B channel is a 64 kbps channel that carries user information streams. No signaling information is carried in the B channel. B-channel user streams include speech encoded at 64 kbps according to ITU G.711, data at or less than 64 kbps, and voice encoded at lower bit rates.

- D Channel—The D channel is used primarily to carry signaling for circuit switching by ISDN networks. D-channel bit rates are different depending on the access method. The D channel also is capable of transmitting user packet data up to 9.6 kbps.

Two types of access methods exist for ISDN:

- BRI
- PRI

BRI

BRI delivers two bi-directional 64 kbps B channels and one bi-directional 16 kbps D channel over standard two-wire telephone lines. Basic rate ISDN service typically is used for residential and small office, home office (SOHO) applications. Each B channel can transmit speech or data; the D channel transmits the signaling or call control messages.

The configuration and reference points for BRI are specified in Figure 3-8.

Figure 3-8 *ISDN BRI Reference Points*

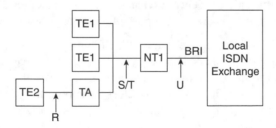

The reference configuration for ISDN is defined in the ITU specification I.411. The reference points specify the transmission medium, interface, and connectors (if used).

- U Reference Point—The U reference point specifies the transmission characteristics of the local loop. For BRI, this two-wire interface operates at 160 kbps (2B + D + 16 kbps for overhead) over standard copper-twisted wires.

- S/T Reference Point—For basic rate access, this interface provides a four-wire connection to ISDN-compatible terminals or terminal adapters. The interface operates at 144 kbps (2B + D) between the ISDN device and the network termination device. You can connect up to eight ISDN devices to the S/T interface.

- R Reference Point—The R reference point provides connection for non-ISDN devices. Such devices connect to the terminal adapter using interfaces such as RS-232 and V.35.

This reference configuration also specifies the set of functions required to access ISDN networks:

— Network Termination 1 (NT1)—Outside the United States, NT1 is on the network side of the defined user-network interface and is considered part of the service provider network. NT1s terminate the two-wire local loop and provide four-wire S/T bus for ISDN terminal equipment (TE).

— TE1—TE1s are ISDN-compatible devices that connect directly to the S/T connector on the NT1.

— TE2—TE2s are non-ISDN compatible devices that require terminal adapter (TA) interconnection.

— TA—TAs provide an ISDN-compliant interface to NT1s and standard interfaces for TE2s. These standard interfaces include RS-232, V.35, RS-449, and X.21.

PRI

PRI corresponds to two primary rates: 1.544 Mbps (T1) and 2.048 Mbps (E1). PRIs typically are used in medium to large business applications. PRI is comprised of B channels and one 64 kbps D channel. The interface structure for T1 is 23B + D (North America and Japan). The interface structure for E1 is 30B + D (Europe).

The configuration and references for PRI are specified in Figure 3-9.

Figure 3-9   *ISDN PRI Reference Points*

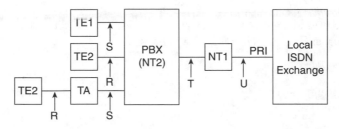

The configuration and reference points for PRI are similar to those for BRI. The differences between the two reference models are discussed here.

- U Reference Point—For PRI, the U interface is four-wire and operates at either T1 (1.544 Mbps) or E1 (2.048 Mbps) PRI rates.

- T Reference Point—For PRI, the T interface provides access to the Network Termination 2 (NT2) device.

- NT2—PBX equipment can provide such NT2 functions as Layer 2 (L2) and Layer 3 (L3) protocol handling as well as multiplexing, switching, interface termination, and maintenance. NT2s also can provide connections to ISDN-compatible TE1s and non-ISDN compatible TE2s.

ISDN L2 and L3 Protocols

ISDN user-network interface L2 and L3 specifications also are referred to as Digital Subscriber Signaling System No. 1 (DSS1). L2 provides error-free and secure connections for two endpoints across the ISDN reference configuration. L3 provides the mechanism for call establishment, control, and access to services. The L2 protocol for ISDN is Q.920/921, and the L3 protocol is Q.930/931. Q.932 enables general procedures for accessing and controlling supplementary services.

The specifications for L2 are referred to as Link Access Procedures on the D channel (LAPD). This protocol provides the reliable transfer of frames between the local exchange and the TE. The specifications for Q.920 and Q.921 are extensive and are available from the Q series of ITU recommendations.

The specifications for L3 define the messages that pass between the local exchange and the TE. These messages are used for call setup, call supervision, call teardown, and supplementary services. The next section discusses the specifics of ISDN messaging.

Q.931 Call Control Messages

The message structure and signaling elements of Q.931 are used in ISDN networks to provide call control capabilities. Q.931 messages are sent from the network to the user and from the user to the network. They are referred to as user-network and network-user messages, as illustrated in Tables 3-11 and 3-12.

Some of the most important Q.931 messages are listed in Table 3-11. The message type field in the general format of the Q.931 message is used to determine the type of message being sent.

Table 3-11   *Q.931 Messages and Type Codes*

Q.931 Message Type	Message Type Value
Setup message (SETUP)	00000101
Setup acknowledgment message (SETACK)	00001101
Call proceeding message (CALPRC)	00000010
Progress message (PROG)	00001111
Alerting message (ALERT)	00000011
Connect message (CONN)	00000101
Connect acknowledgment message (CONACK)	00000111
Disconnect message (DISC)	01000101
Release message (RLSE)	01001101
Release complete message (RLCOM)	01011010
Information message (INFO)	01111011

Source: ITU-T Q.931 3/93

The information or signaling elements of each message type are listed in Table 3-12. Table 3-12 also indicates the mandatory (M) and optional (O) fields for each network-to-user message.

Table 3-12   *User to Network—Information Elements in Q.931 Messages*

Information Elements	SETUP	CALPC	ALERT	CONN	CONAK	DISC	RLSE	RLCOM	INFO
Bearer Capability	M								
Called party number	M								
Calling party number	O								
Called party subaddress	O								
Calling party subaddress	O								
Cause						M	O	O	

continues

Figure 3-11 *Reference Model for Corporate Networks*

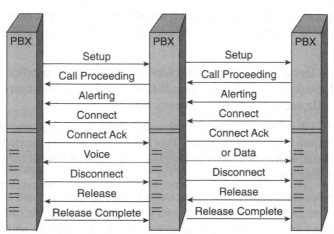

The T reference point defines access to the NT2 device for ISDN PRI. The C reference point is the physical interconnection point to the PBX. It is compatible with many interfaces, including two- and four-wire analog, BRI, PRI, and radio and satellite links. The Q reference point specifies the logical signaling point between two PBXs. This reference point is used to specify signaling-system and related protocols.

QSIG Protocol Stack

The QSIG protocol stack specifies a signaling system at reference point Q and is illustrated in Table 3-14. QSIG has an identical structure to that of ISDN, and at L1 and L2, these protocols can be the same. They differ at L3, however, where QSIG is split into the following three sublayers:

- QSIG BC—With this symmetrical protocol, the interfaces and messages for the user and network sides are identical. The messages and sequences of this protocol are more easily understood and demonstrated in the example at the end of this section.

- QSIG GF—This protocol specifies the control entities for supplementary services and ANFs. This protocol does not have the capability to control these services, but it does provide the generic layer capabilities to enable them. The protocol provides a connection-oriented and connectionless mechanism between the application entities of different PBXs.

- QSIG Supplementary Service and ANF Protocols—These define the procedures for individual or specific services and features. These services and ANFs are defined and detailed in separate specifications. Such organizations as the European Computer Manufacturers Association (ECMA) and the European Telecommunication Standards Institute (ETSI) are developing these protocol standards.

Table 3-14   *QSIG Protocol Stack*

OSI Reference	QSIG Protocol	QSIG Standard
L1	None	Based on interface being used
L2	None	Identical to ISDN L2 (LAPD)
L3	QSIG BC	ECMA 142/143; ETS300* 171/172
	QSIG GF	ECMA 165; ETS300 239
	QSIG protocols for supplementary services	Separate specifications, such as call forward (ECMA 173/174, ETS300 256/257) and call transfer (ECMA 177/178, ETS300 260/261)
L4–L7	Application-based service elements	Transparent to the network

*ETS300 is an ETSI-based standard.

QSIG Basic Call Setup and Teardown Example

The QSIG BC protocol provides the basic capabilities for call setup and teardown. This protocol extends the ISDN access protocol for use in a corporate network or private ISDN. QSIG BC is a symmetrical protocol whereby both the network and user sides of the interface are identical. The message sequence for a basic call is demonstrated in Figure 3-12. The QSIG BC messages are functionally similar to the messages discussed in the "ISDN" section of this chapter.

Figure 3-12 *QSIG BC Message Sequence*

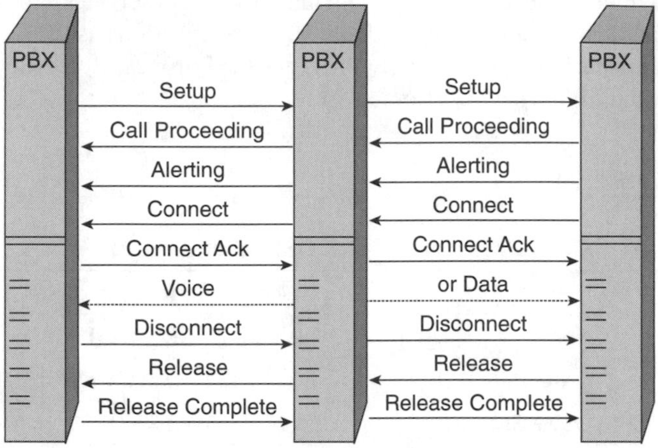

DPNSS

BT and a group of PBX vendors developed DPNSS in the 1980s. They designed this open standard to provide digital private networks at a time when ISDN and QSIG standards were still being defined.

DPNSS has rich services and feature sets and provided the basis for much of the work on the QSIG protocols. Also, interoperability between DPNSS and the QSIG signaling system is specified as part of the inter-working of both protocols.

The ISDN and QSIG protocols became more popular since they were developed, and DPNSS is not as widely used in today's private networks. DPNSS specifications are available from BT Plc and are defined in the following four documents:

- BTNR 188—DPNSS1
- BTNR 188-T—DPNSS1 testing schedule
- BTNR 189—Inter-working between DPNSS1 and other signaling systems
- BTNR 189-I—Inter-working between DPNSS1 and ISDN signaling systems

Summary

The signaling systems discussed in this chapter are wide in scope and exist in many versions. It will take some time before Voice over IP (VoIP) systems fully support all these protocols and their variations. Also, standards bodies such as the Internet Engineering Task

CHAPTER 4

Signaling System 7

Signaling System 7 (SS7) is a common-channel signaling standard developed in the late 1970s by the International Telecommunication Union Telecommunication Standardization Sector (ITU-T), formerly known as the Consultative Committee for International Telegraph and Telephone (CCITT). SS7 was derived from SS6, which was developed in the late 1960s and was the first generation of common-channel signaling. SS7 was initially designed for telephony call-control applications. SS7 applications have greatly expanded since they were first developed, however, and today's SS7 functionality includes database queries, transactions, network operations, and Integrated Services Digital Network (ISDN).

SS7 is used to perform out-of-band signaling in the Public Switched Telephone Network (PSTN). SS7 signaling supports the PSTN by handling call establishment, exchange of information, routing, operations, billing, and support for Intelligent Network (IN) services.

The SS7 protocol is important to Voice over IP (VoIP) and the way it inter-works with the PSTN. This inter-working is critical to the acceptance and, ultimately, the success of VoIP solutions in today's telephone network. Inter-working with a 100-year-old voice infrastructure is not a simple task, and it is naive to think that this is an easy problem to solve. SS7 does provide a common protocol for signaling, messaging, and interfacing for which you can develop VoIP-type devices, however.

SS7's objective was to provide a worldwide standard for telephony network signaling. This did not occur, and many national variants were developed, such as the American National Standards Institute (ANSI) and Bell Communications Research (Bellcore) standards used in North America as well as the European Telecommunication Standards Institute (ETSI) standards used in Europe.

This chapter focuses on the ITU-T-defined standards for SS7 and covers the following aspects:

- SS7 Network Elements and Links
- SS7 Protocol Suite and Messages
- SS7 Examples and Call-flows

The following steps help explain the functions an SSP uses to complete a call. In this case, assume that the originating and destination SSPs are directly attached, as illustrated in Figure 4-2:

1 The SSP uses the called number from the calling party or routing number from the database query to begin circuit connection signaling messages.

2 Then the SSP uses its routing table to determine the trunk group and circuit needed to connect the call.

3 At this point, a signaling setup message is sent to the destination SSP requesting a connection on the circuit specified by the originating SSP.

4 The destination SSP responds with an acknowledgment granting permission to connect to the specified trunk and proceeds to connect the call to the final destination.

STP

STPs, as illustrated in Figure 4-2, are an integral part of the SS7 architecture providing access to the network. STPs route or switch all the signaling messages in the network based on the routing information and destination point code address contained in the message.

The STP provides the logical connectivity between SSPs without requiring direct SSP-to-SSP links. STPs are configured in pairs and are mated to provide redundancy and higher availability. These mated STPs perform identical functions and are considered the home STPs for the directly connected SSP or SCP. The STP also is capable of performing global title translation, which is discussed later in this section.

Circuit-based messages are created on the SSP. Then, they are packetized in SS7 packets and sent from the SSP. Usually they contain requests to connect or disconnect a call. These packets are forwarded to the destination SSP where the call is terminated. It is the STP network's job to properly route such packets to the destination.

Non-circuit based messages that originate from an SSP are database queries requesting additional information needed to complete the call. These packets are forwarded to the destination SCP and are addressed to the appropriate subsystem database. The SCP is the interface to the database that provides the routing number required to complete the call.

STPs also measure traffic and usage. Traffic measurements provide statistics such as network events and message types, and usage measurements provide statistics on the access and number of messages per message type.

Global Title Translation

In addition to performing basic SS7 packet routing, STPs are capable of performing gateway services such as *global title translation*. This function is used to centralize the SCP and database selection versus distributing all possible destination selections to hundreds or thousands of distributed switches. If the SSP is unaware of the destination SCP address, it can send the database query to its local STP. The STP then performs global title translation and re-addresses the destination of the database query to the appropriate SCP.

Global title translation centralizes the selection of the correct database by enabling queries to be addressed directly to the STP. SSPs, therefore, do not have the burden of maintaining every potential destination database address. The term *global title translation* is taken from the term *global title digits*, which is another term for *dialed digits*.

The STP looks at the global dialed digits and through its own translation table to resolve the following:

- The point code address of the appropriate SCP for the database
- The subsystem number of the database

The STP also can perform an intermediate global title translation by using its translation table to find another STP. The intermediate STP then routes the message to the other STP to perform the final global title translation.

STP Hierarchy

STP hierarchy defines network interconnection and separates capabilities into specific areas of functionality. STP implementation can occur in multiple levels, such as:

- Local Signal Transfer Point
- Regional Signal Transfer Point
- National Signal Transfer Point
- International Signal Transfer Point
- Gateway Signal Transfer Point

The local, regional, and national STPs transfer standards-based SS7 messages within the same network. These STPs usually are not capable of converting or handling messages in different formats or versions.

International STPs provide international connectivity where the same International Telecommunication Union (ITU) standards are deployed in both networks.

Gateway STPs can provide the following:

- Protocol conversion from national versions to the ITU standard
- Network-to-network interconnection points
- Network security features such as screening, which is used to examine all incoming and outgoing messages to ensure authorization

You can deploy and install STP functions on separate dedicated devices or incorporate them with other SSP functions onto a single end office or *tandem switch*. Integrating SSP and

STP functions is particularly common in Europe and Australia. This is why fully associated SS7 or CCS7 (CCS7 is the ITU-T version of SS7) networks are prevalent in those areas. *Fully associated SS7* occurs when the same transmission channel carries the bearer's information and the signaling information.

SCP

The SCP, as shown in Figure 4-2, provides the interface to the database where additional routing information is stored for non-circuit based messages. Service-provider SCPs do not house the required information; they do, however, provide the interface to the system's database. The interface between the SCP and the database system is accomplished by a standard protocol, which is typically X.25. The SCP provides the conversion between the SS7 and the X.25 protocol. If X.25 is not the database access protocol, the SCP still provides the capability for communication through the use of primitives.

The database stores information related to its application and is addressed by a subsystem number, which is unique for each database. The subsystem number is known at the SSP level; the request originated within the PSTN contains that identifier. The subsystem number identifies the database where the information is stored and is used by the SCP to respond to the request.

The following databases are the most common in the SS7 network:

- 800 Database—Provides the routing information for special numbers, such as 800, 888, and 900 numbers. The 800 database responds to the special number queries with the corresponding routing number. In the case of 800, 888, and 900 numbers, the routing number is the actual telephone number at the terminating end.

- Line Information Database (LIDB)—Provides subscriber or user information such as screening and barring, calling-card services including card validation and personal identification number (PIN) authentication, and billing. The billing features of this database determine ways you can bill collect calls, calling-card calls, and third-party services.

- Local Number Portability Database (LNPDB)—Provides the 10-digit Location Routing Number (LRN) of the switch that serves the dialed-party number. The LRN is used to route the call through the network, and the dialed-party number is used to complete the call at the terminating SSP.

- Home Location Register (HLR)—Used in cellular networks to store information such as current cellular phone location, billing, and cellular subscriber information.

- Visitor Location Register (VLR)—Used in cellular networks to store information on subscribers roaming outside the home network. The VLR uses this information to communicate to the HLR database to identify the subscriber's location when roaming.

Signaling Links

All signaling points in the SS7 network are connected by signaling links. These full-duplex links simultaneously transmit and receive SS7 messages over the network link. The signaling links are typically 56- and 64 kbps data network facilities, either on standalone lines or extracted on channelized facilities such as structured E1 trunks.

This section covers the following topics:

- Signaling Modes
- Signaling Links and Linksets
- Signaling Routes
- Signaling Link Performance

Signaling Modes

The SS7 network has three modes of signaling:

- Associated Signaling
- Nonassociated Signaling
- Quasi-associated Signaling

Associated signaling, illustrated in Figure 4-3, is the simplest form of signaling, in that the signaling and voice paths are directly connected between the two signaling endpoints. This is not common in North America because end office switches require direct connections to all other end office switches; however, associated signaling is common in Europe, where the signaling path is actually derived within the E1 trunk facilities.

Figure 4-3   *Associated Signaling*

Nonassociated signaling uses a separate logical path for signaling and voice. As illustrated in Figure 4-4, the signaling messages travel through multiple endpoints before reaching the final destination. Alternatively, the voice path can have a direct path to the destination end office switch. Nonassociated signaling is the most common form of signaling in the SS7 network.

- F-links are used to directly interconnect two signaling endpoints, as illustrated in Figure 4-6. These links are used when STPs are not available or when high traffic volumes exist. This is the only link type whose signaling traffic is allowed to follow the same path as the voice circuits. The signaling messages between the two signaling endpoints are associated only with the voice circuits directly connected between the two signaling endpoints. This method is not commonly used in North America; it is common in Europe, however.

Signaling links are grouped together into *linksets* when the links are connected to the same endpoint. Signaling endpoints provide load sharing across all the links in a linkset. *Combined linksets* are used when connecting to mated STP pairs with different point code addresses. In this case, links are assigned to different linksets and are configured as a single combined linkset.

Load sharing across combined linksets occurs when signaling endpoints re-address the messages to adjacent point codes. You can configure alternate linksets to provide redundant paths, increasing reliability over other signaling links such as E- and F-links, as described later in this section.

Signaling Routes

Signaling endpoints have statically predefined routes for destination endpoints. The route is made up of linksets; linksets can be part of more than one route. Groups of routes are called *routesets* and are defined in routing tables to provide alternate routes when the current route is unavailable.

Signaling Link Performance

The availability of signaling in the SS7 network is critical to connect and serve telephone network users. Signaling links provide signaling transmission and access to the SS7 network and, therefore, must be available at all times. If congestion or failure occurs in the network, the links and STP pairs must handle the additional traffic. The STP mated pairs and linkset configurations provide the necessary load sharing and redundancy required to maintain SS7 network reliability.

SS7 Protocol Overview

The SS7 protocol stack and levels differ slightly from the Open Systems Interconnection (OSI) reference model discussed in Chapter 7, "IP Tutorial." A comparison between SS7 protocol levels and the layers of the OSI model is illustrated in Figure 4-8. As you can see, the SS7 protocol has only four levels, and the OSI model has seven. SS7 Levels 1–3 (L1–L3) are identical to OSI L1–L3, and SS7 Level 4 (L4) corresponds to OSI L4–Level 7 (L7).

Figure 4-8   *SS7 Protocol Stack Versus the OSI Model*

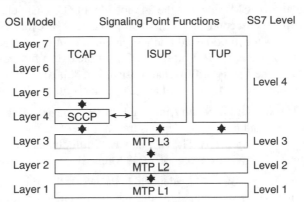

The following sections cover the suite of SS7 protocols identified in Figure 4-8:

- Message Transfer Part (MTP) L1, L2, and L3 provide the transport protocols for all other SS7 protocols. MTP functionality includes network interface specifications, reliable transfer of information, and message handling and routing.

- Signaling Connection Control Part (SCCP) provides end-to-end addressing and routing for L4 protocols such as transaction capabilities application part (TCAP).

- Telephone User Part (TUP) primarily is a link-by-link signaling system used to connect telephone or speech calls as well as facsimile calls.

- ISDN User Part (ISUP) is a circuit-based protocol used to establish and maintain connections for voice and data calls.

- TCAP provides access to remote databases for routing information and enables features in remote network entities.

Physical Layer—MTP L1

The physical layer (L1) of the MTP defines the physical and electrical characteristics of the signaling link. Also called MTP1, this SS7 protocol layer is virtually identical to OSI L1 and does not specify any particular interface. The following list provides some examples of possible MTP1 network interfaces available in networks today:

- T1—The standard in North America, Australia, Hong Kong, and Japan for digital transmission of voice, data, and images. T1 (also known as *DS1*) signals transmit over two pairs of twisted wires with a capacity of 1.544 Mbps. The T1 link has 24 full duplex channels or digital signal level 0s (DS-0s), each consisting of 64 kbps. The payload yields a total of 1.536 Mbps, with the remaining 8 kbps used for framing the T1 link.

- DS-0—The standard speed for digitizing one voice conversation using pulse code modulation (PCM). Each of the 24 individual DS-0 channels is sampled at a rate of 8000 times per second, producing an 8-bit value (1 bit every 125 ms). The 24-channel, 8-bit values are multiplexed into a serial bit stream using time-division multiplexing (TDM) to generate a 192-bit frame. One of the 8kbps framing bits is added as the 193rd bit. The result is a T1 signal consisting of 8000 frames per second, whereby each frame contains one framing bit and 24 channels of 8-bit samples.

- E1—The standard in South America, Europe, and Mexico for digital transmission of voice, data, and images. E1 signals transmit over two pairs of twisted wire with a capacity of 2.048 Mbps. The E1 link has 32 full duplex channels, each consisting of 64 kbps, which yields a total of 2.048 Mbps.

  E1 is made up of 30 DS-0s (identical to the DS-0s found in T1) for voice and data, plus one channel for signaling and one channel for framing.

- 56/64 kbps—The 56- and 64 kbps channels in T1 and E1 systems are DS-0s. The 56- and 64 kbps interface rates are the most commonly used physical interfaces in the SS7 network.

- V.35—The ITU standard for interfacing between a digital service unit (DSU) and a packet/data device. The V.35 interface has defined pin and electrical configurations for a 37-pin connector.

Data Layer—MTP L2

The data layer (L2) of the SS7 protocol is MTP L2, also called MTP2. The MTP2 protocol is used to create reliable point-to-point links between endpoints in a network. MTP2 does not run across the network and, therefore, is not concerned with the final destination of the message. MTP2 has the following mechanisms:

- Error Detection and Correction—Used to maintain data integrity during transmission. The error detection mechanism in MTP2 is provided by cyclic redundancy check (CRC)-16. If CRC-16 detects errors, MTP2 must request a retransmission.

- Sequencing of Packets—Used to identify lost messages during transmission. If lost messages are detected, MTP2 must request a retransmission. Most protocols have a unique message structure to indicate retransmissions. The message structure in SS7 enables the identification of retransmissions in any message. Retransmission requests can be accompanied with the user data of the next message. The user data in a retransmission message can be from another L4 application (that is, SCCP, ISUP, TUP, or TCAP).

- Link Status Indicators—Used to maintain and monitor signaling links as well as monitor remote processor outages.

The MTP2 protocol uses packets called *signal units* to transmit SS7 messages. The signal units are used in the SS7 network to perform error detection, indicate link status, and transfer information messages. Three types of signal units provide MTP2's data layer functions:

- Fill-in Signal Unit (FISU)—Provides link error detection in the SS7 network. As its name signifies, the FISU packets fill in when no traffic is being sent on the network. This enables you to monitor the link at all times, even when no traffic is on the network.

- Link Status Signal Unit (LSSU)—Provides link status on the link between two directly connected signaling elements.

- Message Signal Unit (MSU)—Provides the structure to carry the information messages in the SS7 network. These information messages carry the payload for higher-level messages such as SCCP, TUP, ISUP, and TCAP.

The following sections further discuss these signal units and the role they play in the SS7 network.

FISU

FISUs constantly are transmitted on the signaling links when the LSSU and MSUs are not present. FISUs are sent only between signaling points and are not sent across the SS7 network. The FISU provides error-detection capabilities to the signaling points at both ends of the link. This enables the signaling points to perform error detection to verify link integrity and maintain reliability in the SS7 network.

If the signaling endpoints receive an FISU with errors, the signal unit is discarded. Retransmission of FISUs is not required, as these signal units do not provide any L4 or user information. FISU fields are illustrated in Figure 4-9.

Figure 4-9 *Fill-In Signal Unit Fields*

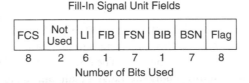

Fill-In Signal Unit Fields

FCS	Not Used	LI	FIB	FSN	BIB	BSN	Flag
8	2	6	1	7	1	7	8

Number of Bits Used

The following list describes the FISU fields (these also are common to the LSSU and MSU):

- The frame check sequence (FCS) is the most important field in the FISU. You use this field to verify the integrity of the link between two adjacent signaling elements. MTP Layer 3 (MTP3) uses the bits in the FCS field to determine whether any errors occurred in the FISU, the LSSU, and the MSU. These bits perform error detection using the CRC-16 mechanism. The originating endpoint calculates FCS bit values

MSU

The MSU provides the structure for transmitting circuit- and non-circuit based messages in the SS7 network. You use circuit-based messages to set up, manage, and release telephone calls. Non-circuit based messages refer to queries for additional routing information and network management data. MSUs originate from MTP3 or from an MTP3 user. MTP3 users include SCCP, ISUP, TUP, and TCAP. These user messages are transferred between two peer L4 protocols in signaling endpoints.

In the case of ISUP, the two endpoints transfer ISUP messages over the SS7 network. An MSU with a routing label carries the ISUP information. The routing label contains the point code addresses of the originating endpoint and destination endpoint.

The originating endpoint passes the ISUP information to MTP3. MTP3 expands the MTP3 message and passes the message to MTP2. MTP2 expands the MTP3 message in an MSU. At this point, the MSU is passed to MTP1 for transmission across the signaling link. The destination endpoint receives the MTP1 message and MTP2 extracts the MTP3 message. The L4 protocol or user data is identified and the message is passed to the ISUP process of the destination endpoint.

The MSU has the same fields as the FISU, with the addition of the SIO and SIF, as illustrated in Figure 4-11.

Figure 4-11 *MSU Fields*

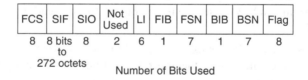

The new MSU fields are defined as follows:

- The SIO identifies the protocol type, such as SCCP, ISUP, TUP, and TCAP, present in the MSU. It also identifies the version of the SS7 protocol. The SIO is an 8-bit (1-octet) value that is broken into two parts: a 4-bit subservice field and a 4-bit service indicator field.

    The 4-bit subservice field identifies the protocol version (national or international) and the MSU priority. The MSU priority bits have four possible options, ranging from a lowest-priority value of 0 to a highest-priority value of 3.

The 4-bit service indicator specifies the MTP3 user or L4 protocol, as indicated in Table 4-1.

Table 4-1   *Service Indicator*

MTP User	Service Indicator Value
Signaling Network Management (SNM) Message	0
Maintenance (MTN) Regular Message	1
Maintenance Special (MTNS) Message	2
SCCP	3
TUP	4
ISUP	5
Data User Part (DUP)—circuit-based messages	6
DUP—facility messages	7

- The Service Information Field (SIF) contains the routing label and control information from upper-level protocols (that is, SCCP, ISUP, TUP, TCAP, or network management). It has a maximum length of 272 octets. Routing labels route the MSU through the network to its final destination and are discussed in the next section. The remaining part of the SIF carries the user message or control data of the higher-level protocols.

Network Layer—MTP3

The network layer of the SS7 protocol is called MTP3. The MTP3 protocol routes SS7 messages and relies on the delivery of messages from MTP2. MTP3 also uses primitives to communicate to L4 protocols such as SCCP, ISUP, TUP, and TCAP as well as to pass and receive information from MTP2.

The MTP3 protocol is divided into two main functions:

- Signaling Message Handling (SMH)—Routes SS7 messages during normal conditions.
- SNM—Reroutes link traffic during network failure conditions.

This section first analyzes the message format of the MTP3 layer and then studies the SMH and SNM processes and functions.

Message Format

The MTP3 message consists of the SIO and SIF. As previously discussed, the SIO identifies the user or protocol type (SCCP, TUP, ISUP, or TCAP) and the version of the SS7 protocol (national or international). The SIF is divided into two parts: the routing label, and the user or L4 message. The user message contains the control information of the upper-level protocols, which are discussed in more detail in the SCCP, ISUP, and TCAP sections of this chapter.

The signaling endpoint MTP3 processes use the routing label (RL) to determine the destination address. The RL contains the Destination Point Code (DPC), Originating Point Code (OPC), and Signaling Link Selector (SLS) fields, as illustrated in Figure 4-12.

Figure 4-12 *MTP3 Message Format*

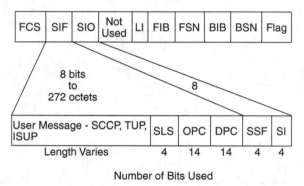

The following list describes the fields in the RL:

- The DPC identifies the point code or address of the destination endpoint and has an address space of 14 bits.

- The OPC identifies the point code or address of the originating endpoint and has an address space of 14 bits.

NOTE   You can provision signaling endpoints with more than one point code address.

- The SLS value identifies the signaling link to which the message is to be routed. MTP users or L4 protocols (SCCP, ISUP, TUP, and TCAP) assign the 4-bit SLS value to each outgoing message. Signaling endpoints use these pre-assigned values to route messages over the appropriate links.

SMH

The SMH function routes SS7 messages during normal conditions. SMH identifies whether the destination address is the receiving endpoint or whether the message needs to be routed.

If the destination address is the receiving endpoint, SMH also identifies the user application (SCCP, ISUP, TUP, or TCAP). If the message needs to be forwarded, SMH identifies the link to which the message is to be forwarded.

The SMH is divided into three processes:

- SMH Message Discrimination—Determines the SS7 message's destination endpoint address. Message discrimination reads the DPC from the routing label in the SIF of the MSU. If it is addressed to the receiving node, message discrimination passes the message to the message distribution function. If it is not addressed to the receiving node, message discrimination passes the message to the message routing function.

- SMH Message Distribution—Identifies the user and delivers the user information (SCCP, TUP, ISUP, TCAP, or network management) in the SS7 message to the upper-level protocol. As previously mentioned, the message distribution process is invoked only when the message is addressed to the receiving endpoint or to itself. The Service Indicator value in the Service Indicator octet field of the MSU determines the user of the message.

  If the user of the message is unavailable for processing, the User Part Unavailable (UPU) message is sent back to the transmitting endpoint. UPU messages sent by the network management process include a cause code that identifies one of the following problems:

  — User part function is not provisioned.

  — User part function is out of service.

  — User part function is unavailable for unknown reasons.

- SMH Message Routing—Interfaces with MTP2 to route messages over the network. The SMH routing process routes messages to the appropriate signaling links. The SMH routing process receives messages from the message discrimination and L4 applications. Message discrimination passes messages to the routing process when the message is destined for another signaling point. Higher-level applications pass messages to the routing process to transport the outgoing messages.

Routing Overview

Service Provider personnel statically maintain signaling endpoint routing tables. The routing table identifies the links, linksets, primary routes, and alternate routes for each DPC. All links in the linkset share the traffic load equally. When a particular destination has more than one linkset, the linksets involved share the traffic load equally.

Priority codes identify primary and alternate routes. The direct, most-direct, or fewest-hop-count route (or link) is always the first choice as the outgoing link. The routes are chosen based on link type (A- to F-links) and signaling endpoint type (SSP, STP, or SCP). An F-link between two SSPs, for example, is the first route choice for messages between these

Congestion Control

MTP2 monitors the level of messages queued in buffers (both output and retransmission) and alerts SNM in case of congestion.

Onset of congestion messages are sent to SNM when the threshold value for the buffers is exceeded. The SNM process considers all destinations across the link to be congested.

Now consider congestion from the signaling endpoint and STP perspective:

- Signaling endpoints (SSP, SCP) receive congestion information from MTP2 *onset of congestion* indications. Excessive higher-layer messages can cause congestion over signal endpoint (SSP and SCP) links. In this case, SNM sends status messages to applications indicating which DPCs are affected. The application should reduce outgoing messages for a period of time. SNM continues to send the *congestion* status message until MTP2 receives the *end of congestion* indication. At this point, SNM stops sending the status messages, and after the timeout period, user applications resume normal activity.

- If the STP SNM process receives an *onset of congestion* alert concerning a particular link, it considers that the route to its adjacent node is congested. When messages are received for the affected node, the STP SNM process sends a Transfer Controlled (TFC) message to the SNM of the transmitting endpoint. The STP indicates the affected node in the TFC message. This enables the signaling endpoint to choose an alternate route to the affected node. When the SNM process receives the *end of congestion* indication, it stops sending the status indications to the transmitting endpoint.

Rerouting

The SNM rerouting process reroutes traffic around an affected node without causing congestion or losing messages. STPs use this process when the route to a specific endpoint is unavailable. SNM uses the Transfer Prohibited (TFP) message to advise all directly connected nodes of the lost route to the specific endpoint. This enables the other STPs to choose an alternate route to the affected node. When the links are restored, Transfer Allowed (TFA) messages alert the directly connected nodes that normal routing procedures can resume.

Changeover and Changeback

You use changeover procedures when signaling links become unavailable and messages need to be diverted over alternate links. You use changeback procedures when the signaling links become available and normal routing needs to be re-established. Changeover and changeback procedures require SNM actions from both signaling points to maintain sequence and minimize loss.

You initiate the changeover procedure using the *changeover order* (COO) message between the signaling points. The COO message indicates the affected link in the SLC field of the MSU. The SMH function does not select the signaling link identified in the SLC field as the outgoing link. SMH selects an alternate route to reach the adjacent signaling point.

When the receiving point receives the COO message, it selects an alternate route and sends a *changeover acknowledgment* (COA) to the transmitting signaling point. The COO and COA messages contain the FSNs of the last message accepted on the unavailable link. Both signaling points retrieve the messages in the output buffers of the unavailable link and move these messages to the output of the alternate link. At this point, all waiting messages are sent in sequence and without loss, completing the changeover procedure.

You use the changeback procedure when the affected link becomes available. Either signaling point can initiate changeback procedures. SNM advises the SMH process that the messages destined for the alternate link should be stored in the *changeback buffer* (CBB) instead. The *changeback declaration* (CBD) is then sent to the adjacent signaling point identifying that the link is now available. The receiving signaling point responds with a *changeback acknowledgment* (CBA). When the signaling point receives the CBA, SNM advises SMH to send the buffered messages out the primary link and resume normal routing procedures.

SCCP

The SCCP provides network services on top of MTP3: The combination of those two layers is called the Network Service Part (NSP) of SS7. TCAP typically uses SCCP services to access databases in the SS7 network. As illustrated in Figure 4-8, the SCCP provides service interfaces to TCAP and ISUP. SCCP routing services enable the STP to perform Global Title Translation (GTT) by determining the DPC and subsystem number of the destination database.

The following SCCP features are covered in the next few sections:

- Connection-Oriented Services
- Connectionless Services and Messages
- SCCP Management Functions

Connection-Oriented Services

SCCP supports connection-oriented services for TCAP and ISUP, however none of these services is used today. As such, this section does not cover SCCP connection-oriented capabilities, messages, or services.

Connectionless Services and Messages

SCCP provides the transport layer for the connectionless services of TCAP (discussed in the section entitled "Transaction Capabilities Applications Part [TCAP]"). TCAP-based services include 800, 888, 900, calling card, and mobile applications. Together, SCCP and MTP3 transfer non-circuit based messages used in these services. The SCCP also enables the STP to perform GTT on behalf of the end office exchange. The end office exchange views the 800 number as a functional address or, in other words, as a global title address. Because global title addresses are not routed, the SCCP in the end office exchange routes query messages to its home STP.

In this section, connectionless services are based on end office exchanges querying a database to obtain the routing number for an 800 number. The following is an example of how this works in the network.

Together, SCCP and MTP3 transport TCAP 800-based queries to centralized databases. The connectionless messages passed between the SCCP and MTP are called *Unitdata Messages (UDTs)* and *Unitdata Service Messages (UDTSs)*.

The SCCP sends a UDT to transfer subsystem information, and it sends a UDT to perform the GTT function. UDTs also are used to query and receive responses from databases. Table 4-2 lists parameters used in the UDT message.

Table 4-2   *UDT Parameters*

Parameter	Type	Length (Octets)
Message Type	M	1
Protocol Class (PRC)	M	1
Called Party Address (CDA)	M	3 minimum
Calling Party Address (CGA)	M	3 minimum
Subsystem Data	M	Variable

Source: ITU-T Q.713 (7/96)

A UDTS is sent to the originating SCCP advising that the receiving SCCP was unable to deliver the UDT to its destination. The return cause parameter indicates why the UDT is being returned. Table 4-3 lists parameters used in the UDTS.

Table 4-3   *UDTS*

Parameter	Type	Length (Octets)
Message Type	M	1
Return Cause	M	1
CDA	M	3 minimum
CGA	M	3 minimum
Subsystem Data	M	Variable

Source: ITU-T Q.713 (7/96)

SCCP Connectionless Example

This example demonstrates ways you can use SCCP services and messages in a typical 800 call:

1 When the end office switch receives a call setup for an 800 number, it launches a query to a database. TCAP passes the calling and called address parameters to SCCP, which then fills the appropriate fields in the UDT and sets the routing indicator bit indicating that a GTT is required. The SCCP addresses the query to the home STP and passes the message to MTP. MTP in the end office switch creates the MSU and forwards the message to the STP.

2 The SCCP function in the STP receives the query and, using its translation tables, re-addresses the message with the Subsystem Number of the database. The SSN includes the DPC and the database subsystem address. The MTP in the STP then forwards the query to the SCP serving the database.

3 The SCCP in the SCP passes the message to TCAP, which queries the database. The database translates the functional number into the routing number and passes the information to the SCCP, which sets the DPC and sends the response back to the originating end office. The SCCP also sets the routing indicator bit indicating to MTP that the routing should be based on the DPC.

SCCP Management Functions

SCCP management functions maintain the transfer of SCCP messages during failure conditions, including network and subsystem failures. SCCP management processes alert SCCP users, such as TCAP or ISUP, during these failure conditions. SCCP management has interfaces to MTP, SCCP connectionless control, and the subsystems (SCCP users). SCCP management uses the unit data connectionless message format.

The following describes a basic call setup and teardown in the SS7 network:

1 The subscriber initiates an off-hook, and the local end office sends the caller a dial tone. The caller dials the desired digits, and the local end office collects the digits dialed.

2 The local end office determines how to connect the call based on its routing tables. The routing tables identify the circuits available to establish an end-to-end connection. The originating office creates and sends an IAM to the switch that provides the first connection (the pass-along method) and indicates the circuit to be used.

3 When it receives the IAM, the intermediate switch responds by sending an ACM to the originating switch. The ACM is a confirmation that the intermediate switch reserved the same circuit that the originating end office designated in the IAM. The ACM also alerts the originating office to provide a ringback tone to the calling party.

4 While sending the ACM, the intermediate switch prepares to set up the next connection by creating an IAM containing the called and calling information provided by the originating end office. The intermediate switch forwards the IAM to the terminating office using its routing tables.

5 Upon receipt of the IAM, the terminating switch determines whether the called party is busy.

If the called party is not busy. the terminating switch responds by sending an ACM to the intermediate switch. Following the ACM, the terminating switch signals the subscriber's (called party) line by ringing the telephone. When the called party answers the call, the terminating office cuts through the voice path and sends an ANM along the same path to the intermediate switch.

6 The intermediate switch in turn cuts through the voice path and sends an ANM to the originating switch. Now the originating switch can connect the voice path and enable the conversation to begin.

7 For this example, the called party goes on-hook first and initiates the release procedures at the terminating exchange. The terminating exchange immediately sends a SUSPEND (SUS) message to the intermediate switch, and in turn, the intermediate switch sends an SUS message to the originating switch.

8 When the calling party goes on-hook, the originating switch sends a Release (REL) message toward the terminating switch using the same path as the other signaling messages. The intermediate and terminating switches acknowledge the release with a RELEASE COMPLETE (RLC) message. The RLC message also signifies that each circuit returned to an idle state.

ISUP Message Format

The message type value in the ISUP message indicates the type of message carried in the MSU and is illustrated in Figure 4-14. The circuit identification code (CIC) identifies the circuit being set up or released.

Figure 4-14 *ISUP Message*

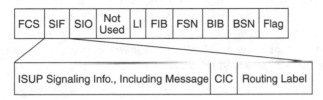

ISUP Call Control Messages

Table 4-4 identifies the most important ISUP call control signaling messages. All ISUP signaling messages contain the ISUP message type parameter.

Table 4-4   *ISUP Messages and Message Types*

ISUP Signaling Message	Message Type Value
IAM	00000001
ACM	00000110
ANM	00001001
REL Message	00001100
RLC Message	00010000
Continuity Test (COT)	00000101
CPG Message	00101100
SUS Message	00001101
Resume (RES) Message	00001110
Forward Transfer (FOT) Message	00001000
INR Message	00000011
INF Message	00000100

Source: ITU-T Q.763 (9/97)

The ISUP call control message formats, including signaling parameters, optional and mandatory fields, and field lengths, are listed in Appendix A, "ISUP Messages/Types Formats."

Each ISUP call control message is explained as follows:

- IAM is the first message used to initiate a call setup. The IAM typically contains the complete called number, also called the *en-bloc address signal*. An *overlap address signal* occurs when the called number is sent in more than one message.

- ACM is a backward message the terminating end office sends to indicate that the end office is ringing the called subscriber. Tandem offices also can send an ACM to signify that an outgoing trunk was seized where ISUP signaling is not supported. The terminating switch sends a *backward message*, whereas the originating switch sends a *forward message*. ANM is a backward message the terminating end office sends to indicate that the called subscriber answered.

- REL is a forward or backward message requesting an immediate release of a connection. The forward and backward nature of the REL message is based on the ability of the called and calling users to initiate a release. You also use the REL message when the tandem or terminating end office cannot set up a call.

- RLC is a forward or backward message indicating that the exchange released the trunk at its end.

- COT is a forward message used to perform a continuity test on an outgoing trunk.

- CPG is a backward message used to report an occurrence, such as an alert, during call setup. The CPG message is sent only after an ACM.

- SUS is a backward message used to suspend a call while its connections are kept intact.

- RES is a message used to resume a suspended call. The SUS and RES messages share the same message format and parameters.

- FOT is a message an outgoing operator uses to request the assistance of an incoming operator.

- INR is a message used to obtain additional call-related information. Usually, the terminating end office sends this message to the originating end office.

- INF is a message used to provide the information requested in the INR.

TCAP

TCAP provides the transaction capabilities carried out by non-circuit based messages used to access remote databases and invoke remote feature capabilities in network elements.

TCAP was first used for 800-number translation. TCAP messages carry the instructions SCPs use to query databases for specific information. TCAP also provides the mechanism to carry the queries and responses from switch to switch. TCAP uses SCCP and MTP protocols to route messages end-to-end. This is different from ISUP, which passes messages from switch to switch. The TCAP protocol provides the means for an application in one signaling point to communicate to an application in another signaling point.

The database information is used for 800, 888, and 900 service, Local Number Portability (LNP), subscriber service such as LIDB, and Mobile Home/Visitor records.

The Intelligent Network (IN) also uses TCAP to invoke features in remote end offices. IN relies on TCAP's services to enable one signaling endpoint to access features in a remote signaling endpoint. IN features such as automatic callback are made possible by TCAP invoke messages that inform the local exchange that the destination party is now available.

The following sections analyze TCAP interfaces, messages, message types, and components. The end of this chapter includes an example of an 800 query using the TCAP protocol.

TCAP Interfaces

TCAP, as illustrated in Figure 4-15, uses SCCP and MTP to route transaction messages in the SS7 network. You use TCAP messages to communicate from one signaling point (Exchange X) to another signaling point (Exchange Y).

Figure 4-15 *TCAP Interfaces and Message Path*

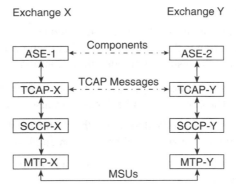

An Application Service Element (ASE) invokes operations at one end, and an ASE executes them at the other end. The ASEs are dedicated to an application, and they peer between remote entities. In the case of an 800 call, Exchange X ASE-1 is the local exchange querying Exchange Y ASE-2, the SCP, for the routing number corresponding to the 800 number.

TCAP messages are contained inside the SCCP portion of the MSU. TCAP messages are comprised of a transaction portion and a component portion.

4 When STP1 receives the IAM, it reads the routing label and routes the IAM to SSP2. The IAM is received and SSP2 determines that it's the serving center. At this point, SSP2 verifies that the called number is idle and returns an ACM (2) to SSP1. At the same time, SSP2 connects the trunk back to SSP1, applies a ringing tone on the trunk, and rings the subscriber line of the called number. When STP2 receives the ACM, it reads the routing label and routes the ACM to SSP1. The ACM indicates that the IAM was received and that SSP2 is the terminating exchange.

5 STP1 receives the ACM and connects the subscriber line of the calling party to the trunk. At this point, the calling subscriber can hear the ringing tone. When the called subscriber answers the call, SSP2 creates and sends an ANM (3) to SSP1. STP2 receives the ANM, reads the routing label, and routes the ANM to SSP1. SSP1 simply verifies that the subscriber and the trunk are connected.

6 If the calling party hangs up the call first, SSP1 creates an REL message (4) addressed to SSP2. The REL message identifies the trunk associated with the call. SSP1 then routes the REL message toward SSP2, where STP1 reads the routing label and routes the REL to SSP2.

7 When SSP2 receives the REL message, it disconnects the trunk from the subscriber line and returns the trunk to an idle state. SSP2 then creates an RLC (5) message, identifying the trunk used for the call. SSP2 addresses the RLC message to SSP1 and routes it toward SSP1. STP2 receives the RLC message, reads the routing label, and routes the message to SSP1. When it receives the RLC message, SSP1 idles the trunk identified in it.

800 Database Query Example

This example demonstrates the steps involved in making an 800 query. The example also shows ways you can use the TCAP protocol for transactions in the SS7 network. Figure 4-17 provides the network topology for this example.

Figure 4-17 *Network for 800 Database Query Example*

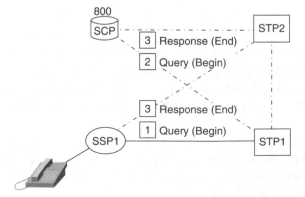

In this example, the analog subscriber connected to SSP1 places an 800 call. The following steps occur when the subscriber on SSP1 places the 800 call:

1 When the subscriber goes off-hook, call processing is initiated in SSP1. Call processing causes SSP1 to enter the *originating call* state and move to the *collecting information* state. SSP1 collects the information or dialed digits from the subscriber.

2 After all the digits are collected, the call enters the *analyzing information* state. SSP1 analyzes the dialed digits and determines that the 800 number is not routable. At this point, the call enters the *wait* state, and the SSP1-TCAP orders the (800) ASE to initiate a transaction with the (800) SCP.

3 SSP1 creates the 800 Query or Begin (1) message that contains the Invoke component requesting the routing number for the specified 800 number. SSP1 then forwards the Query or Begin message to one of its home STPs.

4 STP1 receives the message and determines that it is an 800 query. Next, STP1 selects the appropriate database to process the transaction. STP1 re-addresses the Query or Begin message (2) to the (800) SCP point code (DPC) and the (800) database subsystem number (SSN). STP1 then routes the Query or Begin message to the (800) SCP.

5 When the SCP receives the 800 Query or Begin message, it extracts the request and passes the information to the (800) ASE to execute the database translation. The SCP creates a Response or End message (3) that includes the routing number in the Return Results (Last) component portion of the message. The SCP addresses the message to SSP1 and forwards the message to STP2.

6 When STP2 receives the Response or End message, it reads the routing label and routes the message to SSP1. SSP1 receives the information in the Response message indicating the routing number for the 800 query. At this point, the call enters the *selecting route* state and repeats the same steps as indicated in the "Basic Call Setup and Teardown Example" section of this chapter.

List of SS7 Specifications

The ITU-T standards for SS7 are found in the Q series documents. Table 4-5 lists ITU-T specifications and related Q series document numbers.

Table 4-5   *ITU-T SS7 Specifications*

Title	Doc. Number
Introduction to CCITT Signaling System No. 7	Q.700
Message Transfer Part (MTP)	Q.701–Q.709
Simplified Message Transfer Part	Q.710
Signaling Connection Control Part (SCCP)	Q.711–Q.719
Telephone User Part (TUP)	Q.720–Q.729
Data User Part (DUP)	Q.740–Q.749
Signaling System No. 7 Management	Q.750–Q.759
ISDN User Part (ISUP)	Q.760–Q.769
Transaction Capabilities Application Part (TCAP)	Q.770–Q.779
Intelligent Network (IN)	Q.1200–Q.1999

Summary

SS7/C7 is a complex and important part of the PSTN architecture today. For packet voice to truly be an option for service providers, packet telephony and the SS7 network must integrate.

This chapter covered in detail the four layers of SS7. It also covered the detailed message flows of a common call in SS7. Chapter 13, "Virtual Switch Controller," details ways you can integrate these components into a network also running packet telephony.

The details in this chapter can help those who are deploying SS7 and packet voice networks to better understand how SS7 works. Also, this chapter shows how many details must be covered for packet telephony and the PSTN to successfully integrate. Some of the key areas in which VoIP must inter-work with SS7 include:

- Physical link interconnection of MTP1
- Signal unit termination and acknowledgments of MTP2

- L4 user data extraction from MSUs (for ISUP and TCAP)
- L4 protocol support for call completion- and transaction-based services (ISUP and TCAP, respectively)

These key areas must be addressed for VoIP networks to fit seamlessly into or interface to the PSTN.

- Custom calling features
- Custom Local Area Signaling Service (CLASS) features
- Voice mail

Each feature is discussed in more detail in the following sections.

Custom Calling Features

The services available from custom calling features have been popular since they were introduced in the PSTN. Although you can activate and use each function individually, SPs usually combine features in a single package for simplicity and convenience.

You enable and control custom calling features from within end office switches directly. Signaling System 7 (SS7) messaging and service enablers are not required operate these features. The following list describes some common custom calling features:

- Call forwarding—Enables calls to follow as the subscriber moves from one location to another
- Call waiting—Indicates an incoming call when the subscriber is already involved in a call
- Three-way calling—Enables subscribers to conference a third party in on a conversation
- Speed dialing—Provides a convenient way for subscribers to store frequently used numbers
- Added number—Enables subscribers to add a second line that they can identify by a distinctive ring and call-waiting tones

CLASS Features

CLASS is a popular suite of features available to subscribers. CLASS features provide subscribers with a powerful and convenient tool to control incoming and outgoing calls. Telecordia, formerly known as Bell Communications Research (Bellcore), defined the CLASS standard, which added to the custom calling feature foundation. With CLASS, users interact with the switch software from their own telephone sets and give instructions on which services they want. SS7 messages and functions are then invoked and sent within the network to perform the requested operations.

The following list describes some common CLASS features:

- Customer-originated trace—Enables the subscriber to dial a code after he or she receives a harassing call, which notifies the local law enforcement agency.
- Automatic callback—Used when the subscriber receives a busy signal. This feature notifies the subscriber when the called party line is free by placing the call.
- Automatic recall—Enables the subscriber to easily return a missed call.
- Display features—Requires a display telephone to display the calling name and calling number.
- Calling number blocking—Enables the called party to hide his or her identity when dialing subscribers who have CLASS display capabilities.
- Call screening—Enables subscribers to accept, reject, or forward calls based on a list of received calling numbers.

Voice Mail

PSTN-based voice mail enables SPs to offer an alternative to answering machines. This is attractive because subscribers do not need to purchase or operate any additional equipment. Another benefit of network-based voice mail is that voice messaging is still available even if the called party's line is busy. The two main voice mail services available to residential and small-business users are

- Voice messaging—Enables subscribers to store and play recorded greetings and receive, review, and distribute messages from outside users
- Fax messaging—Enables subscribers to receive faxes and view them at a later time

Integrated Services Digital Network

Integrated Services Digital Network (ISDN) provides the set of digital data and voice services available from today's PSTN. The ISDN network is constructed of standards-based interfaces, protocols, and feature sets. This enables subscribers to connect vendor-compliant devices, which interoperate and provide access to features. ISDN services are made available by ISDN-provisioned exchanges. You also can extend these services through the PSTN network using SS7 and Primary Rate Interface (PRI) trunks. In the case of SS7, ISDN Q.931 messages are mapped into the ISDN User Part (ISUP) and vice versa. The two methods for accessing ISDN, which are discussed in more detail in Chapter 3, "Basic Telephony Signaling," are

- Basic Rate Interface (BRI)—Delivers two 64-kbps bearer (B) channels and one 16-kbps data (D) channel over two-wire copper line loops. The 64-kbps B channels transmit voice and data, and the 16-kbps D channel transmits call control messages and user packet data up to 9.6 kbps.

- PRI—Delivers twenty-three 64-kbps B channels and one 64-kbps D channel over a four-wire T1 line in North America. As in the BRI example, 64-kbps B channels carry data and voice, and the 64-kbps D channel carries call control messages. In PRI, however, the D channel does not support transmission of user packet data. You typically use PRI service to access a Private Branch eXchange (PBX) or routers and gateways used for local-area network (LAN) or dial-up modem access.

See Chapter 3 for a more complete discussion of ISDN and its services.

Business Services

Business services are important to SPs because they represent a large portion of SP's revenue base. Corporate environments require an extensive array of communication services to support their businesses. The following services are described in this section:

- Virtual Private Voice Networks
- Centrex services
- Call center services

Virtual Private Voice Networks

Virtual Private Voice Networks cost-effectively interconnect corporate voice traffic between multiple locations over the PSTN. The alternative to Virtual Private Voice Networks is dedicated tie-lines between locations. Because multiple locations are not typically served by the same exchange, however, Virtual Private Voice Networks are a far more economical solution in such scenarios.

SPs offer cost-competitive Virtual Private Voice Network services by maximizing the private use of public infrastructure. Therefore, public network facilities are somewhat balanced by corporate use during weekdays and residential use during nights and weekends.

Virtual Private Voice Network customers access the public network by interconnecting private network facilities, such as T1 circuits. SS7 facilities, messaging, and inter-working enable VPNs across the public infrastructure. SS7 capabilities also enable corporate and PBX features to be carried transparently across the network. Another benefit of deploying a voice-capable network is to ease the process of adding new and multiple sites to an existing Virtual Private Voice Network. With Virutal Private Voice Networks, this is as easy as adding a new connection to the network and provisioning the appropriate translations and dialing plans. With tie-lines, on the other hand, new end-to-end connections are required between the new location and each existing location, resulting in higher costs to the customer.

Public switching systems identify, process, and route calls based on different protocols and dialing plans. The identity of each Virtual Private Voice Network is made possible by customer-group ID numbers that are maintained and transmitted across the public network through SS7. You use this capability to distinguish and route public calls from private intra-network calls. The customer group identity and other information is inserted in ISUP messages for transmission across the public network.

Dialing plans ensure proper handling of full North American Numbering Plan (NANP) 10-digit station routing and 7-digit on-net to on-net, on-net to off-net, and off-net to on-net routing. The call processing, routing, and dialing capabilities provide uniform dialing plans and access to users at remote locations.

NOTE   Dedicated Access Lines (DALs) connect to the public network. DALs provide both public and private routing of calls and connect through various signaling protocols. These include ISDN, channel-associated signaling (CAS), QSIG (Q Signaling), and Digital Private Network Signaling System (DPNSS), which are detailed in Chapter 3.

Centrex Services

Centrex enables SPs to offer smaller businesses voice and data services similar to those found in larger and more costly private solutions. Centrex services can be delivered by public switching infrastructure and do not require costly customer premise equipment.

The Centrex software loaded in the switch can create a virtual private business network. Centrex services are comparable to on-premise systems and provide call handling, distribution, accounting, and data networking between sites. You can access Centrex services in the following ways:

- POTS—You can designate and use these lines as Centrex lines.

- Feature lines—Equipped with fully featured telephones, these lines can provide additional features and functionality over standard POTS lines, ISDN circuits, or Switched 56/65 circuits.

Centrex offers many features to subscribers. The following list explains some of Centrex's services and capabilities:

- Call handling—Includes call waiting, call forwarding, call park, hunt grouping, and voice mail

- Convenience features—Include automatic dial, speed dialing, ring again, and calling line identification (caller-ID)

- Custom dialing plans—Provide customized plans for each customer group and enable abbreviated dialing for internally placed calls

- Directory assistance—Directory services are available by dialing a three-digit national code or an area-specific code. Directory assistance operators can search for telephone numbers based on directory listings. After the operator finds a match, he or she transfers the call to an audio response unit that quotes the number to the customer. The database search engines available to SPs are extensive and provide effective and timely responses for requesting subscribers.

- Billing services—Operator intervention is still required for about 20 percent of long-distance calls in the U.S. The bulk of this intervention is for collect calls, third-party billing, calling cards, and credit card services. The remaining 80 percent of long-distance calls are handled by automated systems, speech recognition, recording technology, and databases all linked together through an underlying SS7 network.

Summary

Plain old telephone service will not be plain for much longer. With broadband (DSL, cable, wireless) access to the home, voice will simply be another application in everyone's home. The available features listed in the previous list are just the tip of the iceberg. This chapter discussed enhanced services, where the PSTN operators make a hefty portion of their revenue.

The PSTN offers many valuable services to subscribers and is critical to the operation of small, medium, and large businesses. These subscribers and businesses are, however, increasingly relying on the power and value of data networking and the Internet. To this end, the PSTN services discussed in this chapter as well as new voice services will, over time, be delivered over data networks and the Internet.

Voice over IP Technology

ble centers—The capability to "follow the sun" increases the "b
r" costs in a CSCC. *Following the sun* implies that different physi
exist to keep workers working a normal shift. This also is known
g. (When the United States call-center operators are sleeping, f
alian operators can take the calls.)

ntage distribution/overflow routing—The capability to handle ov
ent physical locations increases the profitability in a peak call-flo
verflow mechanism is not properly managed, it can cost more to
an to not service the incoming call.

oyee turnover—Call-center work can be stressful, and, because o
of such work, keeping workers can be difficult.

nal staffing needs—Oftentimes, call centers experience more vo
n periods. As such, they must hire people to accommodate the h
s, and then lay people off when volume drops. (This is a comm
cal support staff during the holiday season, for instance.)

venient busy hours—If the call center does not have a "follow th
t hire staff to work inconvenient hours, such as the night shift, f

nal call-center talent—Having skilled workers come into a brick
y can lower the number of possible workers in the pool of talent. T
t regional workers can work within any geography in a specific
ses the number of workers in the available pool.

are adapting to meet these challenges, as well as meet new den
s to the previously mentioned challenges is increased efficiency
nt, practice the following principles:

uter Telephony Integration (CTI)—One application is for caller
as the caller's name, buying patterns, and address) to be "poppe
s screen so that the agent can handle the call more quickly.

application-based routing—Routing calls to the proper agent ba
cal skills, language, and any other skill can increase the speed by
lled.

ation duplication—Call agents can avoid asking the same quest
rred to a new agent. This is possible due to the information on t
"popping" onto the new agent's screen when the call is transfer

tive Voice Response (IVR)—This enables callers to input basic
s account information) so that calls can be handled more quick

upgrade to an integrated voice and data network initially based
value (which might be hidden to some) is in the value-added s
that can be offered after this enhanced network is in place.

What if your voice mail server was the same as your e-mail server and you could decide whether to download your voice mail over a telephone or use your e-mail client to peruse your voice mail? Those who travel will truly appreciate benefits such as the capability to download voice mail and respond electronically, and to forward voice mail to a group. Such technology exists today and will soon be available and widely used through enterprise and service provider networks.

Packet Telephony Call Centers

In most call centers today, the largest costs are for the brick and mortar holding the building together. You can drastically cut the actual costs of renting a building, putting a phone at each desk, and purchasing the required infrastructure (call-routing technology, PCs, and so on) by using a Packet Telephony Call Center (PTCC).

Each call center is different, but for many call centers, the ability to grow the business as needed (perhaps as discretely as one station at a time) is a great benefit. Currently, call centers must grow in chunks. The size of these chunks depends on how many ports the call centers can purchase for their Private Branch eXchange (PBX) at a time. This is a great disadvantage because call centers usually need to be flexible and be able to grow and shrink as the number of required stations changes.

Many call centers are unable to grow in smaller chunks because the hardware necessary to provide desktop phone services is sold only in larger units (such as growing one to several T1s or E1s at a time, instead of a phone at a time). This prevents the call centers from being able to grow quickly based on seasonal or natural growth.

Circuit-Switching Call Centers (CSCCs) enable users to work from home and still take calls, but this equipment is expensive. With PTCCs, users can log in to a phone no matter where they are and have access to the exact same features as if they were at their desk, and the costs are much lower.

A CSCC currently uses a device known as a PBX Extender, a remote piece of equipment that extends the features of the PBX to the user's premises. A PBX Extender can run upward of $1000 per user, and that's just for the equipment itself. You also have to purchase software that must be added to the central site; the circuit to the worker's residence; and Customer Premise Equipment (CPE) gear, such as the router, for the remote site.

When you use a VoIP network, however, you don't need additional equipment for the remote site. You can take the same phone you use at work and have exactly the same functionality. Of course, the company still has to purchase the circuit to the worker's residence, as well as the CPE equipment.

Nevertheless, VoIP lowers the costs of locating stations anywhere geographically. In doing so, VoIP gives call-center operators a great advantage in terms of hiring skilled or unskilled

---

CHAPTER 6

Voice over IP Benefits and Applications

Now that you have a good understanding of how the Public Switched Telephone Network (PSTN) and Enterprise Telephony (ET) work, you might be asking yourself, "Why put voice on Internet Protocol (IP) networks?" This chapter discusses how the applications currently available in the PSTN, along with other new applications, work in a packet-based voice network. The following issues and applications are addressed:

- Benefits of Voice over IP (VoIP), including cost savings, single infrastructure savings, and new applications
- Using a packet telephony call center versus a circuit-switched call center
- Service provider prepaid calling card applications
- Service provider enhanced services (such as Internet call waiting and click to talk)
- An enterprise VoIP case study

Key Benefits of VoIP

One of the key drivers of combining voice and data networks is monetary savings. If you look strictly at minute-to-minute costs, the savings realized by going with VoIP might not be large enough to justify the expense of rolling out this service.

Price savings can vary based on your geographic location. In countries other than North America, for instance, a minute-to-minute cost comparison between VoIP and the traditional PSTN (a local call in some countries can be around $1 a minute) more than justifies the expense of the new network.

In North America, however, many large corporations pay 3 cents or less per minute for long-distance calls they make within the United States. For such corporations, it is hard to justify to accounting that rolling out a new infrastructure will provide a Return on Investment (ROI) that will pay off quickly—that is, unless they factor in items other than per-minute charges.

For enterprise networks, for instance, consolidating voice and data networks might mean the ET customer can order fewer circuits from the PSTN. Also, an IP infrastructure (utilizing Cisco IP phones) requires fewer adds, moves, and changes than a traditional voice or data network. This is because, with one infrastructure, you can use such data features as

Dynamic Host Configuration Protocol (DHCP). DHCP enables a *device* (a PC or an IP phone) to dynamically receive an IP address (that is, the IP address does not need to be statically configured into the device). So, for instance, if you have an IP phone configured with DHCP, you can move the phone wherever you need and still keep the same phone number. This is similar to moving your laptop from office to office and still being able to log in to the same network server.

Many large enterprises have determined that it costs several hundred dollars just to move a telephone today (this is due to such factors as labor costs and the cost of reconfiguring the switch). Such costs are not incurred in an IP infrastructure, however, because your IP phone profile is set up, and the IP network doesn't care where you are located.

<table>
<tr><td>NOTE</td><td>The Cisco Communication Network is part of Cisco's Enterprise VoIP network. It consists of an IP phone and a Cisco Call Manager. In the Cisco Call Manager, profiles are set up for each individual phone based upon the static Media Access Control (MAC) address of the IP phone. The IP phone simply has to send out a DHCP request when it's plugged into an IP network. The DHCP response includes the IP address that the IP phone is to use, as well as potential Cisco Call Managers to log in to. The IP phone then contacts the Cisco Call Manager and downloads its profile (phone number, features, and so on).</td></tr>
</table>

An additional benefit of VoIP is the ability to have one Information Services (IS) department that supports both voice and data networks (as the networks are now one entity). This can initially cause tension between these two infrastructures, but as with any technological revolution, one must enhance one's skills to survive. This has been the case with the introduction of most new technologies—from the cotton gin to robots.

One benefit of VoIP that enterprises and service providers often overlook is the fact that common infrastructure tools are now no longer needed. These include such tools as physical ports for services such as voice mail. In a circuit-switched voice network, voice mail is sold based on the number of mailboxes and the number of physical ports needed to support simultaneous users. With VoIP, physical circuit-switched ports are not necessary. The voice mail server need only have an IP connection (Ethernet, Asynchronous Transfer Mode [ATM], and so on).

Also, VoIP enables voice mail systems to be put on standards-based platforms (such as PCs and UNIX machines). After a feature is on a standards-based platform, price gouging is much less likely to occur. Voice mail providers today, for example, charge 50 cents to $1.50 per megabyte for hard-drive space because they use a proprietary mechanism to format and store their voice calls. On the other hand, the average price for hard drives at the local PC store is approximately only 3 to 4 cents per megabyte.

workers, as well as growing and shrinking the number of stations needed at in time.

In a packet telephony infrastructure, you can have a group of distributed vir you can locate anywhere, and you can still offer them the same tools that a center offers. Figure 6-1 shows ways you can use a common IP infrastructure various methods, and it showcases one possibility of telecommuters as virt

Figure 6-1   *Virtual Agents*

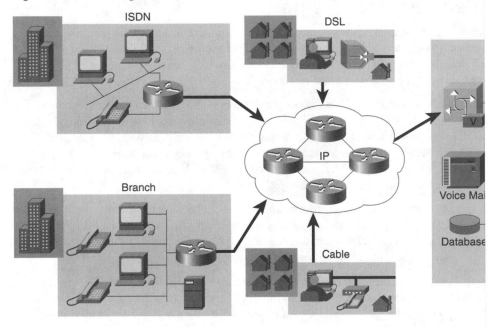

Two of the challenges facing CSCCs today are cost and employee retention of these challenges are as follows:

- Many toll-free numbers—CSCCs must manage the number of circuit uses. Using more circuits increases the cost of operating the CSCC and potentially decrease profits.

- Misrouted/rerouted calls—Each time a call must be routed to a differ (because, for example, an agent might not have the correct skills to a customer's question, or he does not speak a customer's language), re

Some of these services and applications include having both your integrated into one application; using Web-based customer support being able to fax in and out from the desktop (and fax to your e-m able to conduct desktop video conferencing with your customer.

Traditionally, an entire call center revolves around the PBX (as sh such, call centers are held ransom by the number of ports they can in time. Reliance on the PBX also forces the CSCC to deploy appl are compatible with the PBX or when the CTI link enables the fie

Figure 6-2   *Circuit-Switching Call Center*

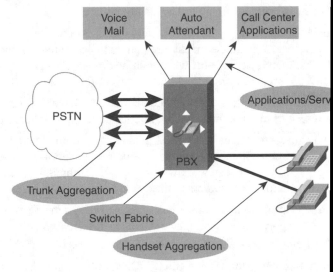

In a PTCC, the network is integrated and standards-based and do component or vendor to provide the entire solution.

This enables the call center to have remote users for a fraction of t (thanks to integrated CPE gear). This also enables the business to that customers need, and enables the business to add new applica collaboration) as needed.

Another important issue with CSCCs is the ability to retain and de Studies show that giving employees options on schedules and "fl increases the retention rates of many companies.

Although Figure 6-2 shows how a CSCC is efficient for a large c CSCC design lacks the flexibility to enable telecommuters, and i into Internet telephony or unified communications (such as fax–t

PTCC enables you to retain a connection into the legacy PBX call center, but it also enables integration into the new network of Web support, Internet telephony, and unified communications. Figure 6-3 shows the components and network design of a PTCC.

This connection to the legacy PBX is accomplished by having an external *call-processing engine* that connects to the PBX and to the Cisco Call Manager through CTI links. The external call-processing engine enables telecommuters and PBX call agents to answer calls as though they are attached to the call center.

Also, with a connection from the legacy CSCC into the IP network, you can use enhanced features such as IP-based IVR systems (also known as Voice Response Units [VRUs]) and unified messaging services such as fax–to–e-mail, text-to-speech, speech-to-text, and so on.

Figure 6-3   *Packet Telephony Call Center*

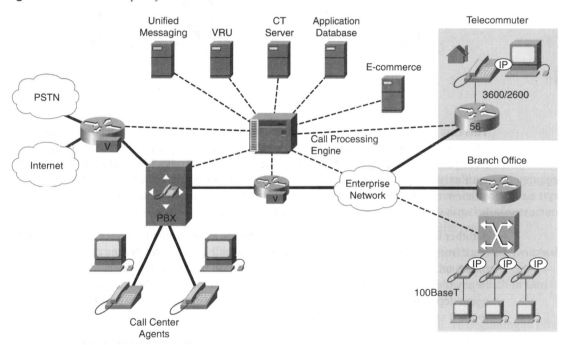

As you can see in Figure 6-3, the Call Center Corporation is no longer tied to physical ports for the VRU, and the entire messaging infrastructure (e-mail, voice mail, applications, and so on) is tied into one common infrastructure.

The call-routing or call-processing engine is now just part of the data network and is removed from the PBX. This enables telecommuters, call-center agents, and branch office agents to have the same access to the same information. Access to a common infrastructure

Figure 6-8   *Call-Flow: Part I*

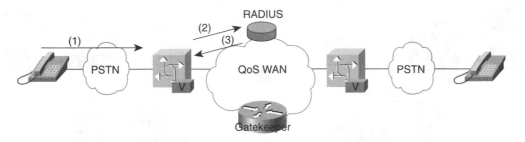

If the ANI is not in the database, the gateway prompts the user for an account number or Personal Identification Number (PIN) and sends this number to the RADIUS server for verification.

The steps illustrated in Figure 6-9 are as follows:

4 The user enters the destination phone number.

5 The gateway consults the gatekeeper on ways he can route the call.

6 The gatekeeper looks up the E.164 address against a table and sends the gateway the IP address of the destination gateway.

Figure 6-9   *Call Flow: Part II*

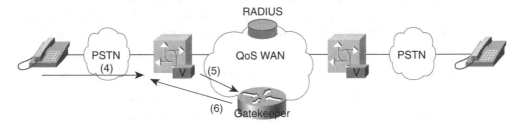

NOTE   The gatekeeper might need to consult a gatekeeper in another zone.

The final steps, illustrated in Figure 6-10, are as follows:

7 The originating gateway places an H.323 call across the IP network to the destination gateway.

8 The destination gateway places a PSTN call to the destination phone.

9 The gateways send start/stop records to the RADIUS server for billing.

Figure 6-10 *Call Flow: Part III*

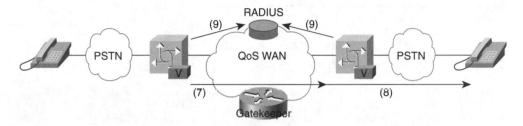

Value-Added Services

After Internet Telephony service providers (ITSPs) have a VoIP network (possibly for a pre- or post-paid application) in place, they can begin to offer value-added services that enable them to charge more than $19.99 per month for standard IS. Two of these value-added applications are Internet Call Waiting (ICW) and Virtual Second Line (V2L).

ICW

ICW is a service that enables subscribers to receive notification of an incoming voice call on their PCs while connected to their ISP. Subscribers are notified of the incoming call through a screen-pop on their PCs, at which point they can do the following:

- Send the call to voice mail.
- Receive the call on the PC using H.323 software (VoIP).
- Drop the Internet session and receive the call on the telephone (PSTN).
- Ignore the call (provide a busy signal or let it ring).

These enhanced services afford benefits to both the service provider and the customer. The service provider can leverage its existing infrastructure to provide more services, and it can have an existing potential customer base with its dial-up customers. The service provider can provide this new service without having to become an official telecommunications provider (such as a Competitive LEC, or CLEC).

The customer benefits in that he does not miss incoming calls while online, does not have to pay for a second line from the telephone company just for Internet access, and can handle incoming calls in many ways. He can still have access to caller-ID, for instance, and he can set up variables such as forwarding to voice mail, ignoring the call, or transferring the call to a cell-phone.

Figure 6-11 details a call-flow between a PSTN (in this case, a Signaling System 7 [SS7] network) and ICW.

Figure 6-11 *ICW Call-Flow*

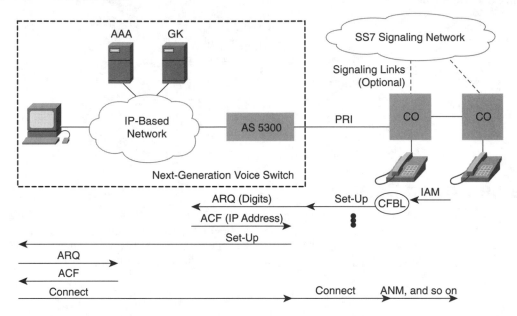

Figure 6-11 shows the Initial Address Message (IAM), "SS7 setup," being passed through to an ISDN setup message. The end office switch has call forwarding turned on so that when the line is busy, the number is forwarded to the AS 5300. The AS 5300 is a VoIP gateway and forwards the call through an Admission Request (ARQ) to an application server.

This application server notifies the PC (using a screen pop), at which point the customer decides whether he wants to accept the call by clicking appropriately. The application server also acts as a gatekeeper and responds to the AS 5300 with an Admission Confirm (ACF) containing the IP address of the PC to which to terminate the call. The PC then verifies that it is okay to talk to the AS 5300 by sending an ARQ and an ACF to the application server, and then it completes the call successfully with a connect message. The messages used in this call-flow are defined in detail in Chapter 10, "H.323."

V2L

V2L is a simple service in that it enables Internet users to place and receive phone calls through their ISP only when they are connected through their Internet connection (modem, cable, digital subscriber line [DSL], and so on). In many V2L cases, the PC is actually assigned a valid E.164 number, although this is not a requirement.

Figure 6-14 *Typical Enterprise Voice and Data Network*

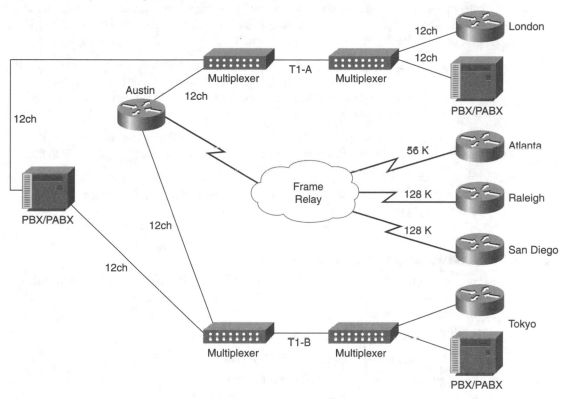

Acme's Current Voice and Data Network

Taking a deeper look into Acme, you need to understand its current network. Acme's headquarters are located in Austin, Texas. Acme has several remote sales and development offices across the United States, as well as in Tokyo and London, where its two largest offices are located. The remaining offices in the U.S. concentrate mainly on sales. Two of Acme's main goals were to cut costs while preparing to deploy a more cost-effective voice network, and to increase bandwidth between sites.

Acme has two intercontinental T1 circuits connected to both London and Tokyo. Multiplexers are used on these circuits to separate 12 channels of each T1 to voice and 12 channels of each T1 to data. The U.S. sites run across a Frame Relay network. The Atlanta

All the benefits of ICW also exist for V2L. One key additional benefit is that service providers can offer outbound traffic, which can, in turn, create significant revenue streams for the service provider. Also, subscribers can save a tremendous amount of money on long-distance charges.

With V2L, ITSPs effectively have a local loop to their customers through their modem access and can offer long-distance services through the Internet. Because the ITSP's IP network is less expensive to build than the PSTN, the ITSP can offer lower long-distance rates to the subscriber. Offering long-distance service provides an additional revenue stream for the ITSP.

Now that you understand how ITSPs can offer value-added applications, it is time to take a look at enterprise networks and how they can take part in packet-based networks.

Enterprise Case Study: Acme Corporation

Chapter 2, "Enterprise Telephony Today," discusses ways you can build enterprise telephone networks. This section discusses ways you can use packet voice technologies not only to save money on long-distance charges, but also to decrease capital expenditures on other recurring charges.

To review, Figure 6-12 shows how numerous enterprise networks have a centralized location with multiple remote sites. The connections between the central site and the remote sites are often called tie-lines. Built to transport voice, tie-lines are permanent 64 Kbps connections that can actually transport voice or data.

Figure 6-12 *Enterprise Telephony*

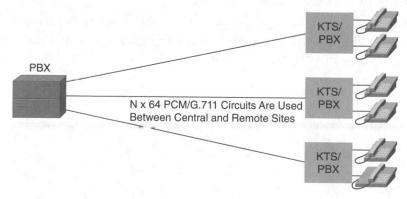

Most enterprise customers also have data networks, a minor modification and enhancement to the data network can enable voice tie-lines to be replaced simply by moving the voice traffic onto the data infrastructure.

This causes the voice and data infrastructure to look something similar to Figure 6-13.

Figure 6-13 *Enterprise Voice and Data Network*

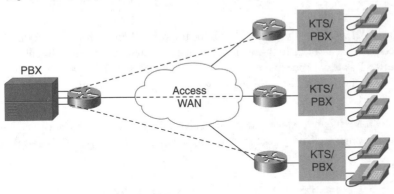

Replacing tie-lines with VoIP and leaving the rest of the infrastructure is just the first step to successful voice and data convergence. Many more steps are necessary.

Acme Corporation, an enterprise customer, wants to converge its voice and data networks to save money in the short term. This book does not provide detailed information on actual monetary savings, but it does highlight some of the areas in which savings can potentially occur.

Having two separate infrastructures for a voice and data network requires that you have leased lines not only for voice, but also for data paths. Figure 6-14 shows a typical enterprise customer with separate networks.

The voice network uses multiplexers to connect voice and data networks across one T1 circuit. When voice is not being used, however, the voice network is still consuming bandwidth across the leased T1 circuit.

site houses a small sales office where from two to five people work at any given time. The Raleigh and San Diego sites have slightly larger regional offices employing both sales people and development staff. Atlanta has a committed information rate (CIR) of 0 and can burst up to 56 K. Raleigh and San Diego both have a 64 K CIR and can burst up to 128 K.

The IS department conducted a study and determined that both data and voice bandwidth needs were growing. The IS department decided to research methods for compressing voice and taking advantage of unused time-division multiplexing (TDM) bandwidth currently utilized by the multiplexing configuration.

The IS department also conducted a study to determine calling patterns. It found that most long-distance calls from all sites are clustered around the various regions in which the corporation has branches.

Acme asked itself several questions to determine whether a combined voice and data network would provide the expected savings.

Acme's Convergence Plan and Goals

It is important to understand where the customer's network stands today and where the customer wants to be when the data/voice networks have converged. Therefore, ask the following questions:

- What is the total expenditure on voice networks and capital equipment?
- What is the primary application for VoIP (toll bypass, call-center, or ICW)?
- How many remote sites does the company have?
- How many people are at each remote site?
- What is the average phone usage in minutes per user per site?
- How many calls are placed to interoffice locations?
- What is the average cost per minute per location?
- What is the customer's expectation of quality (cellular, toll)?
- What is the total number of long-distance minutes between sites?
- What percentage of traffic is expected to be voice/fax?
- Can the existing IP infrastructure support the necessary quality of service (QoS) for voice?

After these questions are answered, enterprise customers can decide whether they can afford to make the voice/data transition.

Acme took the necessary time to plan its network design in phases. Its final network design is shown in Figure 6-15.

Figure 6-15 *Integrated Voice and Data Network*

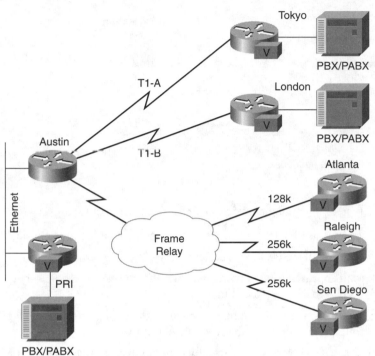

The network design shown in Figure 6-15 is just one step in the path toward voice and data integration. Acme's next step is to slowly replace the key-systems and PBXs at its sites with IP phones. Doing so obviates the need for purchasing additional circuit-switching hardware and provides many additional benefits, including a single infrastructure and support group.

Integration of Voice and Data Networks

The next step for an enterprise customer is to simplify the local-area network (LAN) by implementing a common voice and data network to the desktop. This is accomplished with IP phones, as shown in Figure 6-16.

Figure 6-16 *Voice/Data Integration to the Desktop*

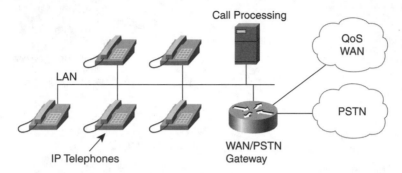

This type of integrated network provides numerous cost savings:

- Phones use DHCP and keep phone numbers regardless of physical location.

- Cabling to the desktop is easier (everything is Ethernet).

- Call appearance remains the same whether the user is at home or at work. This enables fully transparent telecommuting.

- The call-processing engine is now on a standard platform, which provides the enterprise network with greater flexibility.

- Cisco's Call Manager is actually configurable through Hypertext Markup Language (HTML), which simplifies administrative overhead as well as PBX administration.

- Cisco's Call Manager can also support other standards-based interfaces such as Station Message Desk Interface (SMDI) for an interface into a legacy PBX. As an example, you can use this interface to illuminate the message-waiting light.

Putting voice on data networks in enterprise, service provider, and other types of networks affords numerous additional benefits. Some are apparent, and some have yet to be discovered.

Summary

Integrating your voice and data networks is beneficial in many ways. Your costs are reduced due to a single support structure and per-minute, long-distance charges. Also, new applications such as ICW and V2L enable service providers to charge more per subscriber and to differentiate themselves from other service providers.

Call centers offer a great opportunity for voice and data network integration, in that they enable faster customer service. This adds to the call center operator's bottom line and enables applications such as Web line and data/voice collaboration.

Force (IETF) are drafting proposals on ways you can inter-work or backhaul these protocols where appropriate.

The Virtual Switch Controller (VSC), discussed in Chapter 13, "Virtual Switch Controller," provides a centralized mechanism for handling these signaling protocols. So, as standards are accepted and implemented, the inter-working of telephony signaling systems and VoIP systems will become more like "business as usual."

CHAPTER 7

IP Tutorial

Many of the benefits of Voice over IP (VoIP) are derived from the use of Internet Protocol (IP) as the transport mechanism. To truly understand these benefits, you must first understand what IP actually means. What are the behavioral characteristics of IP, and what does an IP packet look like? These questions, and a few others, are answered in this chapter.

Before you can understand what IP can do for you and ways you can run applications through IP, you must first become familiar with the Open Systems Interconnection (OSI) reference model and how it applies to IP.

OSI Reference Model

The International Organization for Standardization (ISO) developed the OSI reference model in the early 1980s, and it is now the standard for developing protocols that enable computers to communicate. Although not all protocols follow this model, many people use it to help them develop and teach new protocols.

The OSI reference model breaks up the problem of intermachine communication into seven layers. Each layer is concerned only with talking to its corresponding layer on the other machine (see Figure 7-1). This means that Layer 5 has to worry only about talking to Layer 5 on the receiving machine, and not what the actual physical medium might be.

In addition, each layer of the OSI reference model provides services to the layer above it (Layer 5 to Layer 6, Layer 6 to Layer 7, and so on) and requests certain services from the layer directly below it (5 to 4, 4 to 3, and so on).

This layered approach enables each layer to handle a small piece of information, make any necessary changes to the data, and add the necessary functions for that layer before passing the data along. Data becomes less human-like and more computer-like the further down the OSI reference model it traverses, until it becomes 1s and 0s (electrical impulses) at the physical layer. Figure 7-1 shows the OSI reference model.

The primary focus of this chapter is to discuss the application, presentation, session, transport, network, data link, and physical layers. Understanding these layers allows you to understand how IP routing works and how IP is transported across various media occurring at Layer 2 and Layer 1.

The Data Link Layer

The data link layer provides reliable transport across a physical link. The link layer has its own addressing scheme. This addressing scheme is concerned with physical connectivity and can transport frames based upon the data link layer address.

Traditional Ethernet switches switch network traffic based upon the data link layer (Layer 2) address. Switching traffic based on a Layer 2 address is generally known as *bridging*. In fact, an Ethernet switch is nothing more than a high-speed bridge with multiple interfaces.

The Physical Layer

The physical layer is concerned with creating 1s and 0s on the physical medium with electrical impulses/voltage changes. Common physical layer communication specifications include the following:

- EIA/TIA-232—Electrical Industries Association/Telecommunications Industry Association specification used for communicating between computer devices. You can use different connectors; this interface is often used for connecting computers to modems.

- V.35—International Telecommunication Union Telecommunication Standardization Sector (ITU-T) signaling mechanism that defines signaling rates from 19.2 Kbps to 1.544 Mbps. This physical interface is a 34-pin connector and also is known as a Winchester Block.

- RS-449—Uses 37 pins and is capable of longer runs than RS-232.

Internet Protocol

IP itself is a connectionless protocol that resides at Layer 3 (the network layer), which means that no reliability mechanisms, flow control, sequencing, or acknowledgments are present. Other protocols, such as TCP, can sit on top of IP (Layer 4, session) and can add flow control, sequencing, and other features.

Given IP's relative position in the OSI reference model, it doesn't have to deal with common data link issues such as Ethernet, Asynchronous Transfer Mode (ATM), Frame Relay, and Token Ring, or with physical issues such as Synchronous Optical Network (SONET), copper, and fiber. This makes IP virtually ubiquitous.

You can run IP into a home or business through any means necessary (for instance, wireless, broadband, or baseband). This doesn't mean that when you design a network you can ignore the lower two layers. It only means that they are independent of any *applications* you put on IP.

IP is considered a *bursty* protocol, which means that the applications residing above IP experience long periods of silence, followed by a need for a large portion of bandwidth. A good example of this is e-mail. If you set your mail package to download e-mail every 20 minutes, about 20 minutes of silence exist during which no bandwidth is needed.

One of the major benefits of IP is the ability to write an application *once* and have it delivered through an assorted type of media *anywhere*, regardless of whether this occurs through a digital subscriber line (DSL) connection in your home or a T1 line in your business.

You can address an IP packet in three general ways: through unicast, multicast, or broadcast mechanisms. Briefly explained, these three mechanisms provide the means for every IP packet to be labeled with a destination address, each in its unique way:

- Unicast is fairly simple, in that it identifies one specific address and only that node is supposed to send the packet to the higher layers of the OSI reference model.

- Broadcast packets are sent to all users on a local subnetwork. Broadcasts can traverse bridges and switches, but they are not passed through routers (unless they are specially configured to do so).

- Multicast packets use a special addressing range that enables a group of users on different subnetworks to receive the same flow. This enables the sender to send only one packet that several disparate hosts can receive.

Unicast, broadcast, and multicast packets each have a significant purpose. Unicast packets enable two stations to communicate with each other, regardless of physical location. Broadcast packets are used to communicate with everyone on a subnetwork simultaneously. Multicast packets enable applications, such as videoconferencing, that have one transmitter and multiple receivers.

Regardless of the type of IP packet used, data link layer addressing is always needed. Data link layer addresses are covered in detail in the next section.

Data Link Layer Addresses

The two types of addresses are data link layer and network layer addresses. Data link layer addresses— also known as Media Access Control (MAC) addresses and physical layer addresses—are unique to every device. In a local-area network (LAN), for instance, each device has a MAC address which identifies itself on the LAN. This enables computers to know who is sending what message. If you look at an Ethernet frame, the first 12 bytes are the destination and source MAC addresses.

If you use an Ethernet LAN switch, the traffic is routed through the switch based on the data link layer address (the MAC address). If you use a repeater or hub to connect the devices to the LAN, the packet is forwarded to all ports, regardless of the MAC address. This is because forwarding through a hub is based upon the *physical* layer and not the data link layer.

When traffic is routed based on the MAC layer address, it is generally referred to as being *switched* or *bridged*. Before routing became prominent in the late 1980s, many companies developed bridges to connect two disparate networks. This enabled a simple and inexpensive method of connecting two networks at the data link layer. Because these bridges did not look at the network layer address, however, unwanted traffic such as broadcasts and multicasts could be transmitted across the bridge, which consumed a large amount of bandwidth.

Most LANs in the 1980s and early 1990s used a hub to connect their Ethernet workstations. This device was known as a *repeater* and replicated the Layer 1 information only. So, if a corporation had an eight-port hub and one of the eight ports received a packet, the packet would be repeated (exactly, errors and all) to the other seven ports.

In the early 1990s, companies began developing LAN switches, which were basically a combination of a hub and bridge. In this scenario, the LAN switch learned which Layer 2 addresses were attached to each of its physical interfaces and forwarded traffic based on the Layer 2 address. If the switch did not have a list of a particular destination Layer 2 address in its switching table, or if the packet were a broadcast packet, the packet was repeated to all other interfaces on the switch.

This transition to network switches enabled networks to make better use of the available bandwidth. This saving in bandwidth was accomplished by preventing unnecessary IP packets from being transmitted on a physical port where the receiving device did not reside.

Now that you understand MAC addresses and how networks use them to route packets, it is time to discuss how networks use IP addressing to further route those packets.

IP Addressing

Of the different addressing schemes, IP addressing is the most important to understand because you must conceptually comprehend how these devices communicate to effectively build networks on top of an IP infrastructure.

Many protocols exist, and each has a different addressing scheme.

Network layer addressing is normally hierarchical. As compared to the Public Switched Telephone Network (PSTN) in the North American Numbering Plan Association (NANPA) network of today, each Numbering Plan Area (NPA) includes a region, with a prefix (Nxx) denoting a sub-region and station identifier (xxxx) denoting the actual phone.

Network layer addressing lies at Layer 3 of the OSI model. This enables a group of computers to be given similar logical addresses. Logical addressing is similar to determining a person's address by looking at his or her country, state, ZIP code, city, and street address.

Routers forward traffic based on the Layer 3 or network layer address. IP addressing supports five network classes. The bits at the far left indicate the network class, as follows:

- Class A networks are intended mainly for use with a few large networks because they provide only seven bits for the network address field.

- Class B networks allocate 14 bits for the network address field and 16 bits for the host address field. This address class offers a good compromise between network and host address space.

- Class C networks allocate 21 bits for the network address field. They provide only 8 bits for the host field, however, so the number of hosts per network can be a limiting factor.

- Class D addresses are reserved for multicast groups, as described formally in RFC 1112. In class D addresses, the four highest-order bits are set to 1, 1, 1, and 0.

- Class E addresses also are defined by IP but are reserved for future use. In class E addresses, the four highest-order bits are set to 1, and the fifth bit is always 0.

IP addresses are written in dotted decimal format—for example, 121.10.3.116. Figure 7-2 shows the address formats for class A, B, and C IP networks. An easy way to think of class addressing is that the more networks you have, the fewer hosts you can have on that network.

Figure 7-2   *Class A, B, and C Address Formats*

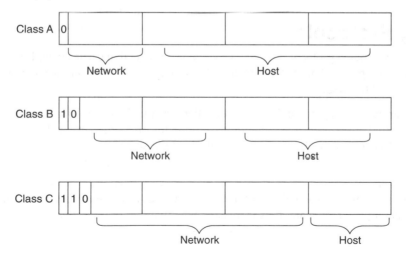

You can also divide IP networks into smaller units called *subnets*. Subnets provide extra flexibility for network administrators. Assume, for example, that a network is assigned a

To simplify router design and operation, IS-IS distinguishes between Level 1 and Level 2 Information Services (ISs):

- Level 1 ISs communicate with other Level 1 ISs in the same area.
- Level 2 ISs route between Level 1 areas and form an intradomain routing backbone.

Hierarchical routing simplifies backbone design because Level 1 ISs only need to know how to get to the nearest Level 2 IS. The backbone routing protocol also can change without impacting the intra-area routing protocol.

OSPF

OSPF is a link-state, Interior Gateway Routing Protocol (IGRP). It was designed to operate in TCP/IP networks and to address the shortcomings of the Router Information Protocol (RIP).

OSPF is derived from a number of sources, including the shortest path first (SPF) algorithm developed by Bolt, Beranek, and Newman, Inc. (BBN), an early version of the OSI IS-IS routing protocol, and other research efforts.

IGRP

IGRP is a robust protocol for routing within an autonomous system having arbitrarily complex topology and consisting of media with diverse bandwidth and delay characteristics.

Cisco Systems developed IGRP in the mid-1980s. It is a distance-vector interior gateway protocol that uses a combination of metrics to make routing decisions.

EIGRP

EIGRP is an enhanced version of the IGRP developed by Cisco Systems.

EIGRP uses the same distance-vector algorithm and distance information as IGRP. EIGRP's convergence properties and operating efficiency are significantly better than those of IGRP.

EIGRP is a distance-vector interior gateway protocol that has the following features:

- It uses a combination of metrics to make routing decisions.
- It uses the Diffusing Update Algorithm (DUAL) to enable routes to converge quickly.
- It sends partial routing-table updates.
- It implements a neighbor discovery mechanism.

RIP

RIP is a distance-vector protocol that uses hop count as its metric. RIP is an Interior Gateway Protocol (IGP); it performs routing within a single autonomous system.

All these various routing protocols are used in different networks based upon their advantages and disadvantages. This book does not discuss in depth when to choose one over the other, but it is important to understand the basics about each protocol to further understand ways you can assemble IP networks.

It also is important to understand the different transport mechanisms that give IP different characteristics. These transport mechanisms are discussed next.

IP Transport Mechanisms

TCP and User Datagram Protocol (UDP) have different characteristics that various applications can use. If reliability is more important than delay, for instance, you can use TCP/IP to guarantee packet delivery. UDP/IP does not utilize packet re-transmissions, however. This can lower reliability, but in some cases a late retransmission is of no use.

To compare various transport layer protocols, you must first understand what makes up an IP packet. Figure 7-4 shows the fields of the IP packet.

Figure 7-4   *IP Packet Fields*

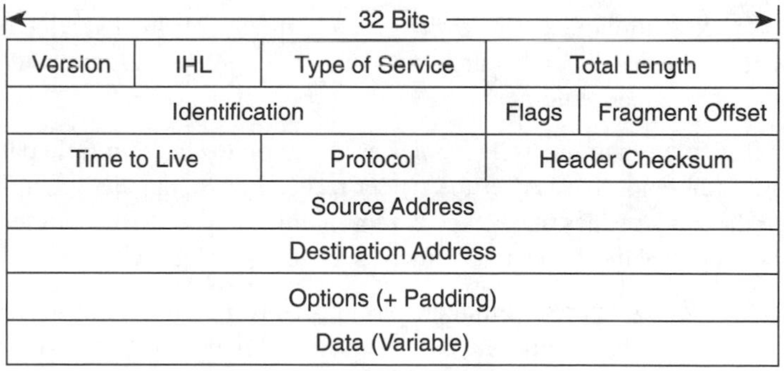

IP packet fields are defined as follows:

- Version—indicates whether IPv4 or IPv6 is being used.

- IP header length (IHL)—Indicates the datagram header length in 32-bit words.

- Type of service—Specifies how a particular upper-layer protocol wants the current datagram to be handled. You can assign packets various quality of service (QoS) levels based on this field.

- Total length—Specifies the length of the entire IP packet, including data and header, in bytes.

- Identification—Contains an integer that identifies the current datagram. This field is used to help piece together datagram fragments.

- Flags—A 3-bit field of which the low-order 2 bits control fragmentation. The high-order bit in this field is not used. One bit specifies whether you can fragment the packet; the second bit specifies whether the packet is the last fragment in a series of fragmented packets.

- Time To Live—Maintains a counter that gradually decrements down to zero, at which point the datagram is discarded. This keeps packets from looping endlessly.

- Protocol—Indicates which upper-layer protocol receives incoming packets after IP processing is complete.

- Header checksum—Verifies that the header is not corrupted.

- Source address—The sending address.

- Destination address—The address to receive the datagram.

- Options—Enables IP to support various options, such as security.

- Data—Contains application data as well as upper-layer protocol information.

TCP

TCP provides full-duplex, acknowledged, and flow-controlled service to upper-layer protocols. It moves data in a continuous, unstructured byte stream where bytes are identified by sequence numbers.

To maximize throughput, TCP enables each station to send multiple packets before an acknowledgment arrives. After the sender receives an acknowledgment for an outstanding packet, the sender slides the packet window along the byte stream and sends another packet. This flow control mechanism is known as a *sliding window.*

TCP can support numerous simultaneous upper-layer conversations. The port numbers in a TCP header identify an upper-layer conversation. Many well-known TCP ports are reserved for File Transfer Protocol (FTP), World Wide Web (WWW), Telnet, and so on.

Within the signaling portion of VoIP, TCP is used to ensure the reliability of the setup of a call. Due to the methods by which TCP operates, it is not feasible to use TCP as the mechanism to carry the actual voice in a VoIP call. With VoIP, packet loss is less important than latency.

The TCP packet fields are as follows:

- Source port and destination port—Identifies the points at which upper-layer source and destination processes receive TCP services.

- Sequence number—Usually specifies the number assigned to the first byte of data in the current message. Under certain circumstances, it also can be used to identify an initial sequence number to be used in the upcoming transmission.

- Acknowledgment number—Contains the sequence number of the next byte of data the sender of the packet expects to receive.

- Data offset—Indicates the number of 32-bit words in the TCP header.

- Reserved—Reserved for future use.

- Flags—Carry a variety of control information.

- Window—Specifies the size of the sender's receive window (that is, buffer space available for incoming data).

- Checksum—Indicates whether the header and data were damaged in transit.

- Urgent pointer—Points to the first urgent data byte in the packet.

- Options—Specifies various TCP options.

- Data—Contains upper-layer information.

UDP

UDP is a much simpler protocol than TCP and is useful in situations where the reliability mechanisms of TCP are unnecessary. UDP also is connectionless and has a smaller header, which translates to minimal overhead.

The UDP header has only four fields: source port, destination port, length, and UDP checksum. The source and destination port fields serve the same functions as they do in the TCP header. The length field specifies the length of the UDP header and data, and the checksum field enables packet integrity checking. The UDP checksum is optional.

UDP is used in VoIP to carry the actual voice traffic (the *bearer channels*). TCP is not used because flow control and retransmission of voice audio packets are unnecessary. Because UDP is used to carry the audio stream, it continues to transmit, regardless of whether you are experiencing 5 percent packet loss or 50 percent packet loss.

If TCP were utilized for VoIP, the latency incurred waiting for acknowledgments and retransmissions would render voice quality unacceptable. With VoIP and other real-time applications, controlling latency is more important than ensuring the reliable delivery of each packet.

TCP is used, on the other hand, for call setup in most VoIP signaling protocols. See Chapter 10, "H.323," Chapter 11, "Session Initiation Protocol," and Chapter 12, "Gateway Control Protocols," for details on VoIP call signaling.

CHAPTER 8

VoIP: An In-Depth Analysis

To create a proper network design, it is important to know all the caveats and inner workings of networking technology. This chapter explains many of the issues facing Voice over IP (VoIP) and ways in which Cisco addresses these issues.

Standard time-division multiplexing (TDM) has its own set of problems, which are covered in Chapter 1, "Overview of the PSTN and Comparisons to Voice over IP," and Chapter 2, "Enterprise Telephony Today." VoIP technology has many similar issues and a whole batch of additional ones. This chapter details these various issues and explains how they can affect packet networks.

The following issues are covered in this chapter:

- Delay/latency
- Jitter
- Digital sampling
- Voice compression
- Echo
- Packet loss
- Voice activity detection
- Digital-to-analog conversion
- Tandem encoding
- Transport protocols
- Dial-plan design

Delay/Latency

VoIP *delay* or *latency* is characterized as the amount of time it takes for speech to exit the speaker's mouth and reach the listener's ear.

Three types of delay are inherent in today's telephony networks: *propagation delay*, *serialization delay*, and *handling delay*. Propagation delay is caused by the speed of light in fiber or copper-based networks. Handling delay—also called processing delay—defines many different causes of delay (actual packetization, compression, and packet switching) and is caused by devices that forward the frame through the network.

Serialization delay is the amount of time it takes to actually place a bit or byte onto an interface. Serialization delay is not covered in depth in this book because its influence on delay is relatively minimal.

Propagation Delay

Light travels through a vacuum at a speed of 186,000 miles per second, and electrons travel through copper or fiber at approximately 125,000 miles per second. A fiber network stretching halfway around the world (13,000 miles) induces a one-way delay of about 70 milliseconds (70 ms). Although this delay is almost imperceptible to the human ear, propagation delays in conjunction with handling delays can cause noticeable speech degradation.

Handling Delay

As mentioned previously, devices that forward the frame through the network cause handling delay. Handling delays can impact traditional phone networks, but these delays are a larger issue in packetized environments. The following paragraphs discuss the different handling delays and how they affect voice quality.

In the Cisco IOS VoIP product, the Digital Signal Processor (DSP) generates a speech sample every 10 ms when using G.729. Two of these speech samples (both with 10 ms of delay) are then placed within one packet. The packet delay is, therefore, 20 ms. An initial look-ahead of 5 ms occurs when using G.729, giving an initial delay of 25 ms for the first speech frame.

Vendors can decide how many speech samples they want to send in one packet. Because G.729 uses 10 ms speech samples, each increase in samples per frame raises the delay by 10 ms. In fact, Cisco IOS enables users to choose how many samples to put into each frame.

Cisco gave DSP much of the responsibility for framing and forming packets to keep router overhead low. The Real-Time Transport Protocol (RTP) header, for example, is placed on the frame in the DSP instead of giving the router that task.

Queuing Delay

A packet-based network experiences delay for other reasons. Two of these are the time necessary to move the actual packet to the output queue (packet switching) and queuing delay.

When packets are held in a queue because of congestion on an outbound interface, the result is *queuing delay*. Queuing delay occurs when more packets are sent out than the interface can handle at a given interval.

Cisco IOS software is good at moving and determining the destination of a packet. Other packet-based solutions, including PC-based solutions, are not as good at determining packet destination and moving the actual packet to the output queue.

The actual queuing delay of the output queue is another cause of delay. You should keep this factor to less than 10 ms whenever you can by using whatever queuing methods are optimal for your network. This subject is covered in greater detail in Chapter 9, "Quality of Service."

The International Telecommunication Union Telecommunication Standardization Sector (ITU-T) G.114 recommendation specifies that for good voice quality, no more than 150 ms of one-way, end-to-end delay should occur, as shown in Figure 8-1. With Cisco's VoIP implementation, *two* routers with minimal network delay (back to back) use only about 60 ms of end-to-end delay. This leaves up to 90 ms of network delay to move the IP packet from source to destination.

Figure 8-1   *End-to-End Delay*

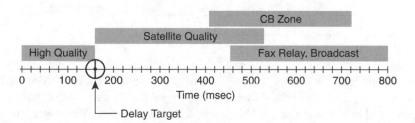

As shown in Figure 8-1, some forms of delay are longer, although accepted, because no other alternatives exist. In satellite transmission, for example, it takes approximately 250 ms for a transmission to reach the satellite, and another 250 ms for it to come back down to Earth. This results in a total delay of 500 ms. Although the ITU-T recommendation notes that this is outside the acceptable range of voice quality, many conversations occur every day over satellite links. As such, voice quality is often defined as what users will accept and use.

In an unmanaged, congested network, queuing delay can add up to two seconds of delay (or result in the packet being dropped). This lengthy period of delay is unacceptable in almost any voice network. Queuing delay is only one component of end-to-end delay. Another way end-to-end delay is affected is through jitter.

Jitter

Simply stated, *jitter* is the variation of packet interarrival time. Jitter is one issue that exists only in packet-based networks. While in a packet voice environment, the sender is expected to reliably transmit voice packets at a regular interval (for example, send one frame every 20 ms). These voice packets can be delayed throughout the packet network and not arrive at that same regular interval at the receiving station (for example, they might not be received every 20 ms; see Figure 8-2). The difference between when the packet is expected and when it is actually received is *jitter*.

Figure 8-2   *Variation of Packet Arrival Time (Jitter)*

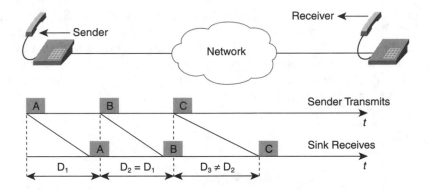

In Figure 8-2, you can see that the amount of time it takes for packets A and B to send and receive is equal (D1=D2). Packet C encounters delay in the network, however, and is received *after* it is expected. This is why a *jitter buffer*, which conceals interarrival packet delay variation, is necessary.

Note that jitter and total delay are *not* the same thing, although having plenty of jitter in a packet network can increase the amount of total delay in the network. This is because the more jitter you have, the larger your jitter buffer needs to be to compensate for the unpredictable nature of the packet network.

If your data network is engineered well and you take the proper precautions, jitter is usually not a major problem and the jitter buffer does not significantly contribute to the total end-to-end delay.

RTP timestamps are used within Cisco IOS software to determine what level of jitter, if any, exists within the network.

The jitter buffer found within Cisco IOS software is considered a dynamic queue. This queue can grow or shrink exponentially depending on the interarrival time of the RTP packets.

Although many vendors choose to use static jitter buffers, Cisco found that a well-engineered dynamic jitter buffer is the best mechanism to use for packet-based voice networks. Static jitter buffers force the jitter buffer to be either too large or too small, thereby causing the audio quality to suffer, due to either lost packets or excessive delay. Cisco's jitter buffer dynamically increases or decreases based upon the interarrival delay variation of the last few packets.

Pulse Code Modulation

Although analog communication is ideal for human communication, analog transmission is neither robust nor efficient at recovering from line noise. In the early telephony network, when analog transmission was passed through amplifiers to boost the signal, not only was the voice boosted but the line noise was amplified, as well. This line noise resulted in an often-unusable connection.

It is much easier for digital samples, which are comprised of 1 and 0 bits, to be separated from line noise. Therefore, when analog signals are regenerated as digital samples, a clean sound is maintained. When the benefits of this digital representation became evident, the telephony network migrated to pulse code modulation (PCM).

What Is PCM?

As covered in Chapter 1, PCM converts analog sound into digital form by sampling the analog sound 8000 times per second and converting each sample into a numeric code. The Nyquist theorem states that if you sample an analog signal at twice the rate of the highest frequency of interest, you can accurately reconstruct that signal back into its analog form. Because most speech content is below 4000 Hz (4 kHz), a sampling rate of 8000 times per second (125 ms between samples) is required.

A Sampling Example for Satellite Networks

Satellite networks have an inherent delay of around 500 ms. This includes 250 ms for the trip up to the satellite, and another 250 ms for the trip back to Earth. In this type of network, packet loss is highly controlled due to the expense of bandwidth. Also, if some type of voice application is already running through the satellite, the users of this service are accustomed to a quality of voice that has excessive delays.

Cisco IOS, by default, sends two 10 ms G.729 speech frames in every packet. Although this is acceptable for most applications, this might not be the best method for utilizing the expensive bandwidth on a satellite link. The simple explanation for wasting bandwidth is that a header exists for every packet. The more speech frames you put into a packet, the fewer headers you require.

If you take the satellite example and use four 10 ms G.729 speech frames per packet, you can cut by half the number of headers you use. Table 8-1 clearly shows the difference between the various frames per packet. With only a 20-byte increase in packet size (20 extra bytes equals two 10 ms G.729 samples), you carry twice as much speech with the packet.

Table 8-1   *Frames per Packet (G.729)*

G.729 Samples per Frame	IP/RTP/UDP Header	Bandwidth Consumed	Latency*
Default (two samples per frame)	40 bytes	24,000 bps	25 ms
Satellite (four samples per frame)	40 bytes	16,000 bps	45 ms
Low Latency (one sample per frame)	40 bytes	40,000 bps	15 ms

* Compression and packetization delay only

Voice Compression

Two basic variations of 64 Kbps PCM are commonly used: μ-law and a-law. The methods are similar in that they both use logarithmic compression to achieve 12 to 13 bits of linear PCM quality in 8 bits, but they are different in relatively minor compression details (μ-law has a slight advantage in low-level, signal-to-noise ratio performance). Usage is historically along country and regional boundaries, with North America using μ-law and Europe using a-law modulation. It is important to note that when making a long-distance call, any required μ-law to a-law conversion is the responsibility of the μ-law country.

Another compression method used often is *adaptive differential pulse code modulation (ADPCM)*. A commonly used instance of ADPCM is ITU-T G.726, which encodes using 4-bit samples, giving a transmission rate of 32 Kbps. Unlike PCM, the 4 bits do not directly encode the amplitude of speech, but they do encode the differences in amplitude, as well as the rate of change of that amplitude, employing some rudimentary linear prediction.

PCM and ADPCM are examples of *waveform* codecs—compression techniques that exploit redundant characteristics of the waveform itself. New compression techniques were developed over the past 10 to 15 years that further exploit knowledge of the source characteristics of speech generation. These techniques employ signal processing procedures that compress speech by sending only simplified parametric information about the original speech excitation and vocal tract shaping, requiring less bandwidth to transmit that information.

These techniques can be grouped together generally as *source* codecs and include variations such as *linear predictive coding (LPC)*, *code excited linear prediction compression (CELP)*, and *multipulse, multilevel quantization (MP-MLQ)*.

Voice Coding Standards

The ITU-T standardizes CELP, MP-MLQ PCM, and ADPCM coding schemes in its G-series recommendations. The most popular voice coding standards for telephony and packet voice include:

- G.711—Describes the 64 Kbps PCM voice coding technique outlined earlier; G.711-encoded voice is already in the correct format for digital voice delivery in the public phone network or through Private Branch eXchanges (PBXs).

- G.726—Describes ADPCM coding at 40, 32, 24, and 16 Kbps; you also can interchange ADPCM voice between packet voice and public phone or PBX networks, provided that the latter has ADPCM capability.

- G.728—Describes a 16 Kbps low-delay variation of CELP voice compression.

- G.729—Describes CELP compression that enables voice to be coded into 8 Kbps streams; two variations of this standard (G.729 and G.729 Annex A) differ largely in computational complexity, and both generally provide speech quality as good as that of 32 Kbps ADPCM.

- G.723.1—Describes a compression technique that you can use to compress speech or other audio signal components of multimedia service at a low bit rate, as part of the overall H.324 family of standards. Two bit rates are associated with this coder: 5.3 and 6.3 Kbps. The higher bit rate is based on MP-MLQ technology and provides greater quality. The lower bit rate is based on CELP, provides good quality, and affords system designers with additional flexibility.

Mean Opinion Score

You can test voice quality in two ways: subjectively and objectively. Humans perform subjective voice testing, whereas computers—which are less likely to be "fooled" by compression schemes that can "trick" the human ear—perform objective voice testing.

Codecs are developed and tuned based on subjective measurements of voice quality. Standard objective quality measurements, such as total harmonic distortion and signal-to-noise ratios, do not correlate well to a human's perception of voice quality, which in the end is usually the goal of most voice compression techniques.

A common subjective benchmark for quantifying the performance of the speech codec is the *mean opinion score (MOS)*. MOS tests are given to a group of listeners. Because voice quality and sound in general are subjective to listeners, it is important to get a wide range of listeners and sample material when conducting a MOS test. The listeners give each sample of speech material a rating of 1 (bad) to 5 (excellent). The scores are then averaged to get the mean opinion score.

In this example, assume that user A is talking to user B. The speech of user A to user B is called G. When G hits an impedance mismatch or other echo-causing environments, it bounces back to user A. User A can then hear the delay several milliseconds after user A actually speaks.

To remove the echo from the line, the device user A is talking through (router A) keeps an inverse image of user A's speech for a certain amount of time. This is called *inverse speech (–G)*. This echo canceller listens for the sound coming from user B and subtracts the –G to remove any echo.

Echo cancellers are limited by the total amount of time they wait for the reflected speech to be received, a phenomenon known as *echo tail*. Cisco has configurable echo tails of 16, 24, and 32 ms.

It is important to configure the appropriate amount of echo cancellation when initially installing VoIP equipment. If you don't configure enough echo cancellation, callers will hear echo during the phone call. If you configure too much echo cancellation, it will take longer for the echo canceller to converge and eliminate the echo.

Packet Loss

Packet loss in data networks is both common and expected. Many data protocols, in fact, use packet loss so that they know the condition of the network and can reduce the number of packets they are sending.

When putting critical traffic on data networks, it is important to control the amount of packet loss in that network.

Cisco Systems has been putting business-critical, time-sensitive traffic on data networks for many years, starting with Systems Network Architecture (SNA) traffic in the early 1990s. With protocols such as SNA that do *not* tolerate packet loss well, you need to build a well-engineered network that can prioritize the time-sensitive data ahead of data that can handle delay and packet loss.

When putting voice on data networks, it is important to build a network that can successfully transport voice in a reliable and timely manner. Also, it is helpful when you can use a mechanism to make the voice somewhat resistant to periodic packet loss.

Cisco Systems developed many quality of service (QoS) tools that enable administrators to classify and manage traffic through a data network. If a data network is well engineered, you can keep packet loss to a minimum.

Cisco Systems' VoIP implementation enables the voice router to respond to periodic packet loss. If a voice packet is not received when expected (the expected time is variable), it is assumed to be lost and the last packet received is replayed, as shown in Figure 8-4.

Because the packet lost is only 20 ms of speech, the average listener does not notice the difference in voice quality.

Figure 8-4   *Packet Loss with G.729*

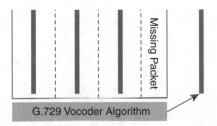

Using Cisco's G.729 implementation for VoIP, let's say that each of the lines in Figure 8-4 represents a packet. Packets 1, 2, and 3 reach the destination, but packet 4 is lost somewhere in transmission. The receiving station waits for a period of time (per its jitter buffer) and then runs a *concealment strategy*.

This concealment strategy replays the last packet received (in this case, packet 3), so the listener does not hear gaps of silence. Because the lost speech is only 20 ms, the listener most likely does not hear the difference. You can accomplish this concealment strategy only if one packet is lost. If multiple consecutive packets are lost, the concealment strategy is run only once until another packet is received.

Because of the concealment strategy of G.729, as a rule of thumb G.729 is tolerant to about five percent packet loss averaged across an entire call.

Voice Activity Detection

In normal voice conversations, someone speaks and someone else listens. Today's toll networks contain a bi-directional, 64,000 bit per second (bps) channel, regardless of whether anyone is speaking. This means that in a normal conversation, at least 50 percent of the total bandwidth is wasted. The amount of wasted bandwidth can actually be much higher if you take a statistical sampling of the breaks and pauses in a person's normal speech patterns.

When using VoIP, you can utilize this "wasted" bandwidth for other purposes when voice activity detection (VAD) is enabled. As shown in Figure 8-5, VAD works by detecting the magnitude of speech in decibels (dB) and deciding when to cut off the voice from being framed.

Figure 8-5 *Voice Activity Detection*

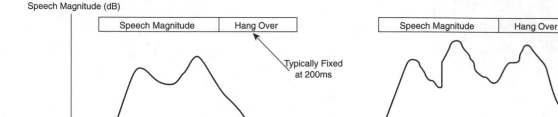

Typically, when the VAD detects a drop-off of speech amplitude, it waits a fixed amount of time before it stops putting speech frames in packets. This fixed amount of time is known as *hangover* and is typically 200 ms.

With any technology, tradeoffs are made. VAD experiences certain inherent problems in determining when speech ends and begins, and in distinguishing speech from background noise. This means that if you are in a noisy room, VAD is unable to distinguish between speech and background noise. This also is known as the *signal-to-noise threshold* (refer to Figure 8-5). In these scenarios, VAD disables itself at the beginning of the call.

Another inherent problem with VAD is detecting when speech begins. Typically the beginning of a sentence is cut off or clipped (refer to Figure 8-5). This phenomenon is known as *front-end speech clipping*. Usually, the person listening to the speech does not notice front-end speech clipping.

Digital-to-Analog Conversion

Digital to analog (D/A) conversion issues also currently plague toll networks. Although almost all the telephony backbone networks in first-world countries today are digital, sometimes multiple D/A conversions occur.

Each time a conversion occurs from digital to analog and back, the speech or waveform becomes less "true." Although today's toll networks can handle at least seven D/A conversions before voice quality is affected, compressed speech is less robust in the face of these conversions.

It is important to note that D/A conversion must be tightly managed in a compressed speech environment. When using G.729, just two conversions from D/A cause the MOS score to decrease rapidly. The only way to manage D/A conversion is to have the network designer design VoIP environments with as few D/A conversions as possible.

Although D/A conversions affect all voice networks, VoIP networks using a PCM codec (G.711) are just as resilient to problems caused by D/A conversions as today's telephony networks are.

Tandem Encoding

As covered in Chapter 1, all circuit-switched networks today work on the premise of switching calls at the data link layer. The circuit switches are organized in a hierarchical model in which switches higher in the hierarchy are called *tandem switches*.

Tandem switches do not actually terminate any local loops; rather, they act as a *higher-layer* circuit switch. In the hierarchical model, several layers of tandem circuit switches can exist, as shown in Figure 8-6. This enables end-to-end connectivity for anyone with a phone, without the need for a direct connection between every home on the planet.

Figure 8-6   *Tandem Switching Hierarchy*

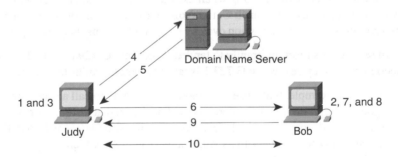

In Figure 8-6, three separate circuit switches are utilized to transport a voice call. A voice call that passes through the two TDM switches and one tandem switch does not incur degradation in voice quality because these circuit switches use 64 Kbps channels.

If the TDM switches compress voice and the tandem switch must decompress and recompress the voice, the voice quality can be drastically affected. Although compression and recompression are not common in the PSTN today, you must plan for it and design around it in packet networks.

RTP

RTP is the standard for transmitting delay-sensitive traffic across packet-based networks. RTP rides on top of UDP and IP. RTP gives receiving stations information that is not in the connectionless UDP/IP streams. As shown in Figure 8-9, two important bits of information are sequence information and timestamping. RTP uses the sequence information to determine whether the packets are arriving in order, and it uses the time-stamping information to determine the interarrival packet time (jitter).

Figure 8-9   *Real-Time Transport Header*

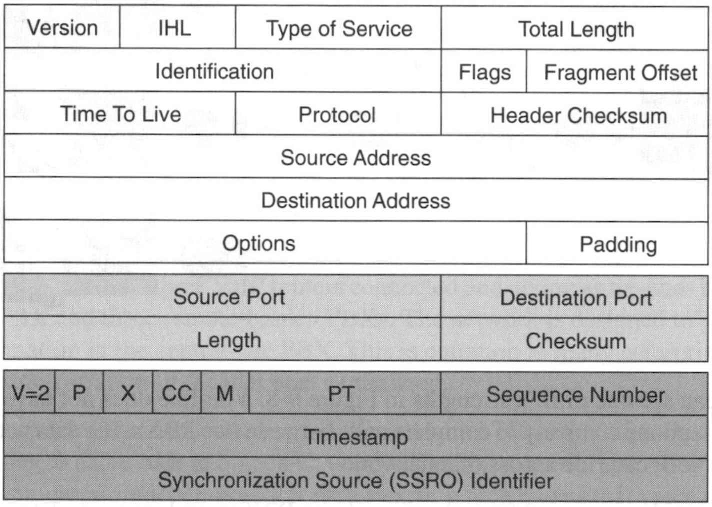

Version	IHL	Type of Service	Total Length	
Identification			Flags	Fragment Offset
Time To Live		Protocol	Header Checksum	
Source Address				
Destination Address				
Options			Padding	
Source Port			Destination Port	
Length			Checksum	
V=2	P	X	CC	M	PT	Sequence Number
Timestamp				
Synchronization Source (SSRO) Identifier				

You can use RTP for media on demand, as well as for interactive services such as Internet telephony. RTP (refer to Figure 8-9) consists of a data part and a control part, the latter called RTP Control Protocol (RTCP).

The data part of RTP is a thin protocol that provides support for applications with real-time properties, such as continuous media (for example, audio and video), including timing reconstruction, loss detection, and content identification.

RTCP provides support for real-time conferencing of groups of any size within an Internet. This support includes source identification and support for gateways, such as audio and video bridges as well as multicast-to-unicast translators. It also offers QoS feedback from receivers to the multicast group, as well as support for the synchronization of different media streams.

Using RTP is important for real-time traffic, but a few drawbacks exist. The IP/RTP/UDP headers are 20, 8, and 12 bytes, respectively. This adds up to a 40-byte header, which is twice as big as the payload when using G.729 with two speech samples (20 ms).

You can compress this large header to 2 or 4 bytes by using RTP Header Compression (CRTP). CRTP is covered in depth in Chapter 9.

Reliable User Data Protocol

Reliable User Data Protocol (RUDP) builds in some reliability to the connectionless UDP protocol. RUDP enables reliability without the need for a connection-based protocol such as TCP. The basic method of RUDP is to send multiples of the same packet and enable the receiving station to discard the unnecessary or redundant packets. This mechanism makes it more probable that one of the packets will make the journey from sender to receiver.

This also is known as *forward error correction* (FEC). Few implementations of FEC exist due to bandwidth considerations (a doubling or tripling of the amount of bandwidth used). Customers that have almost unlimited bandwidth, however, consider FEC a worthwhile mechanism to enhance reliability and voice quality.

Cisco currently utilizes RUDP in its SC2200 product, which enables Signaling System 7 (SS7) to Q.931 over IP conversion. The Q.931 over IP is transmitted over RUDP.

Dial-Plan Design

One of the areas that causes the largest amount of headaches when designing an Enterprise Telephony (ET) network is the *dial plan*. The causes of these head pains might be due to the complex issues of integrating disparate networks. Many of these disparate networks were not designed for integration.

A good data example of joining disparate networks is when two companies merge. In such a scenario, the companies' data networks (IP addressing, ordering applications, and inventory database) must be joined. It is highly improbable that both companies used the same methodologies when implementing their data networks, so problems can arise.

The same problems can occur in telephony networks. If two companies merge, their phone systems (voice mail, billing, supplementary features, and dial-plan addressing) might be incompatible with each other.

These dial-plan issues also can occur when a company decides to institute a corporate dial plan. Consider Company X, for example. Company X grew drastically in the last three years and now operates 30 sites throughout the world, with its headquarters in Dallas. Company X currently dials through the PSTN to all its 29 remote sites. Company X wants to simplify the dialing plan to all its remote sites to enable better employee communication and ease of use.

Company X currently has a large PBX at its headquarters and smaller PBX systems at its remote sites. Several alternatives are available to this company:

- Purchase leased lines between headquarters and all remote sites.

- Purchase a telephony Virtual Private Network (VPN) from the telephone company and dial an access code from anywhere to access the VPN.

- Take advantage of the existing data infrastructure and put voice on the data network.

Regardless of which option Company X chooses, it must face dial-plan design, network management, and cost issues.

Without getting into great detail, most companies must decide on their dial-plan design based on the following issues:

- Plans for growth

- Cost of leased circuits or VPNs

- Cost of additional equipment for packet voice

- Number overlap (when more than one site has the same phone number)

- Call-flows (the call patterns from each site)

- Busy hour (the time of day when the highest number of calls are offered on a circuit)

Depending on the size of the company, the dial plan can stretch from two digits to seven or eight digits. It is important that you not force yourself down a particular path until you address the previous issues.

Company X plans on sustaining 20–30 percent growth and decides on a seven-digit dial plan based on its growth patterns. This choice also cuts down on the number overlap that might be present.

Company X will have a three-digit site code, and four digits for the actual subscriber line. It made this decision because it does not believe it will have more than 999 branch offices.

NOTE   For companies that have hundreds of branch offices, it is common to have more site codes and fewer subscriber lines. If a company has several hundred branch offices and needs thousands of subscriber lines, it must use more digits (that is, it must use an eight- or nine-digit dial plan).

End Office Switch Call-Flow Versus IP Phone Call

To simplify a TDM or end office switch call-flow and an IP call-flow, this section looks at ways you can call your next-door neighbor using both the PSTN and the Internet. Although the Internet today is not the best place to ensure good-quality voice, it is okay for the purposes of showing a call-flow. Figure 8-10 shows a basic call-flow in the PSTN today. Compare this to an IP phone call-flow and notice the similarities of necessary call setup.

Figure 8-10 *Calling My Neighbor with Today's PSTN*

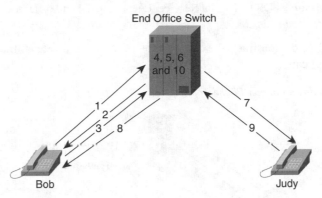

In this example, Bob calls his neighbor Judy. They are both subscribers on the local end office switch, and therefore, no SS7 is needed. The following steps occur:

1 Bob picks up his handset (off hook).

2 The local end office switch gives Bob a dial tone.

3 Bob dials Judy's seven-digit phone number.

4 The end office switch collects and analyzes the seven-digit number to determine the destination of the phone call. The end office switch knows that someone from Bob's house is placing the call because of the specific port that it dedicated to Bob.

5 The switch analyzes the seven-digit called number to determine whether the number is a local number that the switch can serve.

NOTE If the same end office switch does not service Judy, Bob's end office switch looks in its routing tables to determine how to connect this call.

6 The switch determines Judy's specific subscriber line.

7 The end office switch then signals Judy's circuit by ringing Judy's phone.

8 A voice path back to Bob is cut through so that Bob can hear the ring-back tone the end office switch is sending. The ring-back tone is sent to Bob so that he knows Judy's phone is ringing. (The ringing of Judy's phone and the ring-back tone that Bob hears need not be synchronized.)

9 Judy picks up her phone (off hook).

10 The end office switch cuts through the voice path from Bob to Judy. This is a 64 Kbps, full-duplex DS-0 (Digital Service, Level 0) in the end office switching fabric to enable voice transmission.

Figure 8-11 demonstrates the call-flow necessary to complete an Internet phone call using a PC application.

Figure 8-11 *Calling with an Internet-Phone Application*

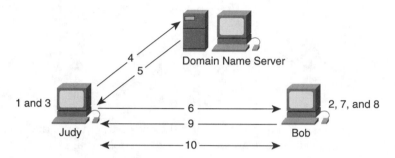

Both Bob and Judy need to be on the Internet or have some other IP network between their homes to talk to each other. Assuming this IP network exists or that both neighbors have a connection to the Internet, you can then follow this possible call-flow:

1 Judy launches her Internet phone (I-phone) application, which is H.323-compatible.

2 Bob already has his I-phone application launched.

3 Judy knows that Bob's Internet "name," or Domain Name System (DNS) entry, is Bob.nextdoorneighbor.com, so she puts that into the "who to call" section in her I-phone application and presses Return.

4 The I-phone application converts Bob.nextdoorneighbor.com to a DNS host name and goes to a DNS server that is statically configured in Judy's machine to resolve the DNS name and get an actual IP address.

5 The DNS machine passes back Bob's IP address.

6 Judy's I-phone application takes Bob's IP address and sends an H.225 message to Bob.

7 The H.225 message signals Bob's PC to begin ringing.

8 Bob clicks on the Accept button, which tells his I-phone application to send back an H.225 connect message.

9 Judy's I-phone application then begins H.245 negotiation with Bob's PC.

10 H.245 negotiation finishes and logical channels are opened. Bob and Judy can now speak to one another through a packet-based network.

This sounds fairly complex. That's because VoIP is complex. The example does not show all the steps and omits some details that a service provider needs to deploy a VoIP network. But despite its complexity, VoIP is beneficial. Because IP is a ubiquitous protocol, as mentioned in Chapter 7, when a call is packetized, it could be destined to your next-door neighbor or to a relative in Norway.

Summary

This chapter brought up many of the issues surrounding VoIP. Many of these issues, such as compression/decompression of the speech frame and propagation delay, are inherent to VoIP, and you can't do much to minimize these effects on VoIP networks.

With careful planning and solid network design, however, you can control and possibly avoid many problematic issues. Some of these issues are jitter, overall latency, handling delay, sampling rates, tandem encodings, and dial-plan design.

References

The following Requests For Comments (RFCs) will help you to continue researching VoIP:

RFC 1889—RTP: A Transport Protocol for Real-Time Applications
RFC 2327—SDP: Session Description Protocol
RFC 2326—RTSP: Real-Time Streaming Protocol
ITU-T Recommendation H.323
ITU-T G. specifications for codecs
ITU-T G.113 Voice Quality Specification
ITU-T P.861 Perceptual Speech Quality Measure(ment), PSQM

CHAPTER 9

Quality of Service

Quality of service (QoS) is an often-used and misused term that has a variety of meanings. In this book, QoS refers to both class of service (CoS) and type of service (ToS). The basic goal of CoS and ToS is to achieve the bandwidth and latency needed for a particular application.

A CoS enables a network administrator to group different packet flows, each having distinct latency and bandwidth requirements. A ToS is a field in an Internet Protocol (IP) header that enables CoS to take place. Currently, a ToS field uses three bits, which allow for eight packet-flow groupings, or CoSs (0-7). New Requests For Comments (RFCs) will enable six bits in a ToS field to allow for more CoSs.

Various tools are available to achieve the necessary QoS for a given user and application. This chapter discusses these tools, when to use them, and potential drawbacks associated with some of them.

It is important to note that the tools for implementing these services are not as important as the end result achieved. In other words, do not focus on one QoS tool to solve all your QoS problems. Instead, look at the network as a whole to determine which tools, if any, belong in which portions of your network.

Keep in mind that the more granular your approach to queuing and controlling your network, the more administrative overhead the Information Services (IS) department will endure. This increases the possibility that the entire network will slow down due to a miscalculation.

QoS Network Toolkit

In a well-engineered network, you must be careful to separate functions that occur on the edges of a network from functions that occur in the core or backbone of a network. It is important to separate edge and backbone functions to achieve the best QoS possible.

Cisco offers many tools for implementing QoS. In some scenarios, you can use none of these QoS tools and still achieve the QoS you need for your applications. In general, though, each network has individual problems that you can solve using one or more of Cisco's QoS tools.

Bandwidth Limitations

The first issue of major concern when designing a VoIP network is bandwidth constraints. Depending upon which codec you use and how many voice samples you want per packet, the amount of bandwidth per call can increase drastically. For an explanation of packet sizes and bandwidth consumed, see Table 9-1.

Table 9-1   *Codec Type and Sample Size Effects on Bandwidth*

Codec	Bandwidth Consumed	Bandwidth Consumed with cRTP (2-Byte Header)	Sample Latency
G.729 w/ one 10-ms sample/frame	40 kbps	9.6 kbps	15 ms
G.729 w/ four 10-ms samples/frame	16 kbps	8.4 kbps	45 ms
G.729 w/ two 10-ms samples/frame	24 kbps	11.2 kbps	25 ms
G.711 w/ one 10-ms sample/frame	112 kbps	81.6 kbps	10 ms
G.711 w/ two 10-ms samples/frame	96 kbps	80.8 kbps	20 ms

After reviewing this table, you might be asking yourself why 24 kbps of bandwidth is consumed when you're using an 8-kbps codec. This occurs due to a phenomenon called "The IP Tax." G.729 using two 10-ms samples consumes 20 bytes per frame, which works out to 8 kbps. The packet headers that include IP, RTP, and User Datagram Protocol (UDP) add 40 bytes to each frame. This "IP Tax" header is *twice* the amount of the payload.

Using G.729 with two 10-ms samples as an example, without RTP header compression, 24 kbps are consumed in each direction per call. Although this might not be a large amount for T1 (1.544-mbps), E1 (2.048-mbps), or higher circuits, it is a large amount (42 percent) for a 56-kbps circuit.

Also, keep in mind that the bandwidth in Table 9-1 does not include Layer 2 headers (PPP, Frame Relay, and so on). It includes headers from Layer 3 (network layer) and above only. Therefore, the same G.729 call can consume different amounts of bandwidth based upon which data link layer is used (Ethernet, Frame Relay, PPP, and so on).

cRTP

To reduce the large percentage of bandwidth consumed by a G.729 voice call, you can use cRTP. cRTP enables you to compress the 40-byte IP/RTP/UDP header to 2 to 4 bytes most of the time (see Figure 9-2).

Figure 9-2   *RTP Header Compression*

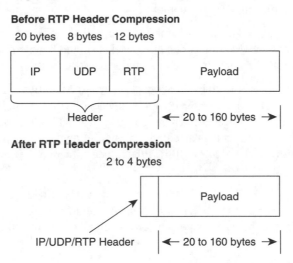

Before RTP Header Compression

20 bytes   8 bytes   12 bytes

IP	UDP	RTP	Payload

Header   ← 20 to 160 bytes →

After RTP Header Compression

2 to 4 bytes

	Payload

IP/UDP/RTP Header   ← 20 to 160 bytes →

With cRTP, the amount of traffic per VoIP call is reduced from 24 kbps to 11.2 kbps. This is a major improvement for low-bandwidth links. A 56-kbps link, for example, can now carry four G.729 VoIP calls at 11.2 kbps each. Without cRTP, only two G.729 VoIP calls at 24 kbps can be used.

To avoid the unnecessary consumption of available bandwidth, cRTP is used on a link-by-link basis. This compression scheme reduces the IP/RTP/UDP header to 2 bytes when UDP checksums are not used, or 4 bytes when UDP checksums are used.

cRTP uses some of the same techniques as Transmission Control Protocol (TCP) header compression. In TCP header compression, the first factor-of-two reduction in data rate occurs because half of the bytes in the IP and TCP headers remain constant over the life of the connection.

The big gain, however, comes from the fact that the difference from packet to packet is often constant, even though several fields change in every packet. Therefore, the algorithm can simply add 1 to every value received. By maintaining both the uncompressed header and the first-order differences in the session state shared between the compressor and the decompressor, cRTP must communicate only an indication that the second-order difference is zero. In that case, the decompressor can reconstruct the original header without any loss of information, simply by adding the first-order differences to the saved, uncompressed header as each compressed packet is received.

Just as TCP/IP header compression maintains shared state for multiple, simultaneous TCP connections, this IP/RTP/UDP compression must maintain state for multiple session contexts. A *session context* is defined by the combination of the IP source and destination addresses, the UDP source and destination ports, and the RTP synchronization source

(SSRC) field. A compressor implementation might use a hash function on these fields to index a table of stored session contexts.

The compressed packet carries a small integer, called the *session context identifier*, or CID, to indicate in which session context that packet should be interpreted. The decompressor can use the CID to index its table of stored session contexts.

cRTP can compress the 40 bytes of header down to 2 to 4 bytes most of the time. As such, about 98 percent of the time the compressed packet will be sent. Periodically, however, an entire uncompressed header must be sent to verify that both sides have the correct state. Sometimes, changes occur in a field that is usually constant—such as the payload type field, for instance. In such cases, the IP/RTP/UDP header cannot be compressed, so an uncompressed header must be sent.

You should use cRTP on any WAN interface where bandwidth is a concern and a high portion of RTP traffic exists. The following configuration tip pertaining to Cisco's IOS system software shows ways you can enable cRTP on serial and Frame Relay interfaces:

```
Leased line
!
interface serial 0
  ip address 192.168.121.18 255.255.255.248
  no ip mroute-cache
  ip rtp header-compression
  encapsulation ppp
!
Frame Relay
!
interface Serial0/0
  ip 192.168.120.10 255.255.255.0
  encapsulation frame-relay
  no ip route-cache
  no ip mroute-cache
  frame-relay ip rtp header-compression
!
```

cRTP Caveats

You should not use cRTP on high-speed interfaces, as the disadvantages of doing so outweigh the advantages. "High-speed network" is a relative term: Usually anything higher than T1 or E1 speed does not need cRTP, but in some networks 512 kbps can qualify as a high-speed connection.

As with any compression, the CPU incurs extra processing duties to compress the packet. This increases the amount of CPU utilization on the router. Therefore, you must weigh the advantages (lower bandwidth requirements) against the disadvantages (higher CPU utilization). A router with higher CPU utilization can experience problems running other tasks. As such, it is usually a good rule of thumb to keep CPU utilization at less than 60 to 70 percent to keep your network running smoothly.

Queuing

Queuing in and of itself is a fairly simple concept. The easiest way to think about queuing is to compare it to the highway system. Let's say you are on the New Jersey Turnpike driving at a decent speed. When you approach a tollbooth, you must slow down, stop, and pay the toll. During the time it takes to pay the toll, a backup of cars ensues, creating congestion.

As in the tollbooth line, in queuing the concept of first in, first out (FIFO) exists, which means that if you are the first to get in the line, you are the first to get out of the line. FIFO queuing was the first type of queuing to be used in routers, and it is still useful depending upon the network's topology.

Today's networks, with their variety of applications, protocols, and users, require a way to classify different traffic. Going back to the tollbooth example, a special "lane" is necessary to enable some cars to get bumped up in line. The New Jersey Turnpike, as well as many other toll roads, has a carpool lane, or a lane that allows you to pay for the toll electronically, for instance.

Likewise, Cisco has several queuing tools that enable a network administrator to specify what type of traffic is "special" or important and to queue the traffic based on that information instead of when a packet arrives. The most popular of these queuing techniques is known as WFQ. If you have a Cisco router, it is highly likely that it is using the WFQ algorithm because it is the default for any router interface less than 2 mbps.

Weighted Fair Queuing

FIFO queuing places all packets it receives in one queue and transmits them as bandwidth becomes available. WFQ, on the other hand, uses multiple queues to separate flows and gives equal amounts of bandwidth to each flow. This prevents one application, such as File Transfer Protocol (FTP), from consuming all available bandwidth.

WFQ ensures that queues do not starve for bandwidth and that traffic gets predictable service. Low-volume data streams receive preferential service, transmitting their entire offered loads in a timely fashion. High-volume traffic streams share the remaining capacity, obtaining equal or proportional bandwidth.

WFQ is similar to time-division multiplexing (TDM), as it divides bandwidth equally among different flows so that no one application is starved. WFQ is superior to TDM, however, simply because when a stream is no longer present, WFQ dynamically adjusts to use the free bandwidth for the flows that are still transmitting.

Fair queuing dynamically identifies data streams or flows based on several factors. These data streams are prioritized based upon the amount of bandwidth that the flow consumes. This algorithm enables bandwidth to be shared fairly, without the use of access lists or other time-consuming administrative tasks. WFQ determines a flow by using the source and destination address, protocol type, socket or port number, and QoS/ToS values.

Fair queuing enables low-bandwidth applications, which make up most of the traffic, to have as much bandwidth as needed, relegating higher-bandwidth traffic to share the remaining traffic in a fair manner. Fair queuing offers reduced jitter and enables efficient sharing of available bandwidth between all applications.

WFQ uses the fast-switching path in Cisco IOS. It is enabled with the **fair-queue** command and is enabled by default on most serial interfaces configured at 2.048 mbps or slower, beginning with Cisco IOS Release 11.0 software.

The weighting in WFQ is currently affected by six mechanisms: IP Precedence, Frame Relay forward explicit congestion notification (FECN), backward explicit congestion notification (BECN), RSVP, IP RTP Priority, and IP RTP Reserve.

The IP Precedence field has values between 0 (the default) and 7. As the precedence value increases, the algorithm allocates more bandwidth to that conversation or flow. This enables the flow to transmit more frequently. See the "Packet Classification" section later in this chapter for more information on weighting WFQ.

In a Frame Relay network, FECN and BECN bits usually flag the presence of congestion. When congestion is flagged, the weights the algorithm uses change such that the conversation encountering the congestion transmits less frequently.

To enable WFQ for an interface, use the **fair-queue** interface configuration command. To disable WFQ for an interface, use the "no" form of this command:

- **fair-queue** [congestive-discard-threshold [dynamic-queues [reservable-queues]]

  — congestive-discard-threshold—(Optional) Number of messages allowed in each queue. The default is 64 messages, and a new threshold must be a power of 2 in the range 16 to 4096. When a conversation reaches this threshold, new message packets are discarded.

  — dynamic-queues—(Optional) Number of dynamic queues used for best-effort conversations (that is, a normal conversation not requiring special network services). Values are 16, 32, 64, 128, 256, 512, 1024, 2048, and 4096. The default is 256.

  — reservable-queues—(Optional) Number of reservable queues used for reserved conversations in the range 0 to 1000. The default is 0. Reservable queues are used for interfaces configured for features such as RSVP.

WFQ Caveats

The network administrator must take care to ensure that the weights in WFQ are properly invoked. This prevents a rogue application from requesting or using a higher priority than he or she intended. How to avoid improperly weighting flows is discussed in the "Packet Classification" section later in this chapter.

WFQ also is not intended to run on interfaces that are clocked higher than 2.048 mbps. For information on queuing on those interfaces, see the " High-Speed Transport" section.

Custom Queuing

Custom queuing (CQ) enables users to specify a percentage of available bandwidth to a particular protocol. You can define up to 16 output queues as well as one additional queue for system messages (such as keepalives). Each queue is served sequentially in a round-robin fashion, transmitting a percentage of traffic on each queue before moving on to the next queue.

The router determines how many bytes from each queue should be transmitted, based on the speed of the interface as well as the configured traffic percentage. In other words, another traffic type can use unused bandwidth from queue A until queue A requires its full percentage.

The following configuration tip shows ways you can enable CQ on a serial interface. You must first define the parameters of the queue list and then enable the queue list on the physical interface (in this case, serial 0):

```
Interface serial 0
ip address 20.0.0.1 255.0.0.0
custom-queue-list 1
!
queue-list 1 protocol ip 1 list 101
queue-list 1 default 2
queue-list 1 queue 1 byte-count 4000
queue-list 1 queue 2 byte-count 2000
!
access-list 101 permit udp any any range 16380 16480 precedence 5
access-list 101 permit tcp any any eq 1720
```

CQ Caveats

CQ requires knowledge of port types and traffic types. This equates to a large amount of administrative overhead. But after the administrative overhead is complete, CQ offers a highly granular approach to queuing, which is what some customers prefer.

Priority Queuing

PQ enables the network administrator to configure four traffic priorities—high, normal, medium, and low. Inbound traffic is assigned to one of the four output queues. Traffic in the high-priority queue is serviced until the queue is empty; then, packets in the next priority queue are transmitted.

This queuing arrangement ensures that mission-critical traffic is always given as much bandwidth as it needs; however, it starves other applications to do so.

Therefore, it is important to understand traffic flows when using this queuing mechanism so that applications are not starved of needed bandwidth. PQ is best used when the highest-priority traffic consumes the least amount of line bandwidth.

The following Cisco IOS configuration tip utilizes **access-list 101** to specify particular UDP and TCP port ranges. **Priority-list 1** then applies **access-list 101** into the highest queue (the most important queue) for PQ. **Priority-list 1** is then invoked on serial 1/1 by the command **priority-group 1**.

```
!
interface Serial1/1
  ip address 192.168.121.17 255.255.255.248
  encapsulation ppp
  no ip mroute-cache
  priority-group 1
!
access-list 101 permit udp any any range 16384 16484
access-list 101 permit tcp any any eq 1720
priority-list 1 protocol ip high list 101
!
```

PQ Caveats

PQ enables a network administrator to "starve" applications. An improperly configured PQ can service one queue and completely disregard all other queues. This can, in effect, force some applications to stop working. As long as the system administrator realizes this caveat, PQ can be the proper alternative for some customers.

CB-WFQ

CB-WFQ has all the benefits of WFQ, with the additional functionality of providing granular support for network administrator-defined classes of traffic. CB-WFQ also can run on high-speed interfaces (up to T3) in 7200 or higher class routers.

CB-WFQ enables you to define what constitutes a class based on criteria that exceed the confines of flow. Using CB-WFQ, you can create a specific class for voice traffic. The network administrator defines these classes of traffic through access lists. These classes of traffic determine how packets are grouped in different queues.

The most interesting feature of CB-WFQ is that it enables the network administrator to specify the exact amount of bandwidth to be allocated per class of traffic. CB-WFQ can handle 64 different classes and control bandwidth requirements for each class.

With standard WFQ, weights determine the amount of bandwidth allocated per conversation. It is dependent on how many flows of traffic occur at a given moment.

With CB-WFQ, each class is associated with a separate queue. You can allocate a specific minimum amount of guaranteed bandwidth to the class as a percentage of the link, or in kbps. Other classes can share unused bandwidth in proportion to their assigned weights. When configuring CB-WFQ, you should consider that bandwidth allocation does not necessarily mean the traffic belonging to a class experiences low delay; however, you can skew weights to simulate PQ.

PQ within CB-WFQ (Low Latency Queuing)

PQ within CB-WFQ (LLQ) is a mouthful of an acronym. This queuing mechanism was developed to give absolute priority to voice traffic over all other traffic on an interface.

The LLQ feature brings to CB-WFQ the strict-priority queuing functionality of IP RTP Priority required for delay-sensitive, real-time traffic, such as voice. LLQ enables use of a strict PQ.

Although it is possible to queue various types of traffic to a strict PQ, it is strongly recommended that you direct only voice traffic to this queue. This recommendation is based upon the fact that voice traffic is well behaved and sends packets at regular intervals; other applications transmit at irregular intervals and can ruin an entire network if configured improperly.

With LLQ, you can specify traffic in a broad range of ways to guarantee strict priority delivery. To indicate the voice flow to be queued to the strict PQ, you can use an access list. This is different from IP RTP Priority, which allows for only a specific UDP port range.

Although this mechanism is relatively new to IOS, it has proven to be powerful and it gives voice packets the necessary priority, latency, and jitter required for good-quality voice.

Queuing Summary

Although a one-size-fits-all answer to queuing problems does not exist, many customers today use WFQ to deal with queuing issues. WFQ is simple to deploy, and it requires little additional effort from the network administrator. Setting the weights with WFQ can further enhance its benefits.

Customers who require more granular and strict queuing techniques can use CQ or PQ. Be sure to utilize great caution when enabling these techniques, however, as you might do more harm than good to your network. With PQ or CQ, it is imperative that you know your traffic and your applications.

Many customers who deploy VoIP networks in low-bandwidth environments (less than 768 kbps) use IP RTP Priority or LLQ to prioritize their voice traffic above all other traffic flows.

Packet Classification

To achieve your intended packet delivery, you must know how to properly weight WFQ. This section focuses on different weighting techniques and ways you can use them in various networks to achieve the amount of QoS you require.

IP Precedence

IP Precedence refers to the three bits in the ToS field in an IP header, as shown in Figure 9-3.

Figure 9-3   *IP Header and ToS Field*

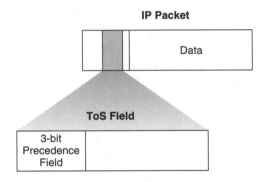

These three bits allow for eight different CoS types (0-7), listed in Table 9-2.

Table 9-2   *ToS (IP Precedence)*

Service Type	Purpose
Routine	Set routine precedence (0)
Priority	Set priority precedence (1)
Immediate	Set immediate precedence (2)
Flash	Set Flash precedence (3)
Flash-override	Set Flash override precedence (4)
Critical	Set critical precedence (5)
Internet	Set internetwork control precedence (6)
Network	Set network control precedence (7)

IP Precedence 6 and 7 are reserved for network information (routing updates, hello packets, and so on). This leaves 6 remaining precedence settings for normal IP traffic flows.

IP Precedence enables a router to group traffic flows based on the eight precedence settings and to queue traffic based upon that information as well as on source address, destination address, and port numbers.

You can consider IP Precedence an in-band QoS mechanism. Extra signaling is not involved, nor does additional packet header overhead exist. Given these benefits, IP Precedence is the QoS mechanism that large-scale networks use most often.

With Cisco IOS, you can set the IP Precedence bits of your IP streams in several ways. With Cisco's VoIP design, you can set the IP Precedence bits based upon the destination phone number (the called number). Setting the precedence in this manner is easy and allows for different types of CoS, depending upon which destination you are calling.

NOTE   To set the IP Precedence using Cisco IOS VoIP, do the following:

```
dial-peer voice 650 voip
 destination-pattern 650
 ip precedence 5
 session target RAS
```

Cisco IOS also enables any IP traffic that flows through the router to have its precedence bit set based upon an access list or extended access list. This is accomplished through a feature known as *policy routing,* which is covered in the "Policy Routing" section later in this chapter.

IP Precedence Caveats

IP Precedence has no built-in mechanism for refusing incorrect IP Precedence settings. The network administrator needs to take precautions to ensure that the IP Precedence settings in the network remain as they were originally planned. The following example shows the problems that can occur when IP Precedence is not carefully configured.

Company B uses WFQ with VoIP on all its WAN links and uses IP Precedence to prioritize traffic on the network. Company B uses a precedence setting of 5 for VoIP and a precedence setting of 4 for Systems Network Architecture (SNA) traffic. All other traffic is assumed to have a precedence setting of 0 (the lowest precedence).

Although in most applications the precedence is 0, some applications might be modified to request a higher precedence. In this example, a software engineer modifies his gaming application to request a precedence of 7 (the highest setting) so that when he and a co-worker in another office play, they get first priority on the WAN link. This is just an example, but it is possible. Because the gaming application requires a large amount of traffic, the company's VoIP and SNA traffic are not passed.

Creating the workaround for this is easy. You can use Cisco IOS to change to 0 any precedence bits arriving from non-approved hosts, while leaving all other traffic intact. This is discussed further in the "Policy Routing" section later in this chapter.

Resetting IP Precedence through Policy Routing

To configure the router to reset the IP Precedence bits (which is a good idea on the edge of a network), you must follow several steps. In this configuration, access-list 105 was created to reset all IP Precedence bits for traffic received from the Ethernet. Only traffic received on the Ethernet interface is sent through the route map. Traffic forwarded out of the Ethernet interface does not proceed through the route map.

```
!
interface Ethernet0/0
 ip address 192.168.15.18 255.255.255.0
 ip policy route-map reset-precedence
!
!
access-list 105 permit ip any any
route-map reset-precedence permit 10
  match ip address 105
  set ip precedence routine
```

Policy Routing

With policy-based routing, you can configure a defined policy for traffic flows and not have to rely completely on routing protocols to determine traffic forwarding and routing. Policy routing also enables you to set the IP Precedence field so that the network can utilize different classes of service.

You can base policies on IP addresses, port numbers, protocols, or the size of packets. You can use one of these descriptors to create a simple policy, or you can use all of them to create a complicated policy.

All packets received on an interface with policy-based routing enabled are passed through enhanced packet filters known as *route maps*. The route maps dictate where the packets are forwarded.

You also can mark route-map statements as "permit" or "deny." If the statement is marked "deny," the packets meeting the match criteria are sent back through the usual forwarding channels (in other words, destination-based routing is performed). Only if the statement is marked "permit" and the packets meet the match criteria are all the set clauses applied.

If the statement is marked "permit" and the packets do not meet the match criteria, those packets also are forwarded through the usual routing channel.

NOTE   Policy routing is specified on the interface that receives the packets, not on the interface that sends the packets.

You can use the IP standard or extended access control lists (ACLs) to establish match criteria, the standard IP access lists to specify the match criteria for source address, and extended access lists to specify the match criteria based upon application, protocol type, ToS, and precedence.

The match clause feature was extended to include matching packet length between specified minimum and maximum values. The network administrator can then use the match length as the criterion that distinguishes between interactive and bulk traffic (bulk traffic usually has larger packet sizes).

The policy routing process proceeds through the route map until a match is found. If no match is found in the route map, or if the route map entry is marked with a "deny" instead of a "permit" statement, normal destination-based routing of the traffic ensues.

NOTE   As always, an implicit "deny" statement is at the end of the list of match statements.

Policy Routing Caveats

You must be careful when choosing the type of policies you route, as you can configure certain policies to force Cisco IOS routers to use the process-switching path (a slower method of forwarding packets). If you are careful, you can avoid this. Also, by default, traffic originating from the router is not sent through the policy route. With a special command, you can send internal traffic (routing updates, VoIP, and so on) through the policy route.

RSVP

RSVP enables endpoints to signal the network with the kind of QoS needed for a particular application. This is a great departure from the network blindly assuming what QoS applications require.

Network administrators can use RSVP as *dynamic access lists*. This means that network administrators need not concern themselves with port numbers of IP packet flows because RSVP signals that information during its original request.

RSVP is an out-of-band, end-to-end signaling protocol that requests a certain amount of bandwidth and latency with each network hop that supports RSVP. If a network node (router) does not support RSVP, RSVP moves onto the next hop. A network node has the option to approve or deny the reservation based upon the load of the interface to which the service is requested.

RSVP works much like an ambulance clearing traffic in front of you. You simply follow behind the ambulance. RSVP, or the ambulance driver, tells each stop (tollbooth, policeman, and so on) that the driver behind him in the 1972 yellow AMC Gremlin is important and needs special privileges. Each stop has the right to decide whether the driver in the 1972 yellow AMC Gremlin is important enough to have these special privileges (for instance, not paying tolls, running traffic lights, or, in the case of IP, having bandwidth and latency bounds).

NOTE   In Cisco IOS, each interface for which you want to enable RSVP must be explicitly configured with RSVP. Also, the network administrator must configure the amount of bandwidth allocated to RSVP on that interface.

Applications receive feedback on whether their request for QoS was approved or denied. Some applications transmit their data to anyone, with no QoS concerns; however, some intelligent applications choose not to transmit, or they choose another route. In the case of VoIP, that route could be the Public Switched Telephone Network (PSTN).

It is interesting to note that the requester of the service levels in RSVP is the receiving station and not the transmitting station. This enables RSVP to scale when IP multicast technology is used. (With IP multicast technology, one transmitter sends to multiple receivers.)

RSVP is not a routing protocol and does not currently modify the IP routing table based upon traffic flows or congestion. RSVP simply traverses IP and enables IP routing protocols to choose the most optimal path. This optimal path might not be the most ideal QoS-enabled path. RSVP cannot adjust the routers to modify that behavior, however.

RSVP Syntax

The syntax of RSVP follows:

```
ip rsvp bandwidth
```

To enable RSVP for IP on an interface, use the **ip rsvp bandwidth** interface configuration command. To disable RSVP, use the "no" form of the command:

```
ip rsvp bandwidth [interface-kbps] [single-flow-kbps]
no ip rsvp bandwidth [interface-kbps] [single-flow-kbps]
```

The command options are defined as follows:

- interface-kbps—(Optional) Amount of bandwidth (in kbps) on interface to be reserved; the range is 1 to 10,000,000.

- single-flow-kbps—(Optional) Amount of bandwidth (in kbps) allocated to a single flow; the range is 1 to 10,000,000.

- Default—75 percent of bandwidth available on interface if no bandwidth (in kbps) is specified.

To display RSVP reservations currently in place, use the **show ip rsvp reservation** command:

```
show ip rsvp reservation [type number]
```

The type number is optional; it indicates interface type and number.

RSVP Caveats

Although RSVP is an important tool in the QoS arsenal, this protocol does not solve all the necessary problems related to QoS. RSVP has three drawbacks: scalability, admission control, and the time it takes to set up end-to-end reservation.

RSVP has yet to be deployed in a large-scale environment. In a worst-case scenario for RSVP, a backbone router must manage several thousand RSVP reservations and queue each flow according to that reservation.

The unknown scalability issues that surround RSVP relegate RSVP toward the edges of the network and force use of other QoS tools for the backbone of the network. In the long term, the Internet Engineering Task Force (IETF) is working on ways to better utilize RSVP and increase the scalability factor.

RSVP works on the total size of the IP packet and does not account for any compression schemes, cyclic redundancy checks (CRCs), or line encapsulation (Frame Relay, PPP, or High-Level Data Link Control [HDLC]).

When using RSVP and G.729 for VoIP, for example, the reservation Cisco IOS software request is 24 kbps, compared to the actual value of ~11 kbps when using cRTP. In other words, on a 56 kbps link, only two 24 kbps reservations are permitted, even though enough bandwidth is available for three 11-kbps VoIP flows.

You can work around this situation by oversubscribing the available bandwidth of the link to enable RSVP to reserve more bandwidth than is actually available. You can use the bandwidth statement on a particular interface to make this reservation. This workaround is permitted as long as the network is properly engineered and you can control network flows.

On a 56-kbps link, for example, the bandwidth statement tells the interface that 100 kbps of bandwidth actually exists. You can then use RSVP to enable 75 percent of the available bandwidth to be used for RSVP traffic. This scenario enables RSVP to reserve the necessary bandwidth for three VoIP G.729 calls. The inherent danger is evident because if cRTP is not used, the link is oversubscribed.

IP RTP Reserve

Cisco IOS has another mechanism for weighting traffic based upon the packet-flow UDP port range. You can compare IP RTP Reserve to a "static" RSVP reservation. When you use IP RTP Reserve, you need not use IP Precedence or RSVP.

Although IP RTP Reserve classifies packets based upon a UDP port range, it also enables you to specify the amount of bandwidth you allow to be prioritized in that port range.

The IP RTP Reserve "static" reservation enables traffic to be classified with a high weight when the "reserved" traffic is present. When this traffic is not present, any other traffic flow can use extra bandwidth not used by this reservation.

The IP RTP Reserve basic configuration is as follows:

```
interface virtual-template 1
ppp multilink
encapsulation ppp
ppp multilink interleave
ppp multilink fragment-delay 20
ip rtp reserve 16384 100 64

ip rtp reserve lowest-UDP-port(16384), range-of-ports (+100 ports),
  maximum-bandwidth (64)
```

This configuration weighs WFQ for all UDP traffic from port 16384 to 16484.

IP RTP Reserve Caveats

IP RTP Reserve is not the most scalable solution available. It allows for a range of only 100 UDP ports, and it does not allow for admission control. Without admission control, any packet flows within the specified IP RTP Reserve range are weighted.

IP RTP Priority

When WFQ is enabled and IP RTP Priority is configured, a strict priority queue is created. You can use the IP RTP Priority feature to enable use of the strict priority queuing scheme for delay-sensitive data.

You can identify voice traffic by its UDP port numbers and classify it into a priority queue. This results in voice that has strict priority service in preference to all other traffic. This is the most recommended classification scheme for VoIP networks on lower-bandwidth links (768 kbps and below).

Traffic Policing

The previous sections covered ways you can queue different flows of traffic and then prioritize those flows. That is an important part of QoS. Sometimes, however, it is necessary to actually regulate or limit the amount of traffic an application is allowed to send across various interfaces or networks.

Cisco has a few tools that enable network administrators to define how much bandwidth an application or even a user can use. These features come in two different flavors: *rate-limiting tools* such as CAR, and *shaping tools* such as GTS or FRTS.

The main difference between these two traffic-regulation tools is that rate-limiting tools drop traffic based upon policing, and shaping tools generally buffer the excess traffic while waiting for the next open interval to transmit the data.

CAR and traffic shaping tools are similar in that they both identify when traffic exceeds the thresholds set by the network administrator.

Often, these two tools are used together. Traffic shaping is used at the edge of the network (customer premises) to make sure the customer is utilizing the bandwidth for business needs.

CAR is often used in service provider networks to ensure that a subscriber does not exceed the amount of bandwidth set by contract with the service provider.

CAR

CAR is a policing mechanism that enables network administrators to set exceed or conform actions. Often you use a conform action to transmit the traffic and an exceed action to drop the packet or to mark it with a lower IP Precedence value.

CAR's rate-limiting mechanism enables a user to

- Control the maximum rate of traffic transmitted or received on an interface
- Give granular control at Layer 3, which enables an IP network to exhibit qualities of a TDM network

You can rate-limit traffic by precedence, Media Access Control (MAC) address, IP addresses, or other parameters. Network administrators also can configure access lists to create even more granular rate-limiting policies.

It is important to note that CAR does not buffer any traffic to smooth out traffic bursts. Therefore, CAR is ideal for high-speed environments, as queuing adds no delay.

To configure CAR and Distributed CAR (DCAR) on Cisco 7000 series routers with RSP7000 or on Cisco 7500 series routers with a VIP2-40 or greater interface processor for all IP traffic, use the following commands, beginning in global configuration mode:

```
Command        Purpose

rate-limit {input | output} bps burst-normal
   burst-max conform-action action exceed-action action
```

The network administrator can specify a basic CAR policy for all IP traffic. See Table 9-3 for a description of conform and exceed action keywords.

For basic CAR and DCAR to be functional, you must define the following criteria:

- Packet direction, incoming or outgoing.

- An average rate, determined by a long-term average of the transmission rate. Traffic that falls under this rate always conforms.

- A normal burst size, which determines how large traffic bursts can be before some traffic is considered to exceed the rate limit.

- An excess burst size.

Traffic that falls between the normal burst size and the excess burst size exceeds the rate limit with a probability that increases as the burst size increases. CAR propagates bursts. It does not smooth or shape traffic.

Conform and exceed actions are described in Table 9-3.

Table 9-3   *Rate-Limit Command Action Keywords*

Keyword	Description
continue	Evaluates the next rate-limit command.
drop	Drops the packet.
set-prec-continue new-prec	Sets the IP Precedence and evaluates the next rate-limit command.
set-prec-transmit new-prec	Sets the IP Precedence and transmits the packet.
transmit	Transmits the packet.

CAR Caveats

You can use CAR and Versatile Interface Processor Distributed CAR (VIP-DCAR) only with IP traffic. Non-IP traffic is not rate-limited.

You can configure CAR or VIP—DCAR on an interface or subinterface. CAR and VIP-DCAR are not supported on the following interfaces, however:

- Fast EtherChannel

- Tunnel
- Primary Rate Interface (PRI)
- Any interface that does not support Cisco express forwarding (CEF)

Traffic Shaping

Cisco IOS QoS software includes two types of traffic shaping: GTS and FRTS. Both traffic-shaping methods are similar in implementation, although their command-line interfaces differ somewhat and they use different types of queues to contain and shape traffic that is deferred.

If a packet is deferred, GTS uses a WFQ to hold the delayed traffic. FRTS uses either a CQ or a PQ to hold the delayed traffic, depending on what you configured. As of April 1999, FRTS also supports WFQ to hold delayed traffic.

Traffic shaping enables you to control the traffic going out of an interface to match its flow to the speed of the remote, target interface and to ensure that the traffic conforms to policies contracted for it. Thus, you can shape traffic adhering to a particular profile to meet downstream requirements, thereby eliminating bottlenecks in topologies with data-rate mismatches.

You use traffic shaping primarily to

- Control usage of available bandwidth
- Establish traffic policies
- Regulate traffic flow to avoid congestion

You can use traffic shaping in the following situations:

- You can configure traffic shaping on an interface if you have a network with different access rates. Suppose one end of the link in a Frame Relay network runs at 256 kbps and the other end runs at 128 kbps. Sending packets at 256 kbps could cause the applications using the link to fail.
- You can configure traffic shaping if you offer a subrate service. In this case, traffic shaping enables you to use the router to partition your T1 or T3 links into smaller channels.

Traffic shaping prevents packet loss. It is especially important to use traffic shaping in Frame Relay networks because the switch cannot determine which packets take precedence and, therefore, which packets should be dropped when congestion occurs.

Moreover, it is of critical importance for VoIP that you control latency. By limiting the amount of traffic and traffic loss in the network, you can smooth out traffic patterns and give priority to real-time traffic.

Differences Between GTS and FRTS

As mentioned, both GTS and FRTS are similar in implementation in that they share the same code and data structures, but they differ in regard to their command-line interfaces and the queue types they use.

Here are two ways in which GTS and FRTS differ:

- FRTS supports shaping based on each data-link connection identifier (DLCI). GTS is configurable per interface or subinterface.

- GTS supports a WFQ shaping queue.

You can configure GTS to behave the same way as FRTS by allocating one DLCI per subinterface and using GTS plus BECN support. The two behave the same, except for the different shaping queues they use.

In versions of software previous to IOS 12.04(T), FRTS and WFQ were not compatible. This limitation was removed, and now both FRTS and GTS work with WFQ. This enables network administrators to choose a more granular QoS mechanism (FRTS and WFQ per DLCI).

Traffic Shaping and Queuing

Traffic shaping smoothes traffic by storing traffic above the configured rate in a queue. When a packet arrives at the interface for transmission, the following happens:

- If the queue is empty, the traffic shaper processes the arriving packet.

  If possible, the traffic shaper sends the packet.

  Otherwise, it places the packet in the queue.

- If packets are in the queue, the traffic shaper sends another new packet in the queue.

When packets are in the queue, the traffic shaper removes the number of packets it can transmit from the queue every time interval.

GTS

GTS applies on a per-interface basis and can use access lists to select the traffic to shape. It works with a variety of Layer 2 technologies, including Frame Relay, ATM, Switched Multimegabit Data Service (SMDS), and Ethernet.

On a Frame Relay subinterface, you can set up GTS to adapt dynamically to available bandwidth by integrating BECN signals, or to simply shape to a pre-specified rate. You also can configure GTS on an ATM interface to respond to RSVPs signaled over statically configured ATM permanent virtual circuits (PVCs).

Most media and encapsulation types on the router support GTS. You also can apply GTS to a specific access list on an interface. Figure 9-4 shows how GTS works.

Figure 9-4   *GTS in Action*

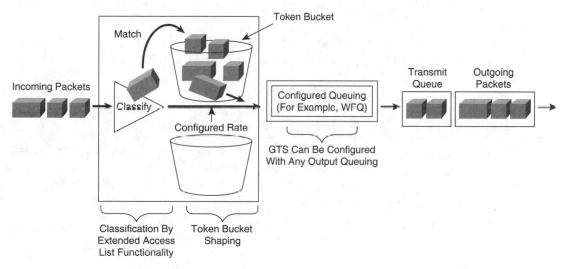

GTS Syntax

To enable traffic shaping for outbound traffic on an interface, use the **traffic-shape rate** interface configuration command. Use the "no" form of this command to disable traffic shaping on the interface.

```
traffic-shape rate bit-rate [burst-size [excess-burst-size]]
no traffic-shape rate
```

The syntax description follows:

- bit-rate—Bit rate that traffic is shaped to, in bits per second (bps). This is the access bit rate you contract with your service provider, or the service level you intend to maintain.

- burst-size—(Optional) Sustained number of bits you can transmit per interval. On Frame Relay interfaces, this is the committed burst size contracted with your service provider; the default is the bit rate divided by 8.

- excess-burst-size—(Optional) Maximum number of bits that can exceed the burst size in the first interval in a congestion event. On Frame Relay interfaces, this is the excess burst size contracted with your service provider; the default is equal to the burst size traffic shape group.

To enable traffic shaping based on a specific access list for outbound traffic on an interface, use the **traffic-shape group** interface configuration command. Use the "no" form of this command to disable traffic shaping on the interface for the access list:

```
traffic-shape group access-list bit-rate [burst-size [excess-burst-size]]
no traffic-shape group access-list
```

Example 9-1

Corporation A wants to limit the output of its Frame Relay circuit to the CIR of the link to prevent packets from being flagged as discard eligible (DE). The Frame Relay circuit is 56 kbps and the CIR is 32 kbps.

```
interface serial 0/0
encapsulation frame-relay
traffic-shape rate 32000 4000 0
```

Example 9-2

Corporation B wants to shape its outbound traffic into its WAN network so that FTP traffic uses only 64,000 bps of its 256-kbps circuit.

```
interface serial 0/0
traffic-shape group 101 64000 8000 0
!
access-list 101 permit tcp any eq ftp any
```

FRTS

Like GTS, FRTS smoothes out traffic spikes by buffering excess traffic. FRTS also can eliminate problems caused by different access rates at the ingress and egress of a Frame Relay network. A central-site Frame Relay network, for instance, often has a high-speed (T1 or greater) connection to the network, and a remote site usually has a connection to the frame network less than 384 kbps.

The central-site router can transmit to the remote router at T1 speeds, but the remote router can receive traffic only at 384 kbps or less. This forces the Frame Relay network to buffer the traffic and can add *seconds* to a packet stream. This renders voice unacceptable in almost any network.

FRTS enables the use of FECN and BECN to dynamically transmit more or less bandwidth.

In Frame Relay networks, BECNs and FECNs indicate congestion. You specify BECN and FECN by bits within a Frame Relay frame.

Using information contained in the BECN-tagged packets received from the network, FRTS also can dynamically throttle traffic. With BECN-based throttling, packets are held in the router's buffers to reduce the data flow from the router into the Frame Relay network.

The throttling is done on each virtual circuit (VC) and the transmission rate is adjusted based on the number of BECN-tagged packets received.

Fragmentation

Both propagation and queuing delay are discussed in previous chapters. The reasoning behind the need for fragmentation is simple. Large packets (1500-byte MTUs) take a long time to move across low-bandwidth links (768 kbps and less). Fragmentation breaks larger packets into smaller packets. You can accomplish this at either layer 2 or layer 3 of the Open Systems Interconnection (OSI) reference model.

In many data applications, latency caused by low-bandwidth links does not matter to the end user. In real-time applications, however, this can cause many problems (choppy voice quality, missed frames, dropped calls, and so on).

A 1500-byte packet moving across a 56-kbps circuit, for example, takes 214 ms to traverse the circuit. The ITU-T recommendation for uni-directional maximum voice latency is less than 150 ms. Therefore, *one* 56-kbps circuit and *one* 1500-byte packet consume the entire VoIP delay budget.

Fragmentation in itself is not enough to remove the latency problem on low-bandwidth circuits. The router must also be able to queue based upon fragments or smaller packets instead of by the original (prefragmented) packet.

Cisco Systems' VoIP implementation enables users to modify the number of samples per packet. By default with G.729, two 10-ms speech samples are put into one frame. This gives you a packet every 20 ms. This means you need to be able to transmit a VoIP packet out of the router every 20 ms.

This 20-ms distance between each frame can change based upon the number of speech samples you decide to put in each frame. Also, this number is important because it enables you to determine the size of fragmentation needed.

As shown in Figure 9-5, you can determine your fragment size depending on the speed of the link and the samples per frame.

Figure 9-5   *Fixed-Frame Propagation Delay*

		Frame Size						
		1 Byte	64 Byte	128 Byte	256 Byte	512 Byte	1024 Byte	1500 Byte
Link Speed	56 kbps	143 us	9 ms	18 ms	36 ms	72 ms	144 ms	214 ms
	64 kbps	125 us	8 ms	16 ms	32 ms	64 ms	128 ms	187 ms
	128 kbps	62.5 us	4 ms	8 ms	16 ms	32 ms	64 ms	93 ms
	256 kbps	31 us	2 ms	4 ms	8 ms	16 ms	32 ms	46 ms
	512 kbps	15.5 us	1 ms	2 ms	4 ms	8 ms	16 ms	23 ms
	768 kbps	10 us	640 us	1.28 ms	2.56 ms	5.12 ms	10.24 ms	15 ms
	1536 kbps	5 us	320 us	640 us	1.28 ms	2.56 ms	5.12 ms	7.5 ms

Blocking

Fragmentation helps to eliminate "blocking" issues. *Blocking* is the amount of time you allow another packet to consume available WAN bandwidth and force other real-time packets to be queued. Blocking directly affects your delay budget. You can use different rules of thumb, but generally, you want to keep the blocking delay at 80 percent of your total voice packet size.

If you have two 10-ms speech samples in one 20-ms packet, for example, you want a maximum blocking delay of approximately 16 ms. Assuming your WAN link is 56 kbps and using Figure 9-5 as an example, you want your packets to be fragmented to about 128 bytes. If you want an exact figure, the algorithm to use to determine your packet fragmentation size is as follows:

WAN bandwidth × blocking delay = fragment size in bits

Utilizing this algorithm to compute the exact delay based on the preceding recommendations:

WAN bandwidth (56 kbps) × blocking delay (16 ms) = 896 bits per second
(112 Bytes per second)

MCML PPP

When this section was written, the MCML extension to multilink PPP was in draft stage. The extension was being drafted to provide a mechanism that enabled fragmentation to occur at the link layer, yet remain oblivious to upper layers. Multilink PPP already had a fragmentation mechanism that enabled packets to be sent down two different physical circuits and be reassembled at the receiving side. A method for using multilink PPP on a single physical medium and applying different queues, which enabled packets to be de-queued based upon the fragment and not upon the entire packet, was required, however.

MCML PPP still requires fragments to be classified by IP Precedence and RSVP, and to be queued by WFQ, as shown in Figure 9-6.

Figure 9-6   *Multi-Class, Multilink PPP*

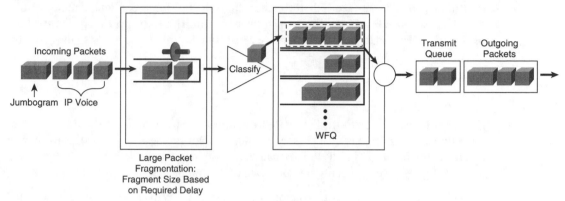

Incoming Packets

Jumbogram   IP Voice

Classify

Transmit
Queue

Outgoing
Packets

WFQ

Large Packet
Fragmentation:
Fragment Size Based
on Required Delay

MCML Caveats

You can use MCML only on interfaces that can run PPP, which immediately rules out a
large portion of WAN networks (Frame Relay, ATM, and so on).

MCML specifies only the fragmentation method; it does not specify the queuing technique
needed to prioritize the fragments.

MCML PPP Syntax

You can use MCML only on a dialer interface. Therefore, on a leased-line interface, you
must use a virtual template.

```
interface Serial0
 bandwidth 56
 no ip address
 encapsulation ppp
 no ip route-cache
 no ip mroute-cache
 bandwidth 56
 no fair-queue
 ppp multilink
 multilink-group 1
interface Multilink 1
 ip address 10.1.1.2 255.255.255.252
 no ip directed-broadcast
 ip rtp priority 16384 16383 26
 no ip route-cache
 no ip mroute-cache
 fair-queue 64 256 1000
 ppp multilink
 ppp multilink fragment-delay 10
 ppp multilink interleave
 multilink-group 1
```

In this configuration, **PPP multilink** is configured on the serial 0 interface. A new **multilink-group 1** interface is then created with IP RTP Priority configured along with MCML PPP and WFQ. Under the serial 0 interface, **multilink-group 1** maps to **interface Multilink 1**. This enables all the **interface Multilink 1** attributes to apply to the serial 0 interface.

FRF.12

FRF.12 is a specification by the Frame Relay Forum Technical Committee, and you can find it at http://www.frforum.com. This specification enables Frame Relay networks to operate in a manner similar to MCML PPP. Because this fragmentation also happens at the link layer, the upper-layer protocols are not aware of the fragmentation.

As with MCML PPP, packets are fragmented at entry to the WAN network and reassembled when the destination router receives them.

FRF.12 also specifies the interworkings between Frame Relay and ATM. This enables packets fragmented by FRF.12 on the Frame Relay side of the circuit to be reassembled on the ATM side of the circuit.

IP MTU and MTU

On WAN interfaces that do not support MCML PPP or FRF.12, you can set the interface or protocol MTU to a lower value, which then forces fragmentation.

The MTU on a serial interface is usually 1500 bytes. With FRF.12 and MCML PPP, you can change the actual packet size sent on the interface without disturbing the actual packet flow. When you lower the MTU or IP MTU size, the packet changes for the duration of that packet's trip.

The IP MTU configuration is as follows:

```
interface Serial0/0
 ip mtu 300
 no ip address
 encapsulation frame-relay
 fair-queue 64 256 1000
 !
interface Serial0/0.1 point-to-point
 ip mtu 300
 ip address 40.0.0.7 255.0.0.0
```

The MTU configuration is as follows:

```
interface Serial0/0
  mtu 300
  no ip address
  ip rsvp bandwidth 1158 1158
  encapsulation frame-relay
fair-queue 64 256 1000
 !
interface Serial0/0.1 point-to-point
```

```
mtu 300
ip address 40.0.0.7 255.0.0.0
```

IP MTU Caveats

Changing the size of the IP packet for its entire life can cause many problems. The receiving station's overall performance is affected, for instance, because it handles many smaller packets more slowly than one big packet. Also, the header of the packet needs to be duplicated for *each* fragment.

Consider one 1500-byte packet that includes a 40-byte header. If you fragment the 1460-byte payload into 100-byte frames, you get 14 packets with 100 bytes and one packet with 60 bytes. You now need to put a 40-byte header back onto each of the 15 packets. In doing so, you increase the header size from 40 bytes to 600 bytes.

Another major problem with IP MTU and MTU sizing is that if the Do Not Fragment (DNF) bit is set on a packet, that packet is discarded. Many applications set this bit to prevent intermediary devices (routers and other network elements) from breaking their packet into many pieces. One reason the DNF bit might be set is to keep the receiving station from being burdened by having to put the fragments back into the proper order.

MTU Caveats

MTU sizing changes the size of *all* packets exiting that interface, including IP, Internetwork Packet eXchange (IPX), AppleTalk, and routing updates. This can be a problem for routing updates, Frame Relay Local Management Interface (LMI) updates, and other protocols that don't support fragmentation.

Edge QoS Wrap-Up

At this point, you should understand the basics of packet classification, fragmentation, queuing, bandwidth, and policing mechanisms. It is important to note that you can use some or many of these mechanisms concurrently in a given environment.

As a rule of thumb, you always need to use packet classification and queuing mechanisms. Based upon bandwidth constraints and administrative policies, you might need to use compression and fragmentation methods as well.

Backbone Networks

The backbone of the network is completely different than the edge of the network, and you should not treat it with the same QoS mechanisms. Although the classification mechanisms for both might be the same or similar, the queuing, fragmentation, and bandwidth mechanisms are usually either not used or different.

High-Speed Transport

You can define high-speed transport as any interface higher than T1 speed. Although most people refer to digital signal level 3 (DS-3) interfaces and above as high-speed networks, just as with microprocessors what is considered high speed today will be outdated in the future.

It is necessary to focus on different QoS mechanisms with high-speed transports. It is usually not feasible to apply all the same rules and policies on a high-speed interface as you would on a lower-speed interface. This is mainly because the more policies and QoS mechanisms you apply, the longer the router must take to forward a packet. Although this is usually okay on lower-speed interfaces, higher-speed interfaces cannot spend as much time identifying and queuing each packet.

As customers move to higher-speed interfaces (such as OC-48), however, it is important to provide them with options so that they can determine how to properly enable QoS on their networks.

POS

With the capability for IP to travel directly on a Synchronous Optical Network (SONET) infrastructure came the need to prioritize traffic on this high-speed interface. Before putting IP directly on SONET, people used ATM as the transport mechanism. Although you can use ATM QoS tools to provide the necessary priority schemes, new IP QoS mechanisms had to be developed, however, to handle QoS on interfaces up to OC-48.

Modified Deficit Round Robin

Cisco 12000 Gigabit Switch Routers (GSRs) are currently the only Cisco IP Routing products that have an IP OC-48 interface. Modified Deficit Round Robin (MDRR) extends Deficit Round Robin (DRR) to provide priority for real-time traffic such as VoIP. Within MDRR, IP packets are mapped to different CoS queues based on precedence bits.

All the queues are serviced in round-robin fashion except for one: the priority queue used to handle voice traffic.

DRR provides queuing similar to WFQ but for higher-speed interfaces from OC-3 to OC-48. MDRR extends the DRR protocol to include a high-priority queue that is treated differently from the other queues associated with service classes.

For each set of CoS queues supported, MDRR includes a low-latency, high-priority (LLHP) queue for VoIP or other real-time traffic. Except for the LLHP queue, MDRR services all queues in round-robin fashion.

This enables service providers or others with a need for high-speed queuing to ensure that VoIP is prioritized above all other traffic.

IP and ATM

Many networks today use ATM as the Layer 2 transport, with IP, TDM, and other traffic traversing a single ATM network. Because of this, it is necessary to map IP QoS onto an ATM network.

You can map IP prioritization onto ATM in two ways. The first method simply maps the precedence values on an IP packet to different ATM PVCs. This enables the network administrator to have different PVCs, allocating important traffic over a variable bit rate (VBR) ATM circuit and less important traffic over an unspecified bit rate (UBR) ATM circuit.

You also can have PVCs of varying speeds and purposely send data down a congested PVC while sending voice and other real-time traffic down a less-congested PVC.

The second method maps IP prioritization onto ATM using queuing techniques such as WFQ to prioritize between different flows per PVC.

Congestion Avoidance

As discussed previously, WFQ, PQ, and CQ mechanisms manage existing congestion and prioritize the traffic that is of highest importance.

Congestion avoidance works on a similar problem from a completely different angle. Instead of managing the existing congestion, congestion avoidance works to avoid congestion to begin with. In simplistic terms, you avoid congestion by dropping packets from different flows, which causes applications to slow the amount of traffic being sent. This avoids what is known as *global synchronization*, which occurs when many IP TCP flows begin transmitting and stop transmitting at the same time. This is caused by the lack of QoS in a service provider's backbone.

WRED

Random Early Detection (RED) is a congestion avoidance mechanism (as opposed to a congestion management mechanism) that is potentially useful, especially in high-speed transit networks. Sally Floyd and Van Jacobson proposed it in various papers in the early 1990s.

The theory behind WRED, simply, is that most data transports are somehow sensitive to loss and at least momentarily slow down if some of their traffic gets dropped.

To signal a TCP station to stop transmitting, you simply drop some of the sending station's traffic. WRED is Cisco's implementation of dropping traffic to avoid global synchronization.

WRED combines the capabilities of the RED algorithm with IP Precedence. This combination provides for preferential traffic handling for higher-priority packets. It can selectively discard lower-priority traffic when the interface starts to get congested and provide differentiated performance characteristics for different classes of service.

WRED also is RSVP aware, and it can provide an IS controlled-load QoS service. To fully comprehend how WRED works, you must understand TCP packet loss behavior.

TCP

A stream of data sent on a TCP connection is delivered reliably and in order to the destination. Transmission is made reliable through the use of sequence numbers and acknowledgments. Conceptually, each octet of data is assigned a sequence number. The sequence number of the first octet of data in a segment is the sequence number transmitted with that segment and is called the *segment sequence number*.

Segments also carry an acknowledgment number, which is the sequence number of the next expected data octet of transmissions in the reverse direction. When the TCP transmits a segment, it puts a copy on a retransmission queue and starts a timer; when the acknowledgment for that data is received, the segment is deleted from the queue. If the acknowledgment is not received before the timer runs out, the segment is retransmitted.

An acknowledgment by TCP does not guarantee that the data was delivered to the end user, only that the receiving TCP took the responsibility to do so.

To govern the flow of data into a TCP, you employ a flow control mechanism. The data-receiving TCP reports a window to the sending TCP. This window specifies the number of octets, starting with the acknowledgment number that the data-receiving TCP is currently prepared to receive.

When a user sends a TCP packet and a dropped segment is detected, the user's machine sends the first segment on its awaiting-acknowledge list (to restart the flow of data) and enters a slow-start phase. The user's machine tests the network to find a rate at which it can send without dropping data.

In a network that does not utilize RED, the buffers fill up and packets are tail-dropped. A tail-drop occurs when the router cannot receive packets because its queues are full. This causes multiple TCP sessions to restart their slow-start mechanism. This scenario eventually causes the network traffic to come in surges as TCP window sizes increase.

The router can use RED to manage the TCP slow-start mechanism to throttle back an individual TCP flow, measure the effect, and then drop packets from more TCP flows, if necessary.

NOTE	To enable WRED, use the following command:

```
random-detect [weighting]
```

weighting—(Optional) Exponential weighting constant in the range 1 to 16 used to determine the rate packets are dropped when congestion occurs; the default is 10 (that is, drop 1 packet every 210 packets).

WRED is useful in high-speed TCP/IP networks to avoid congestion by dropping packets at a controlled rate.

Backbone QoS Wrap-Up

It is important to note that both edge QoS and backbone QoS must work together to achieve the proper QoS for the various applications which might be traversing a network.

As a rule of thumb, it is wise to use high-speed congestion avoidance techniques in the backbone as well as some form of high-speed transmission, such as POS/Synchronous Digital Hierarchy (SDH) or IP + ATM inter-working. You can achieve IP QoS using several different mechanisms. The actual transport mechanism you choose is not as important as verifying that all the tools you need are present to service your applications.

Rules of Thumb for QoS

Before implementing QoS on the edge of a network, ask the following questions:

1   Do you have a low-bandwidth WAN circuit?

    If yes, use cRTP.

    Also, choose a fragmentation method. (FRF.12 is recommended first for Frame Relay networks. MCML PPP is recommended first for all other networks. MTU and IP MTU sizing are *not* recommended.)

2   Does your traffic need to be prioritized on your WAN circuits?

    If yes, use some form of queuing. (LLQ is recommended first, followed by IP RTP Priority and CB WFQ.)

3   Have you chosen CB-WFQ?

    If yes, select a method of classifying your traffic flows. (IP RTP Priority is recommended first, followed by IP Precedence.) It is generally useful to use both IP RTP Priority and IP Precedence, as some networks use IP Precedence for weighting (usually backbone networks).

4   Do you have a hub-and-spoke Frame Relay network or another need for shaping your traffic flows?

    If yes, select traffic shaping. (GTS is recommended first, followed by FRTS.)

Before implementing QoS on the backbone of a network, ask the following questions:

1 Have you chosen your high-speed networking technology?

2 Have you ensured that the edge QoS is compatible with the backbone QoS or CoS? (IP Precedence is recommended first.)

3 Have you utilized a congestion avoidance mechanism on highly utilized high-speed circuits? These circuits must have a high percentage of loss-tolerable protocols (such as TCP).

Cisco Labs' QoS Testing

Cisco conducted the following tests to show not only VoIP quality, but also how Cisco QoS tools work under load.

For the testbed, Cisco used a simple network with two Cisco VoIP gateways and one 56-kbps WAN. It completed two tests:

- Test A consisted of testing with and without QoS enabled while steadily increasing the saturation of the WAN link.

- Test B consisted of testing with and without QoS enabled while sending traffic across the WAN link in a bursty nature.

When no QoS was used, FIFO queuing was implemented. When QoS was used, MCML PPP, WFQ, and IP Precedence were utilized.

Cisco sent the traffic through two in-house traffic generation tools. It measured latency and voice quality using a voice-quality test tool that utilizes the ITU-T PSQM recommendation P.861.

When measuring PSQM, the higher the score the worse the voice quality. Table 9-4 shows the results from Test A.

Table 9-4   *Results for Test A*

Bandwidth Saturation (Percent)	Delay (ms)	PSQM	Delay/QoS (ms)	PSQM/QoS
0	76	1.43	76	1.43
40	233	1.94	106	1.5
60	242	2.1	104	1.43
75	280	7	102	1.51
90	300	9	104	1.51
100	350	10	105	1.51

To better understand the difference QoS can make, see Figure 9-7.

Figure 9-7   *Graph of Test A Results*

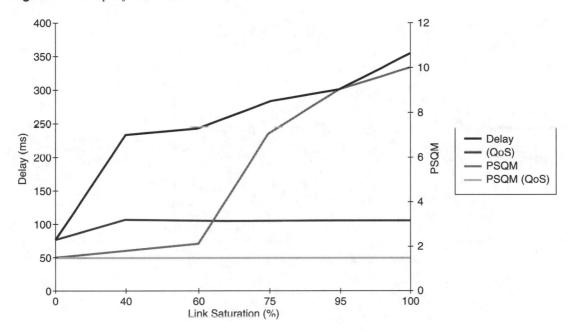

Results for Test B are just as dramatic and appear in Figure 9-8. Cisco IOS software QoS tools, when implemented properly, can definitely affect the caliber and stability of voice quality.

Figure 9-8 *Graph of Test B Results*

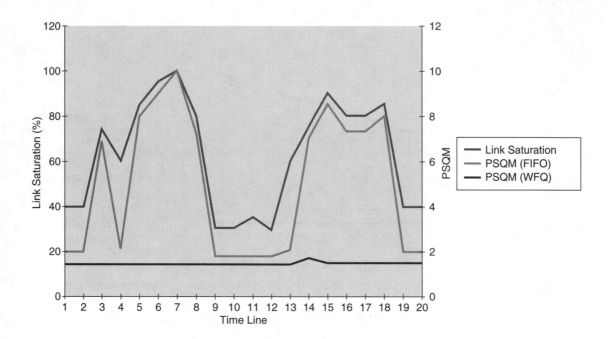

Summary

This chapter covered a broad topic called QoS. The concept of receiving a packet at the instant the sender wants it to be received is complex. Indeed, building a network to run VoIP is complex. Proper QoS is the most important step in ensuring good voice quality.

Cisco offers a variety of tools to enable network administrators to create the proper environment for VoIP. Although it is unlikely that you will use all these tools, it is important to understand how all of them can affect your network.

Cisco has plenty of experience with prioritizing delay-sensitive traffic over an IP network. This started many years ago when Cisco put SNA onto IP networks. Even then, due to latency and packet loss concerns, few customers believed SNA could possibly run over an IP network. Today, however, a good portion of SNA traffic is transported over IP networks.

The same thing is happening with voice. Many skeptics do not believe IP can give the proper QoS for such a real-time application, but with the proper network design and the right tools, it is possible.

This chapter also covered different queuing techniques, such as WFQ, CB-WFQ, LLQ, PQ, and CQ, to give readers an understanding of how these tools evolved over time. Currently it is highly recommended that you use LLQ if you plan to deploy a VoIP network. If you cannot upgrade your IP network to the latest version of code, it is better to use other queuing techniques, such as PQ and CQ, to give you better QoS performance than none at all.

With queuing comes prioritization. Although some queuing techniques, such as LLQ, have built-in prioritization, it is important to ensure that you have all the correct tools turned on. Even if you use LLQ, for instance, you should still enable IP Precedence in case a backbone network uses that tool to prioritize dropped packets. Other components such as bandwidth-saving techniques and backbone tools are part of the arsenal a network administrator has to provide the correct QoS. Each network is different and requires not only attention to detail but also a knowledgeable administrator who knows how to tune the network to provide optimal QoS.

QoS will continue to evolve over time, and in the future, IP might become the de-facto transport method. So, not only will your voice be transmitted over IP, but TDM circuits as well.

IP Signaling Protocols

CHAPTER 10

H.323

H.323 is an International Telecommunication Union Telecommunication Standardization Sector (ITU-T) specification for transmitting audio, video, and data across an Internet Protocol (IP) network, including the Internet. When compliant with H.323, vendors' products and applications can communicate and interoperate with each other. The H.323 standard addresses call signaling and control, multimedia transport and control, and bandwidth control for point-to-point and multipoint conferences. The *H* series of recommendations also specifies H.320 for Integrated Services Digital Network (ISDN) and H.324 for plain old telephone service (POTS) as transport mechanisms.

The H.323 standard consists of the following components and protocols:

Feature	Protocol
Call Signaling	H.225
Media Control	H.245
Audio Codecs	G.711, G.722, G.723, G.728, G.729
Video Codecs	H.261, H.263
Data Sharing	T.120
Media Transport	RTP/RTCP

The H.323 system is discussed in the following three sections:

- H.323 elements
- H.323 protocol suite
- H.323 call-flows

H.323 Elements

Figure 10-1 illustrates the elements of an H.323 system. These elements include terminals, gateways, gatekeepers, and multipoint control units (MCU).

Often referred to as endpoints, terminals provide point-to-point and multipoint conferencing for audio and, optionally, video and data. Gateways interconnect to Public Switched Telephone Network (PSTN) or ISDN networks for H.323 endpoint interworking. Gatekeepers provide admission control and address translation services for terminals or gateways. MCUs are devices that allow two or more terminals or gateways to conference with either audio and/or video sessions.

Figure 10-1 *Elements of H.323 Networking*

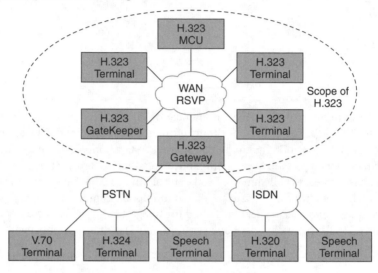

Terminal

The network element illustrated in Figure 10-2 is defined in H.323 as a *terminal*. H.323 terminals must have a system control unit, media transmission, audio codec, and packet-based network interface. Optional requirements include a video codec and user data applications.

Figure 10-2 *Relationships of H.323 Components*

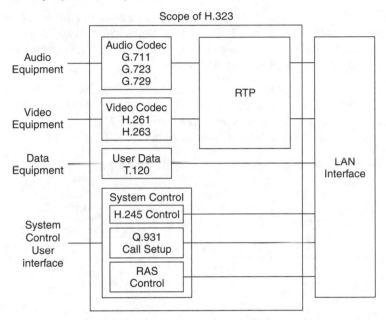

The following functions and capabilities are within the scope of the H.323 terminal:

- System Control Unit—Provides H.225 and H.245 call control, capability exchange, messaging, and signaling of commands for proper operation of the terminal.

- Media Transmission—Formats the transmitted audio, video, data, control streams, and messages onto network interface. Media transmission also receives the audio, video, data, control streams, and messages from the network interface.

- Audio Codec—Encodes the signal from the audio equipment for transmission and decodes the incoming audio code. Required functions include encoding and decoding G.711 speech and transmitting and receiving a-law and μ-law formats. Optionally, G.722, G.723.1, G.728, and G.729 encoding and decoding can be supported.

- Network Interface—A packet-based interface capable of end-to-end Transmission Control Protocol (TCP) and User Datagram Protocol (UDP) unicast and multicast services.

- Video Codec—Optional, but if provided, must be capable of encoding and decoding video according to H.261 Quarter Comment Intermediate Format (QCIF).

- Data Channel—Supports applications such as database access, file transfer, and *audiographics conferencing* (the capability to modify a common image over multiple users' computers simultaneously), as specified in Recommendation T.120.

Gateway

The H.323 gateway reflects the characteristics of a Switched Circuit Network (SCN) endpoint and H.323 endpoint. It translates between audio, video, and data transmission formats as well as communication systems and protocols. This includes call setup and teardown on both the IP network and SCN.

Gateways are not needed unless interconnection with the SCN is required. Therefore, H.323 endpoints can communicate directly over the packet network without connecting to a gateway. The gateway acts as an H.323 terminal or MCU on the network and an SCN terminal or MCU on the SCN, as illustrated in Figure 10-3.

Figure 10-3 *Elements of an H.323 Gateway*

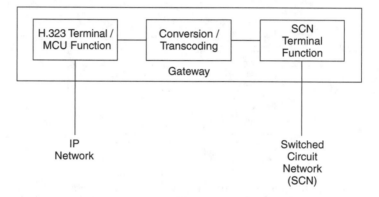

Gatekeeper

An optional function, the gatekeeper provides pre-call and call-level control services to H.323 endpoints. Gatekeepers are logically separated from the other network elements in H.323 environments. If more than one gatekeeper is implemented, inter-communication is accomplished in an unspecified manner.

New versions of H.323—such as H.323 version 3, which was scheduled to be finalized on paper by the end of 1999—will attempt to recommend a gatekeeper inter-communication specification. The Gatekeeper can use a simple query/response sequence (Location Request [LRQ] or Location Confirmation [LCF]) to remotely locate users. To exchange some information, H.323 version 3 also uses Annex G for database query or exchange. Yet another protocol, the Open Settlements Protocol (OSP), also specified as European Telecommunication Standards Institute (ETSI) TS 101 321, is used largely for intra-domain interactions from both the gateway and gatekeepers.

If a gatekeeper is present in an H.323 system, it must perform the following:

- Address Translation—Provides endpoint IP addresses from H.323 aliases (such as pc1@cisco.com) or E.164 addresses (standard phone numbers).

- Admissions Control—Provides authorized access to H.323 using the Admission Request/Admission Confirm/Admission Reject (ARQ/ACF/ARJ) messages, discussed in the "RAS Signaling" section later in this chapter.

- Bandwidth Control—Consists of managing endpoint bandwidth requirements using Bandwidth Request/Bandwidth Confirm/Bandwidth Reject (BRQ/BCF/BRJ) messages, discussed in the "RAS Signaling" section later in this chapter.

- Zone Management—Provided for registered terminals, gateways, and MCUs and discussed further in the "RAS Signaling" section later in this chapter.

Optionally, the gatekeeper can provide the following functionality:

- Call Control Signaling—Uses the Gatekeeper Routed Call Signaling (GKRCS) model, reviewed in the "Call Control Signaling (H.225)" section later in this chapter.

- Call Authorization—Enables the gatekeeper to restrict access to certain terminals and gateways or to restrict access based on time-of-day policies.

- Bandwidth Management—Enables the gatekeeper to reject admission if the required bandwidth is not available.

- Call Management—Services include maintaining an active call list that you can use to indicate that an endpoint is busy.

The MCU and Elements

The multipoint controller (MC) supports conferences between three or more endpoints in a multipoint conference. MCs transmit the capability set to each endpoint in the multipoint conference and can revise capabilities during the conference. The MC function can be resident in a terminal, gateway, gatekeeper, or MCU.

The multipoint processor (MP) receives audio, video, and/or data streams and distributes them to endpoints participating in a multipoint conference.

The MCU is an endpoint that supports multipoint conferences and, at a minimum, consists of an MC and one or more MPs. If it supports centralized multipoint conferences, a typical MCU consists of an MC and an audio, video, and data MP.

H.323 Proxy Server

An H.323 proxy server is a proxy specifically designed for the H.323 protocol. The proxy operates at the application layer and can examine packets between two communicating applications. Proxies can determine the destination of a call and perform the connection if desired. The proxy supports the following key functions:

- Terminals that don't support Resource Reservation Protocol (RSVP) can connect through access or local-area networks (LANs) with relatively good quality of service (QoS) to the proxy. Pairs of proxies can then negotiate adequate QoSs to tunnel across the IP network. Proxies can manage QoS with RSVP and/or IP precedence bits.

- Proxies support the routing of H.323 traffic separate from ordinary data traffic through application-specific routing (ASR).

- A proxy is compatible with network address translation, enabling H.323 nodes to be deployed in networks with private address space.

- A proxy deployed without a firewall or independently of a firewall provides security so that only H.323 traffic passes through it. A proxy deployed in conjunction with a firewall enables the firewall to be simply configured to pass all H.323 traffic by treating the proxy as a trusted node. This enables the firewall to provide data networking security and the proxy to provide H.323 security.

H.323 Protocol Suite

The H.323 protocol suite is based on several protocols, as illustrated in Figure 10-4. The protocol family supports call admissions, setup, status, teardown, media streams, and messages in H.323 systems. These protocols are supported by both reliable and unreliable packet delivery mechanisms over data networks.

Although most H.323 implementations today utilize TCP as the transport mechanism for signaling, H.323 version 2 does enable basic UDP transport. Also, other standards bodies are investigating the use of other reliable UDP mechanisms to create more scalable signaling methods.

Figure 10-4 *Layers of the H.323 Protocol Suite*

Reliable TCP Delivery			Unreliable UDP Devlivery		
H.245	H.225		Audio/Video Streams		
	Call Control	RAS	RTCP		RTP
TCP			UDP		
IP					
Data/Physical Layers					

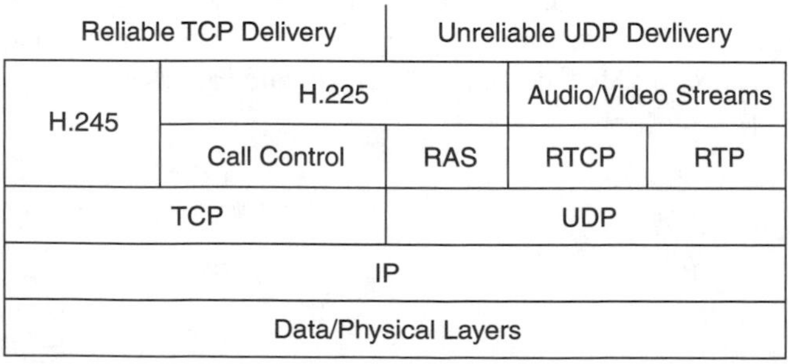

The H.323 protocol suite is split into three main areas of control:

- Registration, Admissions, and Status (RAS) Signaling—Provides pre-call control in H.323 gatekeeper-based networks.

- Call Control Signaling—Used to connect, maintain, and disconnect calls between endpoints.

- Media Control and Transport—Provides the reliable H.245 channel that carries media control messages. The transport occurs with an unreliable UDP stream.

The remainder of this section focuses on these three key signaling functions.

RAS Signaling

RAS signaling provides pre-call control in H.323 networks where gatekeepers and a zone exist. The RAS channel is established between endpoints and gatekeepers across an IP network. The RAS channel is opened before any other channels are established and is independent of the call control signaling and media transport channels. This unreliable UDP connection carries the RAS messages that perform registration, admissions, bandwidth changes, status, and disengage procedures.

Gatekeeper Discovery

Gatekeeper discovery is a manual or automatic process endpoints use to identify which gatekeeper to register with. In the manual method, endpoints are configured with the gate-keeper's IP address and, therefore, can attempt registration immediately, but only with the predefined gatekeeper. The automatic method enables the relationship between endpoints and gatekeepers to change over time and requires a mechanism known as *auto discovery*.

Auto discovery enables an endpoint, which might not know its gatekeeper, to discover its gatekeeper through a multicast message. Because endpoints do not have to be statically configured or reconfigured for gatekeepers, this method has less administrative overhead. The gatekeeper discovery multicast address is 224.0.1.41, the gatekeeper UDP discovery port is 1718, and the gatekeeper UDP registration and status port is 1719. The following three RAS messages are used for H.323 gatekeeper auto discovery:

- Gatekeeper Request (GRQ)—A multicast message sent by an endpoint looking for the gatekeeper.

- Gatekeeper Confirm (GCF)—The reply to an endpoint GRQ indicating the transport address of the gatekeeper's RAS channel.

- Gatekeeper Reject (GRJ)—Advises the endpoint that the gatekeeper does not want to accept its registration. This is usually due to a configuration on the gateway or gatekeeper.

Figure 10-5 illustrates the messaging and sequencing processes for auto discovery.

Figure 10-5 *Gatekeeper Auto Discovery*

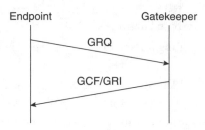

For redundancy purposes, the gatekeeper can identify alternative gatekeepers in GCF messages. You can use alternative gatekeepers when the primary gatekeeper fails.

Registration

Registration is the process that enables gateways, endpoints, and MCUs to join a zone and inform the gatekeeper of their IP and alias addresses. A necessary process, registration occurs after the discovery process, but before you can attempt any calls. You can use the following six messages to enable an endpoint to register and cancel registration:

- Registration Request (RRQ)—Sent from an endpoint to the gatekeeper RAS channel address

- Registration Confirm (RCF)—Sent by the gatekeeper and confirms an endpoint registration

- Registration Reject (RRJ)—Sent by the gatekeeper and rejects an endpoint registration

- Unregister Request (URQ)—Sent from an endpoint or gatekeeper to cancel a registration

- Unregister Confirm (UCF)—Sent from the endpoint or gatekeeper to confirm an unregistration

- Unregister Reject (URJ)—Indicates that the endpoint was not preregistered with the gatekeeper

Figure 10-6 illustrates the messaging and sequencing processes for endpoint registering and endpoint and gatekeeper unregistering.

Figure 10-6 *Endpoint Registering and Endpoint and Gatekeeper Unregistering*

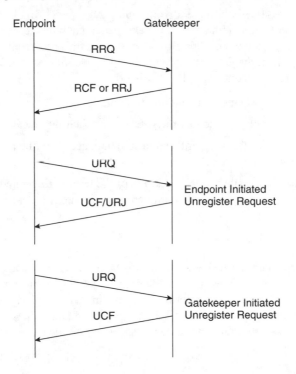

Endpoint Location

Endpoints and gatekeepers use *endpoint location* to obtain contact information when only alias information is available. Locate messages are sent to the gatekeeper's RAS channel address or are multicast to the gatekeeper's discovery multicast address. The gatekeeper responsible for the requested endpoint replies by indicating its own or the endpoint's contact information.

The endpoint or gatekeeper can include one or more E.164 addresses outside the zone in the request. You can use the following three messages to locate endpoints:

- LRQ—Sent to request the endpoint or gatekeeper contact information for one or more E.164 addresses.

- LCF—Sent by the gatekeeper and contains the call signaling channel or RAS channel address of itself or the requested endpoint. It uses its own address when GKRCS is used and the requested endpoint's address when Directed Endpoint Call Signaling is used.

- Location Reject (LRJ)—Sent by gatekeepers that receive an LRQ for which the requested endpoint is not registered or has unavailable resources.

Admissions

Admission messages between endpoints and gatekeepers provide the basis for call admissions and bandwidth control. Gatekeepers authorize access to H.323 networks by confirming or rejecting an admission request. An admission request includes the requested bandwidth, which the gatekeeper can reduce in the confirmation. The following messages provide admissions control in H.323 networks:

- ARQ—An attempt by an endpoint to initiate a call
- ACF—An authorization by the gatekeeper to admit the call
- ARJ—Denies the endpoint's request to gain access to the network for this particular call

The ACF message contains the IP address of the terminating gateway or gatekeeper and enables the originating gateway to immediately initiate call control signaling procedures.

Status Information

The gatekeeper can use the RAS channel to obtain status information from an endpoint. You can use this message to monitor whether the endpoint is online and offline due to a failure condition. The typical polling period for status messages is 10 seconds. During the ACF, the gatekeeper also can request that the endpoint send periodic status messages during a call. You can use the following three messages to provide status on the RAS channel:

- Information Request (IRQ)—Sent from the gatekeeper to the endpoint requesting status.
- Information Request Response (IRR)—Sent from the endpoint to the gatekeeper in response to an IRQ. This message also is sent from an endpoint if the gatekeeper requests periodic status updates.
- Status Enquiry—Sent outside the RAS channel on the call signaling channel. An endpoint or gatekeeper can send Status Enquiry messages to another endpoint to verify call state. Gatekeepers typically use these messages to verify whether calls are still active.

Bandwidth Control

Bandwidth control is initially managed through the admissions exchange between an endpoint and the gatekeeper within the ARQ/ACF/ARJ sequence. The bandwidth can change during a call, however. You can use the following messages to change bandwidth:

- BRQ—Sent by an endpoint to the gatekeeper requesting an increase or decrease in call bandwidth
- BCF—Sent by the gatekeeper confirming acceptance of the bandwidth change request

- BRJ—Sent by the gatekeeper rejecting the bandwidth change request (sent if the requested bandwidth is not available)

NOTE   Bandwidth control is limited in scope to only the gatekeeper and gateways and does not take into account the state of the network itself. The gatekeeper currently looks only at its static bandwidth table to determine whether to accept or reject the bandwidth request.

Call Control Signaling (H.225)

In H.323 networks, call control procedures are based on International Telecommunication Union (ITU) Recommendation H.225, which specifies the use and support of Q.931 signaling messages. A reliable call control channel is created across an IP network on TCP port 1720. This port initiates the Q.931 call control messages between two endpoints for the purpose of connecting, maintaining, and disconnecting calls.

The actual call control and keepalive messages move to ephemeral ports after initial call setup. But 1720 is the well-known port for H.323 calls. H.225 also specifies the use of Q.932 messages for supplementary services. The following Q.931 and Q.932 messages are the most commonly used signaling messages in H.323 networks:

- Setup—A forward message sent by the calling H.323 entity in an attempt to establish connection to the called H.323 entity. This message is sent on the well-known H.225 TCP port 1720.

- Call Proceeding—A backward message sent from the called entity to the calling entity to advise that call establishment procedures were initiated.

- Alerting—A backward message sent from the called entity to advise that called party ringing was initiated.

- Connect—A backward message sent from the called entity to the calling entity indicating that the called party answered the call. The connect message can contain the transport UDP/IP address for H.245 control signaling.

- Release Complete—Sent by the endpoint initiating the disconnect, which indicates that the call is being released. You can send this message only if the call signaling channel is open or active.

- Facility—A Q.932 message used to request or acknowledge supplementary services. It also is used to indicate whether a call should be directed or should go through a gatekeeper.

Figure 10-7 illustrates the signaling messages for call setup. Interaction with the gatekeeper is limited to RAS messages for call permission and, possibly, on status messages.

Figure 10-7 *Call Setup Signaling Messages*

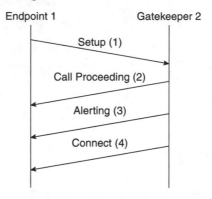

You can route the call signaling channel in an H.323 network in two ways: through Direct Endpoint Call Signaling and GKRCS. In the Direct Endpoint Call Signaling method, call signaling messages are sent directly between the two endpoints, as illustrated in Figure 10-8.

Figure 10-8 *Direct Endpoint Call Signaling*

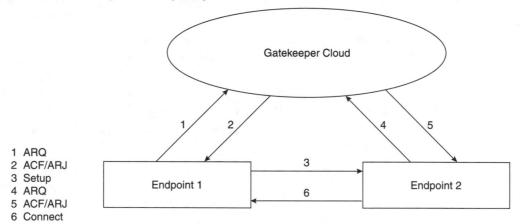

In the GKRCS method, call signaling messages between the endpoints are routed through the gatekeeper, as illustrated in Figure 10-9.

Figure 10-9 *Gatekeeper Routed Call Signaling*

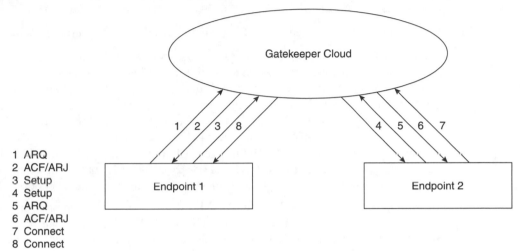

1 ARQ
2 ACF/ARJ
3 Setup
4 Setup
5 ARQ
6 ACF/ARJ
7 Connect
8 Connect

NOTE   In Figures 10-8 and 10-9, the Setup and Connect messages are call signaling channel messages, whereas the remaining messages are RAS channel messages.

You can offer supplementary services through the GKRCS method if the call signaling channel is left open during the call. Gatekeepers also can close the call signaling channel after call setup is complete.

Media Control and Transport (H.245 and RTP/RTCP)

H.245 handles end-to-end control messages between H.323 entities. H.245 procedures establish logical channels for transmission of audio, video, data, and control channel information. An endpoint establishes one H.245 channel for each call with the participating endpoint. The reliable control channel is created over IP using the dynamically assigned TCP port in the final call signaling message.

The exchange of capabilities, the opening and closing of logical channels, preference modes, and message control take place over this control channel. H.245 control also enables separate transmit and receive capability exchange as well as function negotiation, such as determining which codec to use.

If you use Gatekeeper Routed call signaling, you can control channel routing in two ways. You can use *Direct H.245 Control*, which occurs directly between two participating endpoints. Or, you can use *Gatekeeper Routed H.245 Control*, which occurs between each endpoint and its gatekeeper.

You can use the following procedures and messages to enable H.245 control operation:

- Capability Exchange—Consists of messages that securely exchange the capabilities between two endpoints, also referred to as terminals. These messages indicate the terminal's transmit and receive capabilities for audio, video, and data to the participating terminal. For audio, capability exchange includes speech transcoding codecs such as G-series G.729 at 8 kbps, G.728 at 16 kbps, G.711 at 64 kbps, G.723 at 5.3 or 6.3 kbps, or G.722 at 48, 56, and 64 kbps. It also includes International Organization for Standardization (ISO) series IS.11172-3 with 32-, 44.1-, and 48 kHz sampling rates, and IS.13818-3 with 16-, 22.05-, 24-, 32-, 44.1-, and 48 kHz sampling rates; and GSM full-rate, half-rate, and enhanced full-rate speech audio codecs.

- Master-Slave Termination—Procedures used to determine which endpoint is master and which endpoint is slave for a particular call. The relationship is maintained for the duration of the call and is used to resolve conflicts between endpoints. Master-slave rules are used when both endpoints request similar actions at the same time.

- Round-Trip Delay—Procedures used to determine delay between the originating and terminating endpoints. The RoundTripDelayRequest message measures the delay and verifies whether the remote H.245 protocol entity is alive.

- Logical Channel Signaling—Opens and closes the logical channel that carries audio, video, and data information. The channel is set up before the actual transmission to ensure that the terminals are ready and capable of receiving and decoding information. The same signaling messages establish both uni-directional and bidirectional channels. After logical channel signaling is successfully established, the UDP port for the RTP media channel is passed from the terminating to the originating endpoint. Also, when using the Gatekeeper Call Routed model, this is the point at which the gatekeeper can divert the RTP streams by providing the actual UDP/IP address of the terminating endpoint.

Fast Connect Procedures

The two procedures available to establish media channels between endpoints are H.245 and Fast Connect. Fast Connect enables media connection establishment for basic point-to-point calls with one round-trip message exchange. These procedures dictate that the calling endpoint include the *faststart* element in the initial setup message.

The faststart portion consists of logical channel sequences, media channel capabilities, and the necessary parameters to open and begin media transmission. In response, the called endpoint returns an H.225 message (call proceeding, progress, alerting, or connect) containing a faststart element that selects the accepted terminal capabilities. At this point, both the calling and called endpoints can begin transmitting media if the setup sequence based on H.225 reached the connected state.

Tunneling H.245

You can encapsulate or tunnel H.245 messages within the H.225 call signaling channel instead of creating a separate H.245 control channel. This method improves call setup time and resource allocation, and it provides synchronization between call signaling and control. You can encapsulate multiple H.245 messages in any H.225 message. Also, at any time either endpoint can switch to a separate H.245 connection.

Call Termination

Either endpoint participating in a call can initiate call termination procedures. First, the endpoint must cease media transmissions (such as audio, video, or data) and close all logical channels. Next, it must end the H.245 session and send a release complete message on the call signaling channel, if it's still open or active. At this point, if no gatekeeper is present, the call is terminated. When a gatekeeper is present, the following messages are used on the RAS channel to complete call termination:

- Disengage Request (DRQ)—Sent by an endpoint or gatekeeper to terminate a call
- Disengage Confirm (DCF)—Sent by an endpoint or gatekeeper confirming disconnection of the call
- Disengage Reject (DRJ)—Sent by the endpoint or gatekeeper rejecting call disconnection

Media Transport (RTP/RTCP)

RTP provides media transport in H.323. More specifically, RTP enables real-time, end-to-end delivery of interactive audio, video, and data over unicast or multicast networks. Packetization and transmission services include payload identification, sequencing, timestamping, and monitoring.

RTP relies on other mechanisms and lower layers to ensure on-time delivery, resource reservation, reliability, and QoS. RTCP monitors data delivery as well as controls and identifies services. The media channel is created using UDP, where RTP streams operate on an even port number and the corresponding RTCP stream operates on the next-higher (odd) port number.

H.323 Call-Flows

The call-flows outlined in this section demonstrate ways the H.323 family of protocols provides call setup between two endpoints. Assume these are speech calls and that all endpoints already completed registration with the appropriate gatekeeper. The call setup examples include two different gatekeeper implementations as well as two different call signaling methods.

Figure 10-12 *Direct Endpoint Signaling—Two Gatekeepers*

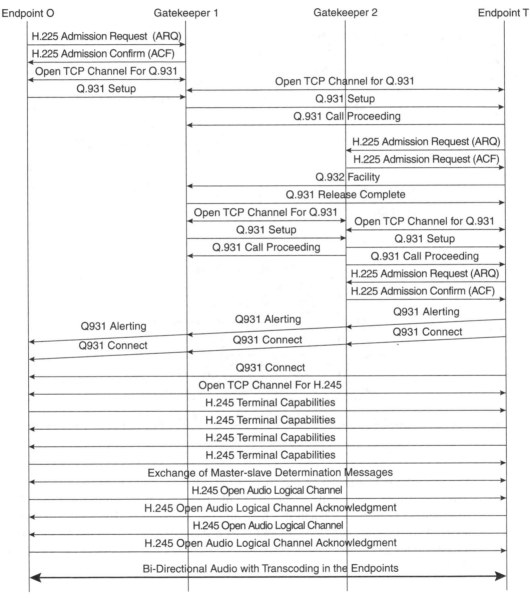

The final H.323 call-flow example demonstrates call setup procedures for the GKRCS method, whereby each endpoint has a different gatekeeper. This enables LRQs and LCFs to be sent between the two gatekeepers, which enables control of billing records at the gatekeeper as all the setup and control messages pass through the gatekeeper.

Figure 10-13 *Gatekeeper Routed Call Signaling—Two Gatekeepers*

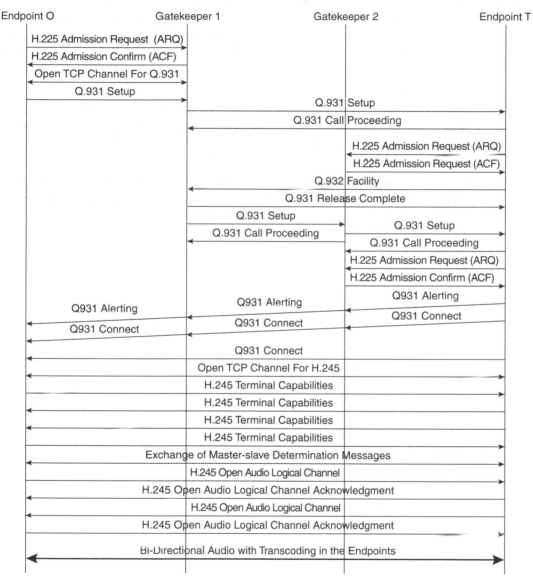

CHAPTER 11

Session Initiation Protocol

The Session Initiation Protocol (SIP) is an application-layer signaling-control protocol used to establish, maintain, and terminate multimedia sessions. Multimedia sessions include Internet telephony, conferences, and other similar applications involving such media as audio, video, and data.

You can use SIP invitations to establish sessions and carry session descriptions. SIP supports unicast and multicast sessions as well as point-to-point and multipoint calls. You can establish and terminate communications using the following five SIP facets: user location, user capability, user availability, call setup, and call handling.

SIP, on which Request For Comments (RFC) 2543 is based, is a text-based protocol that is part of the overall Internet Engineering Task Force (IETF) multimedia architecture. The IETF also includes the Resource Reservation Protocol (RSVP; RFC 2205), Real-Time Transport Protocol (RTP; RFC 1889), Real-Time Streaming Protocol (RTSP; RFC 2326), Session Announcement Protocol (SAP; internet draft), and SDP (Session Description Protocol; RFC 2327). SIP's functions are independent, however, so it does not depend on any of these protocols. It is important to note that SIP can operate in conjunction with other signaling protocols, such as H.323.

Internet Protocol (IP) telephony is still being developed and will require additional signaling capabilities in the future. The extensibility of SIP enables such development of incremental functionality. SIP message headers are versatile, and you can register additional features with the Internet Assigned Numbers Authority (IANA). SIP message flexibility also enables elements to construct advanced telephony services, including mobility type services.

As of the writing of this chapter, the IETF has not yet ratified SIP, so this chapter focuses on the basics of SIP and does not discuss extensibility or services. The following issues are covered in this chapter:

- SIP overview—Components, addressing, and invitations
- Messages—Headers, requests, and responses
- Basic operation—Proxy and redirect server operation

SIP Overview

This section describes the basic functionality and key elements of SIP. The two components in a SIP system are *user agents* and *network servers.* Calling and called parties are identified by *SIP addresses;* parties need to locate *servers* and *users. SIP transactions* also are covered as part of this overview.

User Agents

User agents are client end-system applications that contain both a user-agent client (UAC) and a user-agent server (UAS), otherwise known as *client* and *server*, respectively.

- Client—Initiates SIP requests and acts as the user's calling agent.

- Server—Receives requests and returns responses on behalf of the user; acts as the user-called agent.

Network Servers

Two types of SIP network servers exist: *proxy servers* and *redirect servers.* Functional examples of these servers are provided in the section "Basic Operation of SIP," later in this chapter.

- Proxy server—Acts on behalf of other clients and contains both client and server functions. A proxy server interprets and can rewrite request headers before passing them on to other servers. Rewriting the headers identifies the proxy as the initiator of the request and ensures that replies follow the same path back to the proxy instead of the client.

- Redirect server—Accepts SIP requests and sends a redirect response back to the client containing the address of the next server. Redirect servers do not accept calls, nor do they process or forward SIP requests.

Addressing

SIP addresses, also called SIP Universal Resource Locators (URLs), exist in the form of users @ hosts. Similar to e-mail addresses, a SIP URL is identified by user@host. The user portion of the address can be a user name or telephone number, and the host portion can be a domain name or network address. You can identify a user's SIP URL by his or her e-mail address. The following example depicts two possible SIP URLs:

sip:ciscopress@cisco.com
sip:4085262222@171.171.171.1

Locating a Server

A client can send a SIP request either directly, to a locally configured proxy server, or to the IP address and port of the corresponding SIP URL. Sending a SIP request directly is relatively easy, as the end-system application knows the proxy server. Sending a SIP request in the second manner is somewhat more complicated, for the following reasons:

- The client must determine the IP address and port number of the server for which the request is destined.

- If the port number is not listed in the requested SIP URL, the default port is 5060.

- If the protocol type is not listed in the request SIP URL, the client must first attempt to connect using User Datagram Protocol (UDP) and then Transmission Control Protocol (TCP).

- The client queries the Domain Name System (DNS) server for the host IP address. If it finds no address records, the client is unable to locate the server and cannot continue with the request.

SIP Transactions

After addressing is resolved, the client sends one or more SIP requests and receives one or more responses from the specified server. All the requests and responses associated with this activity are considered part of a SIP transaction. For simplicity and consistency, the header fields in all request messages match the header fields in all response messages.

You can transmit SIP transactions in either UDP or TCP. In the case of TCP, you can carry all request and response messages related to a single SIP transaction over the same TCP connection. You also can carry separate SIP transactions between the two entities over the same TCP connection. If you use UDP, the response is sent to the address identified in the header field of the request.

Locating a User

The called party might move from one to several end systems over time. He or she might move from the corporate local-area network (LAN) to a home office connected through his or her Internet service provider (ISP), or to a public Internet connection while attending a conference, for example. Therefore, for location services, SIP needs to accommodate the flexibility and mobility of IP end systems. The locations of these end systems might be registered with the SIP server or with other location servers outside the scope of SIP. In the latter case, the SIP server stores the list of locations based on the outside location server that is returning multiple host possibilities.

The action and result of locating a user depends on the type of SIP server being used. A SIP redirect server simply returns the complete list of locations and enables the client to locate the user directly. A SIP proxy server can attempt the addresses in parallel until the call is successful.

- CANCEL—This request enables user agents and network servers to cancel any in-progress request. This does not affect completed requests in which final responses were already received.
- REGISTER—This method is used by clients to register location information with SIP servers.

Message Responses

SIP message responses are based upon the receipt and interpretation of a corresponding request. They are sent in response to requests and indicate call success or failure, including the status of the server. The six classes of responses, their status codes, and explanations of what they do are provided in Table 11-3. The two categories of responses are *provisional,* which indicates progress, and *final,* which terminates a request. In Table 11-3 informational responses are provisional, and the remaining five are final responses.

Table 11-3   *SIP Responses*

Class of Response	Status Code	Explanation
Informational	100	Trying
	180	Ringing
	181	Call is being forwarded
	182	Queued
Success	200	OK
	300	Multiple choices
	301	Moved permanently
	302	Moved temporarily
	303	See other
	305	Use proxy
	380	Alternative service
Client-Error	400	Bad request
	401	Unauthorized
	402	Payment required
	403	Forbidden
	404	Not found
	405	Method not allowed
	406	Not acceptable
	407	Proxy authentication required

Table 11-3   *SIP Responses (Continued)*

Class of Response	Status Code	Explanation
Client-Error	408	Request timeout
	409	Conflict
	410	Gone
	411	Length required
	413	Request entity too large
	414	Requested URL too large
	415	Unsupported media type
	420	Bad extension
	480	Temporarily not available
	481	Call leg or transaction doesn't exist
	482	Loop detected
	483	Too many hops
	484	Address incomplete
	485	Ambiguous
	486	Busy here
Server-Error	500	Internal server error
	501	Not implemented
	502	Bad gateway
	503	Service unavailable
	504	Gateway timeout
	505	SIP version not supported
Global Failure	600	Busy everywhere
	603	Decline
	604	Does not exist anywhere
	606	Not acceptable

Basic Operation of SIP

SIP servers handle incoming requests in two ways. This basic operative is based on inviting a participant to a call. The two basic modes of SIP server operation described in this section are the following:

- Proxy servers
- Redirect servers

Proxy Server Example

The communication exchange for the INVITE method using the proxy server is illustrated in Figure 11-1.

Figure 11-1 *Proxy Mode of Operation*

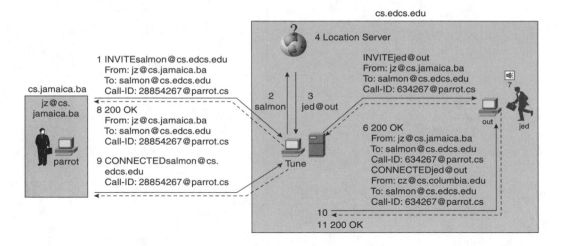

Source: Henning Schulzrinne, Columbia University

The operational steps in the proxy mode needed to bring a two-way call to succession are as follows:

1 The proxy server accepts the INVITE request from the client.

2 The proxy server identifies the location by using the supplied addresses and location services.

3 An INVITE request is issued to the address of the location returned.

4 The called party user agent alerts the user and returns a success indication to the requesting proxy server.

5 An OK (200) response is sent from the proxy server to the calling party.

6 The calling party confirms receipt by issuing an ACK request, which is forwarded by the proxy or sent directly to the called party.

Redirect Server Example

The protocol exchange for the INVITE request using the redirect server is shown in Figure 11-2.

Figure 11-2 *Redirect Mode of Operation*

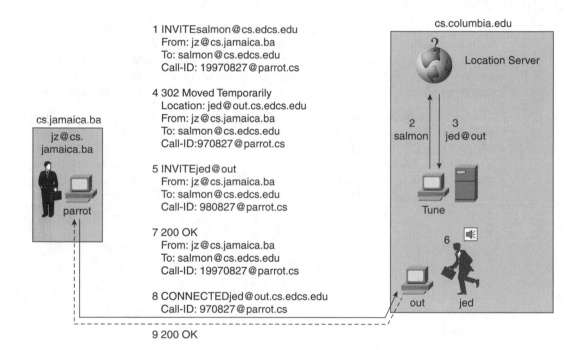

Source: Henning Schulzrinne, Columbia University

The operational steps in the redirect mode to bring a two-way call to succession are as follows:

1 The redirect server accepts the INVITE request from the calling party and contacts location services with the supplied information.

2   After the user is located, the redirect server returns the address directly to the calling party. Unlike the proxy server, the redirect server does not issue an INVITE.

3   The user agent sends an ACK to the redirect server acknowledging the completed transaction.

4   The user agent sends an INVITE request directly to the address returned by the redirect server.

5   The called party provides a success indication (200 OK), and the calling party returns an ACK.

Summary

SIP is an IETF standards-based signaling protocol for multimedia applications with one or more participants. The IETF's approach is to create a layered and functional architecture in which specific features and functionality are realized by highly optimized protocols. SIP is a flexible protocol that has extension capabilities for additional features and services. This chapter provides foundational concepts and does not specify SIP's full suite of possibilities.

The International Telecommunication Union Telecommunication Standardization Sector (ITU-T) H.323 signaling standard discussed in Chapter 10, "H.323," differs from the IETF SIP protocol. SIP boasts some advantages over H.323, such as quicker call set-up times and less-complex, HTTP-like implementation with a modular architecture containing functions that reside in separate protocols. SIP implementation also is stateless, meaning that all servers need not maintain call state.

RFC 2543

Handley, et al.

CHAPTER 12

Gateway Control Protocols

This chapter covers two Internet Engineering Task Force (IETF) gateway control protocols that are used to control Voice over IP (VoIP) gateways from external call-control elements: Simple Gateway Control Protocol (SGCP) and Media Gateway Control Protocol (MGCP).

It also covers another device control specification that has a significant impact on the packet telephony industry: Internet Protocol Device Control (IPDC), which was fused with SGCP to form MGCP. All three gateway control protocols were designed to support gateways that have external intelligence (that is, external call-control elements). Therefore, their use is prevalent in large trunking gateways and residential gateways.

Simple Gateway Control Protocol

Simple Gateway Control Protocol (SGCP) enables call-control elements to control connections between trunking, residential, and access-type VoIP gateways. Although these gateways target different market segments, all of them convert time-division multiplexing (TDM) voice to packet voice. Call-control elements are generally referred to as Media Gateway Controllers (MGCs) or call agents.

SGCP assumes an architecture whose call-control intelligence is outside of the gateway and is handled by external call-control elements, called *call agents*. In this model, one or more call agents can participate in constructing a call. Synchronization among these call agents is assumed and is not covered by SGCP.

SGCP is used to establish, maintain, and disconnect calls across an Internet Protocol (IP) network. This is accomplished by controlling the required connections between desired and corresponding endpoints. Authorization of calls and connections is outside the scope of this protocol. SGCP does not contain a security mechanism for unauthorized call setup or interference. The specification does, however, state that it is the expectation that all transactions are carried over secure Internet connections.

Security for these connections is provided by the IP Security Architecture as defined in Request For Comments (RFC) 1825 and using either IP Authentication Header (RFC 1826) or IP Encapsulating Security Payload (RFC 1827).

Relation to Other Standards

In SGCP, call agents handle call signaling functions and gateways provide audio translation functions. Call agents also can implement H.323 signaling capabilities and establish calls using the Gatekeeper Routed Call Signaling (GKRCS) model. In this case, call agents can connect calls between gateways using SGCP and between terminals using H.323 procedures.

IETF produced standards for multimedia applications. They include Session Description Protocol (SDP; RFC 2327), Service Advertising Protocol (SAP), Session Initiation Protocol (SIP, discussed in more detail in Chapter 11, "Session Initiation Protocol"), and Real-Time Streaming Protocol (RTSP; RFC 2326).

The last three standards provide alternative signaling techniques to SGCP, however all four standards use SDP for session description and Real-time Transport Protocol (RTP) to transmit audio. The call agent also can convert between alternative signaling techniques and direct the RTP streams between corresponding elements.

Session Description Protocol

Session Description Protocol (SDP) describes session parameters such as IP addresses, the User Datagram Protocol (UDP) port, RTP profiles, and multimedia conference capabilities. SGCP follows the conventions of SDP as defined in RFC 2327, and implementations are expected to conform. SGCP, however, limits its first multimedia use of SDP to the setting of one media type: audio circuits in telephony gateways.

Call agents use the following SDP parameters to provision telephony gateways:

- IP Addresses—Specify remote gateway, local gateway, or multicast audio conference addresses used to exchange RTP packets
- UDP Port—Indicates the transport port used to receive RTP packets from the remote gateway
- Audio Media—Specify audio media, including codec

Transmission over UDP

SGCP's request messages are sent to IP addresses of specified endpoints using UDP. Response messages also are sent through UDP back to the originator's source IP address. UDP provides connectionless service over IP and, therefore, might be subjected to packet losses. SGCP handles lost or delayed responses by repeating requests. To accomplish these requests, SGCP entities are expected to maintain a list of currently executing transactions as well as all responses sent within the last 30 seconds.

This list enables the entity to compare the transaction identifier of incoming requests to transaction identifiers of the latest responses. Therefore, if an entity receives a request with a transaction identifier matching one of the cached responses, it resends the response. The onus is on the requesting entity to provide suitable timeouts, provide timely retries, clear pending connections, and seek redundant services.

SGCP Concepts

The basic constructs of SGCP are *endpoints* and *connections*. Groups of connections constitute a *call*, which is set up by one or more call agents. Another key concept covered in this section is the use of *digit maps* for collecting digits at gateways.

Endpoints

Endpoints are sources or sinks of data that physically or logically exist within an entity. Trunk circuits connecting gateways and telephone switches are physical endpoints, whereas announcements stored in audio devices are logical endpoints. Endpoints are identified by two components: the domain name of the entity where the endpoint exists, and the local name specifying the individual endpoint.

In the case of trunk circuits, call agents have Signaling System 7 (SS7) interconnection where circuits are identified by trunk group and circuit number. Therefore, when the call agent is creating a connection, the following identifies the endpoint:

domain name / interface / circuit number

The domain name and the interface represent the gateway and link where the endpoint exists. The circuit represents the physical digital signal level 0 (DS-0) where the call is terminated.

Connections

Connections exist in either point-to-point or multipoint form. You use several point-to-point connections to construct a call and to transfer data between endpoints. Multipoint connections connect an endpoint to a multipoint session. The gateway identifies the connection when instructed to create a connection. These connection identifiers represent the connection between the endpoint and the call.

This is a good place to cover the concept of connection modes before delving deeper into each request function. A mode parameter determines and qualifies how to handle audio received on connections. The connection's operation is described by the connection modes illustrated in Table 12-3.

Table 12-3 *Connection Modes*

Mode	Operation
sendonly	Gateway should only send packets.
recvonly	Gateway should only receive packets.
sendrecv	Gateway should send and receive packets.
inactive	Gateway should not send or receive packets.
loopback	Gateway should place circuit in loopback mode.
conttest	Gateway should place circuit in test mode.

NotificationRequest

The *NotificationRequest* command advises the gateway to notify the originator when a specified event occurs in an endpoint. The call agent downloads a list of events to the gateway that's requesting the detection and reporting certain events. The notification request typically contains the following fields:

- Endpoint ID—Indicates the endpoint in the gateway where the request executes.

- Notified Entity—If present, specifies where notification should be sent. If not present, indicates that notification should be sent to the originator.

- Request Identifier—Correlates request to notification that is triggered.

- Digit Map—Enables the call agent to download a digit map that only returns digits for subsequent notifications. An optional parameter.

- Requested Events—Contains the list of events the gateway is requested to detect and report on to the call agent. Possible events in the list include fax and modem tones, continuity tone and detection, on-hook and off-hook transition, flash hook, channel-associated signaling (CAS), wink, and DTMF or pulse digits. In addition, each event has an associated action such as "notify the event immediately," "swap audio for call waiting and three-way calling," "accumulate according to digit map," and "ignore the event."

- Signal Requests—Specifies a set of endpoint actions that the gateway is requested to perform. The list of actions includes ringing and distinctive ringing, as well as ring back, dial, intercept, busy, answer, call waiting, off-hook warning, and continuity tones.

The requested event refers to the detection of an event, and the signal event refers to the resulting action. If off-hook is the requested event, for example, dial tone is the signal event.

Notification

The gateway sends a *Notification* based on requested events in the notification request and on the occurrence of these observed events. The *Notification* command contains the following parameters:

- Endpoint ID—This parameter indicates the endpoint in the gateway that is issuing the notification.

- Notified Entity—This optional parameter is equal to the same parameter in the corresponding notification request.

- Requested Identifier—This parameter is equal to the same parameter in the notification request and correlates the request to the notification.

- Observer Events—This parameter contains the actual observed data based on the requested event parameter in the notification request.

CreateConnection

As its name indicates, this function creates a connection between two endpoints. The following *CreateConnection* parameters provide the necessary information to build a gateway's view of a connection:

- Call ID—All connections related to a call share this network-wide or global unique identifier.

- Endpoint ID—Identifies the endpoint in the gateway where the *CreateConnection* command is executed.

- Notified Entity—Optional parameter specifying where notifications should be sent.

- Local Connection Options—Describes data communication characteristics used to execute the *CreateConnection* command. The fields in this parameter include encoding method, packetization period, bandwidth, type of service (ToS), and use of echo cancellation. By default, echo cancellation is always performed; however, this field enables these operations to be turned off.

- Mode—Dictates the mode of operation for the connection. The options are full duplex, receive only, send only, inactive, and loopback.

- Remote Connection Descriptor—Indicates the local connection options sent to the remote gateway.

- Requested Events, Request Identifier, Digit Map, Signal Requests—The call agent can use these optional parameters to transmit a notification request that can be executed as a connection is created.

- CDB—Common Database providing authorization and routing information
- ACC—Accounting Gateway collecting start and end accounting information

Figure 12-1 *Basic RGW-to-TGW Call*

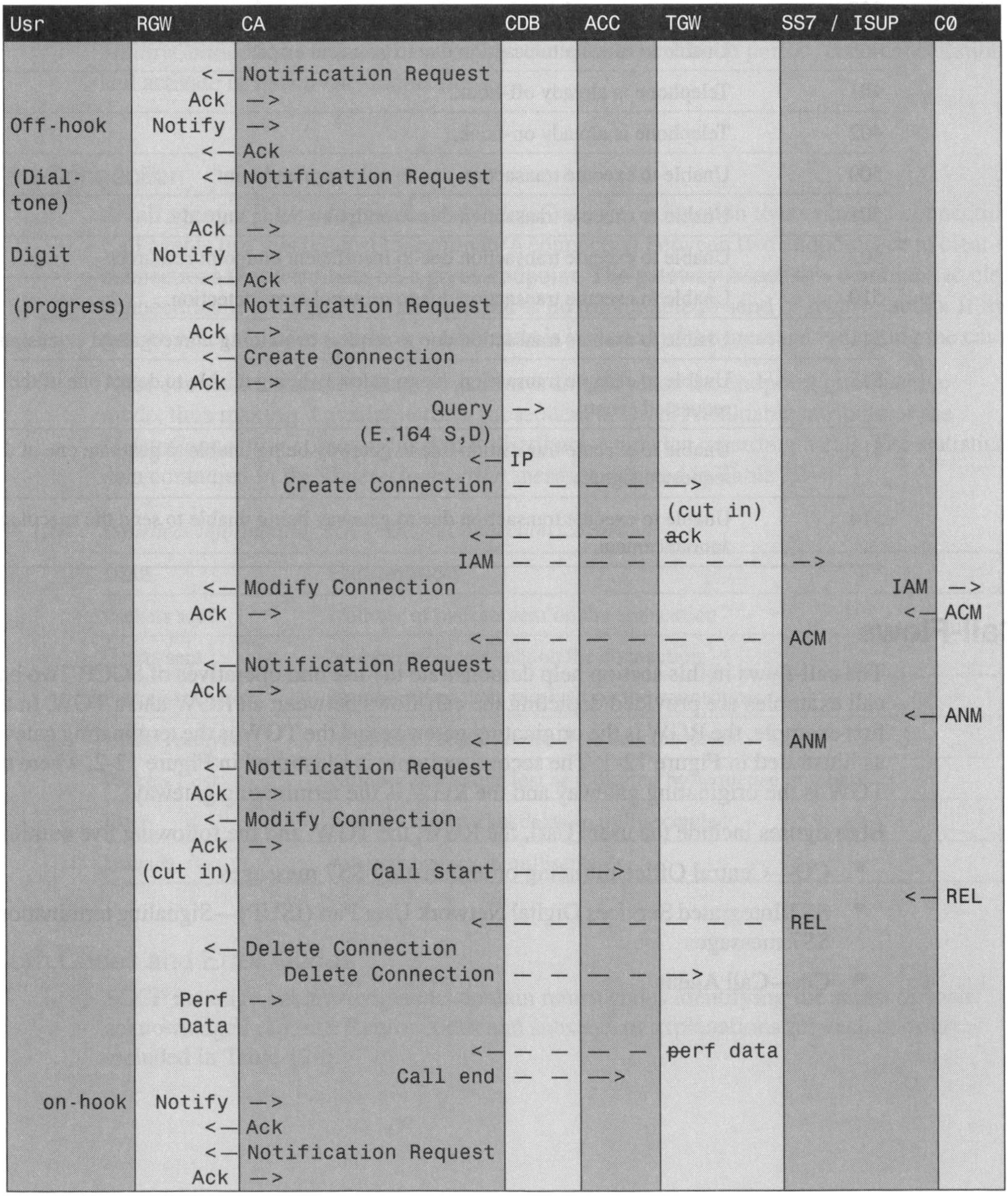

```
Usr          RGW      CA                    CDB    ACC    TGW       SS7 / ISUP    C0

                      <─ Notification Request
             Ack  ─>
Off-hook     Notify ─>
                      <─ Ack
(Dial-                <─ Notification Request
tone)
             Ack  ─>
Digit        Notify ─>
                      <─ Ack
(progress)            <─ Notification Request
             Ack  ─>
                      <─ Create Connection
             Ack  ─>
                              Query   ─>
                              (E.164 S,D)
                                      <─ IP
                      Create Connection  ─ ─ ─ ─ ─>
                                             (cut in)
                                      <─ ─ ─ ─ ─   ack
                              IAM  ─ ─ ─ ─ ─ ─ ─ ─ ─>
                      <─ Modify Connection                        IAM  ─>
             Ack  ─>                                                   <─ ACM
                                      <─ ─ ─ ─ ─ ─ ─ ─   ACM
                      <─ Notification Request
             Ack  ─>
                                                                      <─ ANM
                                      <─ ─ ─ ─ ─ ─ ─ ─   ANM
                      <─ Notification Request
             Ack  ─>
                      <─ Modify Connection
             Ack  ─>
             (cut in)     Call start  ─ ─ ─>
                                                                      <─ REL
                                      <─ ─ ─ ─ ─ ─ ─ ─   REL
                      <─ Delete Connection
                          Delete Connection  ─ ─ ─ ─ ─>
             Perf ─>
             Data
                                      <─ ─ ─ ─ ─   perf data
                          Call end  ─ ─ ─>
on-hook      Notify ─>
                      <─ Ack
                      <─ Notification Request
             Ack  ─>
```

Figure 12-2 *Basic TGW-to-RGW Call*

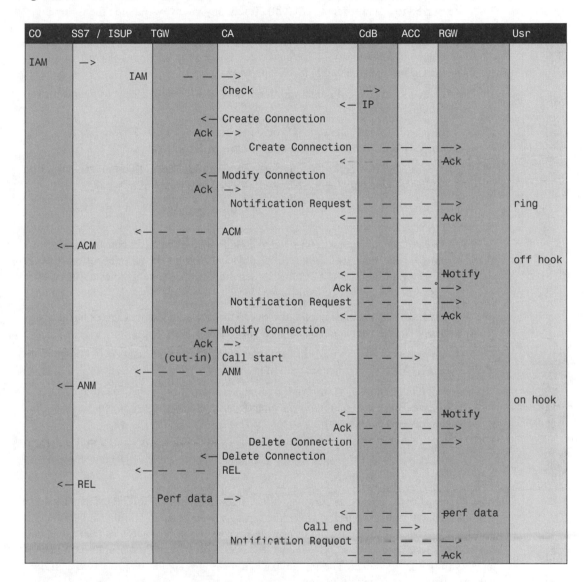

Media Gateway Control Protocol

Media Gateway Control Protocol (MGCP) controls VoIP through external call-control elements. The first version of MGCP was based on the fusion of SGCP and IPDC. Therefore, this section concentrates on the differences between MGCP and SGCP, which are largely due to functionality inspired by IPDC.

MGCP enables telephony gateways to be controlled by external call-control elements (MGCs; referred to as call agents in SGCP). Telephony gateways include the following:

- Trunk Gateways—The interface between the telephone network and VoIP network
- Voice over ATM Gateways—The interface between the telephone network and Asynchronous Transfer Mode (ATM) network
- Residential Gateways—Enable traditional analog telephone access to inter-work across the VoIP network
- Business and Access Gateways—Provide an analog or digital Private Branch eXchange (PBX) and soft-switch interface to a VoIP network
- Network Access Servers—The interface that provides access to the Internet through the Public Switched Telephone Network (PSTN) and modems
- Circuit or Packet Switches—Offer call-control access to external call-control elements

MGCP utilizes the same connection model as SGCP, where the basic constructs are endpoints and connections. Endpoints can be physical or logical, and connections can be point-to-point or multipoint. MGCP, however, enables connections to be established over several types of bearer networks, as follows:

- IP Networks—Transmission of audio over Transmission Control Protocol/Internet Protocol (TCP/IP) networks using RTP and UDP
- ATM Networks—Audio transmission over an ATM network using ATM adaptation Layer 2 (AAL2) or another adaptation layer
- Internal Connections—Transmission of packets across the TDM backplane or bus of the gateway (such as *hairpinning*, which occurs when a call is not sent out into the packet network but is sent back to the PSTN)

The remainder of this section covers some simple differences between SGCP and MGCP. This section also provides a primer for the two larger sections covering MGCP event packages and control functions.

MGCP uses SDP to provision gateways with IP addresses and UDP/RTP profiles identical to SGCP. MGCP utilizes SDP for two media types, however: audio circuits and data access circuits. Also, MGCP messages are transmitted across the packet network over UDP, but they can piggyback messages. MGCP enables several messages to be sent to the same gateway in one UDP packet. These piggybacked messages should be processed as if they were received as several simultaneous messages.

A formal wildcard structure, inspired from IPDC, is introduced in MGCP. MGCs or call agents can use the wildcard convention when sending commands to gateways. The wildcard enables the call agent to identify any or all the arguments in the command.

If a multipoint call is completed and a number of connections need to be disconnected, for example, the call agent can send one *DeleteConnection* request using the *all of* argument to specify all connections related to the specified endpoint.

Additional call-flows are not provided in this section, given that MGCP has the same call-control functions, messages, and sequencing features as SGCP.

Event Packages

Inspired from IPDC, MGCP events and signals are grouped into packages. Each package supports the typical events and signals required for a particular type of endpoint. One package might group events and signals related to a trunking gateway, for example, and another package might group events and signals related to an analog access-type line. The term *event name* refers to events and signals contained in an event package. The package name and event, separated by a slash ("/"), identify the event name. Table 12-6 lists the 10 basic packages defined in MGCP.

Table 12-6   *Basic Packages*

Package	Name
Generic Media Package	G
DTMF Package	D
MF Package	M
Trunk Package	T
Line Package	L
Handset Package	H
RTP Package	R
Network Access Server Package	N
Announcement Server Package	A
Script Package	Script

NOTE   Implementers can define additional packages and event names and register these additions with the Internet Assigned Numbers Authority (IANA).

As mentioned previously, each package contains specific events and signals related to endpoint type. The following information is required for each event:

- Description of event, actual user signal generated, and user-observed result. For example, one possible event is an off-hook transition. This event occurs when a user goes off-hook and detects dial tone.

A summary of control commands and corresponding codes is listed in Table 12-9.

Table 12-9 *MGCP Commands*

Command	Code
EndpointConfiguration	EPCF
NotificationRequest	RQNT
Notify	NTFY
CreateConnection	CRCX
ModifyConnection	MDCX
DeleteConnection	DLCX
AuditEndpoint	AUEP
AuditConnection	AUCX
RestartIn-Progress	RSIP

EndpointConfiguration

EndpointConfiguration commands enable the call agent to specify the encoding of signals received by the endpoint. This is particularly useful in international circumstances where both μ-law and A-law encoding techniques are used. This command passes this information to the gateway with the following two parameters:

- Endpoint ID—Identifies the name of the endpoint in the gateway. If the *all of* wildcard convention is used, this parameter identifies all endpoints matching the wildcard.

- Bearer Information—Identifies the coding technique for the data received on the line side of the endpoint identified. Currently, the only subparameters defined are A-law and μ-law.

NotificationRequest

The *NotificationRequest* command in MGCP differs slightly from that in SGCP in that it contains the following three new parameters:

- Quarantine Handling—An optional parameter that specifies whether quarantined events should be processed or discarded and whether one or multiple notifications to this request are required. A *quarantined event* is a mechanism for MGCP to queue events while another event is being notified to the call agent.

- Detect Events—An optional parameter specifying the list of quarantined events for detection during the quarantine period. Possible events up for detection include in-line ringback and quality alert. A detected event is the detection that needs to be performed during a quarantine.

- Embedded Endpoint Configuration—If embedded, this parameter can insert the parameters carried after the notification request and can specify the encoding technique for the line side of the endpoint.

Notifications

The *Notify* command is the same in MGCP as it is in SGCP. Gateways use the *Notify* command to advise the call agent of events.

CreateConnection

MGCP's version of the *CreateConnection* command has some modifications and additional parameters over the SGCP version. The following three parameters outline the differences:

- Second Endpoint ID—Used instead of the Remote Connection descriptor to create a connection between two endpoints in the same gateway. This command specifies local connections over resident TDM backplanes or bus interconnections.

- Embedded Notification Request—Enables the call agent to transmit the optional requested events, request identifier, digit map, and signal requests, as well as handle quarantines and detect events parameters within the embedded request.

- Embedded Endpoint Configuration—Inserts the parameters carried after the notification request and specifies the encoding technique for the line side of the endpoint.

NOTE   You can use the *CreateConnection* command for IP, ATM, and local connections as specified by the SDP parameters.

ModifyConnection

The parameters used in the *ModifyConnection* command are the same as those used in the *CreateConnection* request.

DeleteConnection

The *DeleteConnection* command basically falls under the same theme as the other requests, whereby the embedded notification and embedded endpoint configuration requests augment the existing SGCP framework.

As indicated in the SGCP section of this chapter, statistical data accompanies the response to a *DeleteConnection* command. The difference in MGCP is in reporting the statistics for ATM and local-type connections. The data fields are the same; however, the explanation for ATM and local-based statistics differs, as indicated in Tables 12-10 and 12-11.

Table 12-10 *ATM Statistical Information: MGCP DeleteConnection Command*

Data	Explanation—ATM Connection
Packets sent	Total number of cells sent over the ATM connection
Octets sent	Total number of payload octets sent in ATM cells
Packets received	Total number of cells received on the ATM connection
Octets received	Total number of payload octets received in ATM cells
Packets lost	Total number of cells lost
Jitter	Inter-arrival jitter between ATM cells
Latency	Not determined if this parameter is feasible

Table 12-11 *Local Statistical Information: MGCP DeleteConnection Command*

Data	Explanation—Local Connection
Packets sent	Not relevant
Octets sent	Total number of payload octets sent over the local connection
Packets received	Not relevant
Octets received	Total number of octets received over the local connection
Packets lost	Not relevant
Jitter	Not relevant
Latency	Not relevant

NOTE   The call agent can use the *all of* wildcard convention to delete all connections belonging to an endpoint, such as in the case of multipoint connections.

AuditEndpoint

The call agent can use the *AuditEndpoint* command to determine the status of an endpoint. This request contains an Endpoint ID parameter identifying the endpoint being audited and a Requested Information parameter containing the following subparameters:

- Endpoint List—Identifies the endpoint being audited. You can use the *all of* wildcard to indicate all endpoints matching the wildcard.
- Notified Entity—Currently notified entity for active notification requests.
- Requested Events—List of currently requested events.
- Digit Map—Currently used by endpoint.
- Signal Requests—List of signal requests applied to endpoint.
- Request Identifier—The last received notification request.
- Connection Identifiers—List of the current connections existing for the specified endpoint.
- Detect Events—List of events currently being detected in quarantine mode.
- Local Connection Options—List of all current values, such as codec and packetization period. You also can use this command to request the current event packages supported on the specified endpoint.

AuditConnection

Call agents use the *AuditConnection* command to retrieve information about connections. This command contains the Endpoint ID and Connection ID indicating the location and connection being audited. The Requested Information subparameters contain the following information:

- Call ID—Unique identifier of the call for which one of its connections is being audited
- Notified Entity—Currently notified entity for the connection
- Local Connection Options—Options supplied for this connection
- Mode—Current mode of connection
- Remote Connection Descriptor—Supplied to the gateway for the connection
- Local Connection Descriptor—The gateway used for the connection
- Connection Parameters—Current value of connection parameters for the connection

RestartIn-Progress

The gateway uses the *RestartIn-Progress* command to inform the call agent that an endpoint or group of endpoints was taken out of service or is back in service. The *RestartIn-Progress* command contains the following parameters:

- Endpoint ID—Identifies the endpoint. Using the *all of* wildcard convention, it identifies the group of endpoints being taken into or out of service.

- Restart Method—Specifies one of three types of restarts. The *graceful* restart method indicates that specified endpoints will be taken out of service after a specified time and that the call agent should not attempt to establish new connections. The *forced* restart method indicates that endpoints were abruptly taken out of service and connections were lost. The *restart* method indicates when endpoints with no existing connections will be put back in service.

- Restart Delay—Used to express delay in number of seconds.

Return Codes and Error Codes

MGCP requests are acknowledged and responses contain return and error codes similar to that of SGCP. Table 12-12 indicates codes identical to SGCP and new codes specific to MGCP.

Table 12-12 *MGCP Return and Error Codes*

Return Code	Explanation
200–514	Same as SGCP.
515	Transaction refers to an incorrect Connection ID.
516	Transaction refers to an unknown Call ID.
517	Unsupported mode.
518	Unsupported event package.
519	Gateway does not have a digit map.
520	Unable to complete transaction due to endpoint restarting.
522	No such event or signal.
523	Unknown action or combination of actions.
524	Inconsistent with Local Connection Options.

Summary

SGCP and MGCP are vital components used during the transition from a network whose components are in one monolithic platform to a network whose components are distributed. SGCP and MGCP form the basis for call agents and gateways to communicate. This is one of the keys to a distributed packet network.

As this is a new and evolving industry, these protocols have room to develop over time to suit industry needs. In fact, as of this writing, another protocol—known as MEGACO and as H.248—is making its way through the standards process. Currently, however, dozens of vendors have written to the MGCP standard, so deployment of this technology is imminent.

Although this protocol might seem complex, it is actually a simple, yet powerful, protocol that will be the basis for packet-based voice networks for many years to come.

CHAPTER 13

Virtual Switch Controller

This chapter focuses on Cisco's Virtual Switch Controller (VSC), which is a key architectural component of the virtual switch. The concept of a virtual switch is based on today's voice networks moving from a time-division multiplexing (TDM) infrastructure to a new packet-based, voice service infrastructure. This new infrastructure consists of the following distributed network elements:

- Media gateways (MGs)
- Packet networks
- Signaling, services, and call control
- Service provisioning and management

The collection of these elements constitutes a virtual switch where intercommunication is accomplished using open and standards-based protocols. Cisco's VSC provides the virtual switch's call-control functions. Drawing upon analogies of existing TDM switches, the VSC implements the functions of the software components found in a Service Switching Point (SSP). Other VSC-equivalent terms include Media Gateway Controller (MGC), call agent, soft-switch, and software-based SSP.

Overview of the Virtual Switch

The virtual-switch concept evolves the current paradigm of TDM switches into a distributed architecture. This concept is realized through the use of the:

- Packet-based multiservice access methods, equivalent to Public Switched Telephone Network (PSTN) line cards
- Distributed packet-bearer switching networks, analogous to TDM switch fabric
- Call-control servers such as VSC, analogous to SSP functionality

In addition to functions commonly found in a traditional SSP, however, the VSC adds additional capabilities that cater to applications such as H.323 and Session Initiation Protocol (SIP). The VSC operates in a UNIX environment with the goal of providing customers a high degree of open interfaces and programmability. Cisco's realization of the virtual switch is a component of the Cisco Open Packet Telephony (OPT) architecture.

- Endpoint client multimedia applications
- Corporate voice on-net and off-net services
- Voice over IP (VoIP) local/end office applications on cable infrastructure

Figure 13-2 depicts a generic packet voice application and illustrates various architectural components as well as how they fit and interact with each other.

Figure 13-2 *Packet Voice Network Architecture*

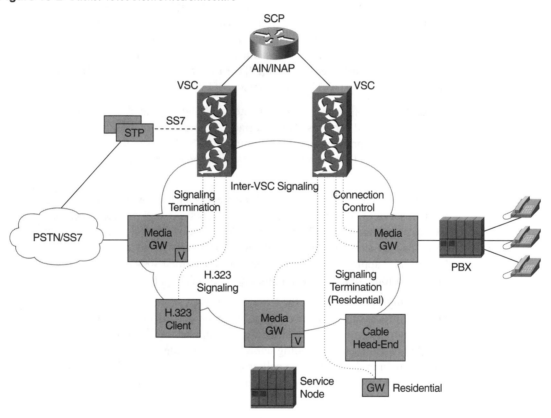

Network Elements

This section reviews each network element identified in Figure 13-2. These elements include the following:

- VSC
- MG
- SCP

- Service node
- Cable head end
- Residential gateway
- H.323 endpoint/client

Virtual Switch Controller

At a high level, the virtual switch controller (VSC) provides the following core capabilities:

- Call-signal processing including Integrated Services Digital Network (ISDN) Level 3 (Q.931), SS7 Level 4 (ISDN User Part [ISUP]), H.323, and Multi-Frequency/channel-associated signaling (MF/CAS), as well as call signaling toward devices located at residential gateways connected through cable or digital subscriber line (DSL) Customer Premise Equipment (CPE); also includes the capability to translate between different signaling types on different call legs

- Address resolution, call routing, resource management, connection control, and Call Detail Record (CDR) generation

- Service access functions for accessing services executing on external server platforms (such as SCP or Service node)

- Management interfaces using Simple Network Management Protocol (SNMP) for faults, performance, and configuration; Web-based configuration tool and element management system

Media Gateway

Media Gateway (MG) performs the following high-level functions:

- Physical T1/E1 TDM facility termination from the PSTN or Private Branch eXchanges (PBXs)

- Communication with the VSC for call setup and teardown using SGCP or MGCP

- Echo cancellation into the circuit-switched network

- Balancing the jitter buffers

- Voice activity detection (VAD), such as silence suppression and comfort noise regeneration

- Voice compression using International Telecommunication Union (ITU) recommendations such as G.711, G.723.1, and G.729

- Tone generation, which generates dial, busy, ring-back, and congestion tones

- Dual-Tone Multi-Frequency (DTMF) transport, which enables use of touch tones for voice mail applications with codecs that support DTMF detection/transport

- µ-law and a-law transcoding when required
- Quality of service (QoS) support

Service Control Point

The SCP provides the execution environment for service logic. The SCP is responsible for processing transaction requests and returning a response. A typical transaction request in the voice world is a number translation.

Examples of this service include 800 (toll-free) service and Local Number Portability (LNP). A toll-free application running on the SCP, for example, has a sophisticated logic that enables the end user to control how incoming calls are routed. You can base toll-free call routing on dialed number, time of day, day of week, geographic point of origination, and even on how busy a terminating automatic call distribution (ACD) might be at a given moment. Customers or the service provider (SP) can own the SCP.

Service Node

The service node component of Cisco's voice architecture is realized by Cisco's open, programmable switch of the VCO. The VCO/4k is modular and scalable. It incorporates compatible generic software, universal network interfaces, and service resources and employs advanced technologies such as SS7, ISDN, hierarchical call control, and SNMP network management. In addition, the VCO/4k are Central Office (CO)-compliant, and you can deploy them in fully redundant or nonredundant environments.

Cable Head End

The Universal Broadband Router is an integrated cable modem termination system (CMTS) and Cisco 7200 series router utilizing radio frequency (RF) line cards. The Universal Broadband Router provides a single integrated solution with CMTS functionality, the capability to terminate the Data-over-Cable Service Interface Specifications (DOCSIS) protocol, and the capability to perform all the data routing functions required. Instantiation of this component also includes a Digital Subscriber Line Multiplexer (DSLAM).

Residential Gateway

The residential gateway is a voice/data CPE device that provides from two to four ports of plain old telephone service (POTS) capability. The device runs the DOCSIS protocol to provide packet data and telephony services over the hybrid fiber-coaxial (HFC) cable to the CMTS. Another example of this component also includes a DSL modem.

H.323 Endpoint/Client

The H.323 client represents a broad range of voice/multimedia applications that are hosted natively on the IP network. The H.323 endpoint is covered in detail in Chapter 10, "H.323."

Network Interfaces

The four main VSC network interfaces are signaling termination, inter-VSC signaling, connection control, and services control, as illustrated in Figure 13-3.

Figure 13-3 *Network Interfaces*

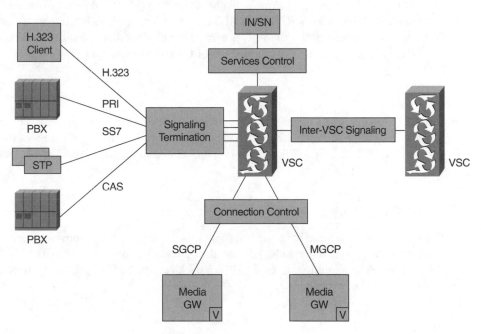

Each VSC network interface is discussed in the following sections.

Signaling Termination

The signaling termination capability enables the VSC to mediate between many signaling variants, such as SS7, Primary Rate Interface (PRI), CAS, and H.323, to name a few.

SS7 Links

Several mechanisms are available to terminate SS7 signaling traffic on the VSC:

- Nonassociated signaling (A-links)—Terminated directly on the VSC using either a V.35 or T1/E1 physical interface. Optionally, to increase reliability characteristics, you can configure a set of Signaling Link Terminals (SLTs) to handle the lower layers of SS7. The SLTs are implemented using Cisco 2600 series routers fronting Sun servers that host the VSC application.

- Fully associated signaling (F-links)—Carry bearer traffic and are terminated on the packet gateway. The packet gateway is responsible for executing Message Transfer Parts (MTPs) 1 and 2, encapsulating MTP Layer 3 (MTP L3) protocol data units and sending them to the VSC for MTP L3 and ISUP processing. The transport between the packet gateway and the VSC is carried out using Reliable User Data Protocol (RUDP), a thin-reliability layer on top of User Data Protocol (UDP).

PRI Links

The PRI links carry a D channel and terminate directly on the voice gateway. The voice gateway peripherals execute Level 1 (L1) and Level 2 (L2)—the lower layers of the PRI interface (Q.921). Layer 3 (L3; Q.931) is encapsulated in the RUDP packet and sent to the VSC for call processing.

CAS Links

CAS links terminate directly on the voice gateway. Low-level CAS protocols (for example, line and address signaling) are handled by the gateway periphery. You use a CAS Application Programming Interface (API) to backhaul the call-processing events over IP to the VSC for call handling.

H.323

The VSC handles the precall-level Registration, Admissions, and Status (RAS) requests as well as call-level Q.931 requests originated from the H.323 clients. This signaling termination follows delivery procedures described in the H.323 standard. In other words, the VSC has H.225 RAS/Q.931 capabilities, however it does not have H.323 gatekeeper functionality.

Inter-VSC Signaling

The VSC-to-VSC protocol scales the network by distributing control over multiple VSC platforms. A modified ISUP protocol called Enhanced ISUP (E-ISUP) exchanges call-control information between the VSCs over an IP network using RUDP. MTP information is not required and is, therefore, not transported.

The E-ISUP messages also carry Session Description Protocol (SDP) elements in ISUP generic digits information elements, which the VSC uses to specify connection attributes in SGCP and MGCP.

NOTE   The industry is moving toward using SIP or a variant of SIP, known as SIP+, for an inter-MGC communication protocol.

Connection Control: SGCP/MGCP

End-to-end voice connections in the packet network are established using SGCP or MGCP, an open mechanism to set up connections in IP networks. SGCP and MGCP are UDP-based transaction protocols that permit manipulation of the connections represented by physical or logical endpoints. The connections are described using attributes such as IP addresses, codecs, and so on. SGCP and MGCP manage call setup requests and connections from phones connected to gateways such as cable or DSL modems. SGCP/MGCP provide a mechanism to specify grammar sent by the VSC to the residential gateway instructing it how to relay voice events.

The VSC also supports a Virtual Switch Interface (VSI) into the Cisco BPX wide-area switch. The VSI is a Cisco-defined interface that enables an external device to control a Cisco BPX wide-area switch. As the controller, the VSC implements the VSI-master functionality. The VSC audits the current connections on the BPX against the current connections on the VSC. The underlying interface between the VSC and the BPX is ATM adaptation Layer 5 (AAL5).

In VSI, the controller (the VSC) requests that the switch (the BPX) create, delete, and change connections. The switch is required to notify the controller of changes to its synchronization state (active session-id) and/or changes to its logical interfaces (loading changes, state changes, and so on).

Services Control

Access to service can follow two paths:

- IN (AIN/INAP/convergence sublayer-1 [CS-1]) platforms such as SCPs interface initially over standards-based AIN/INAP interfaces transported over the SS7 network, with future migration to IP-based transport.

- Service node services (such as calling cards and voice mail) initially connect over TDM PRI interfaces. In the future, the service node platforms will transition to IP networks to avoid unnecessary TDM/IP inter-working.

VSC Architecture and Operations

Figure 13-4 depicts the major functional blocks of Cisco's VSC platform.

Figure 13-4 *Functional Components of the VSC*

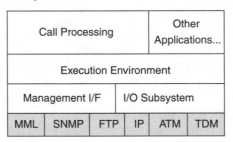

Cisco's VSC is an open platform and is built to host third-party developed applications through a set of powerful application/protocol building tools and associated APIs.

These tools include:

- Application Toolkit—The VSC Application Toolkit enables users to customize protocols and their inter-working features. The toolkit also provides powerful language tools and an API to develop state- and event-driven applications that reside on the VSC platform.

- Conversion Analyzer—The Conversion Analyzer generates output reports using traces in the inter-working engine. Information in the report includes message input, conversion, and output.

- Simulator—The simulator enables users to create message sets and run them through a mirrored inter-working engine to determine/diagnose application or protocol errors. Detailed reports include message input, conversion, and output.

VSC-Supported Protocols

A great VSC feature is the fact that its architecture supports multiple access and network protocols. New protocols and variations of existing protocols continue to be added to the library. Table 13-1 provides a comprehensive list of protocols.

Table 13-1   *SC-Supported Protocols*

ANSI ISUP (SS7)	ITU Q.931 PRI	Belgian Q761 ISUP
BTNUP	ETSI ISUP V2	Alcatel 4400 PRI
BTNUP NRC	ETSI Q.SIG	NI-2 (Bell-1268)
China TUP	ITU Q.767 ISUP	NI-2+ (Bell-1268-C3)
DNPSS	French ISUP	Polish ISUP
Dutch ISUP	German ISUP	Finland Q761 ISUP
ETSI PRI	Hong Kong Q761 ISUP	Australian Q761 ISUP

Execution Environment

The Execution Environment (XE) provides common services to application programs running on the signaling host. The major goals of the XE are the following:

- Provide application programs with a flexible, stable, and consistent infrastructure

- Enable new applications to be more easily integrated with existing applications running on the same platform

- Minimize the amount of work that application developers must do to create a new application

- Provide a simplified interface to operating system services so that third parties can develop custom applications that can run in a process on the VSC

Services provided by the XE include the following:

- Process Management—Enables processes to be managed by the XE. This includes orderly startup, shutdown, and monitoring of process health. Process management also is used to implement the cut-over to a new version of a process with minimal interruption of service.

- Alarms—Enable processes to register, set, and clear alarms. Alarm sets and clears are automatically reported to processes that request this service. You can use this capability to report alarms to attached management interfaces, enabling such processes to implement necessary recovery action.

Figure 13-5 *Route Selection Process*

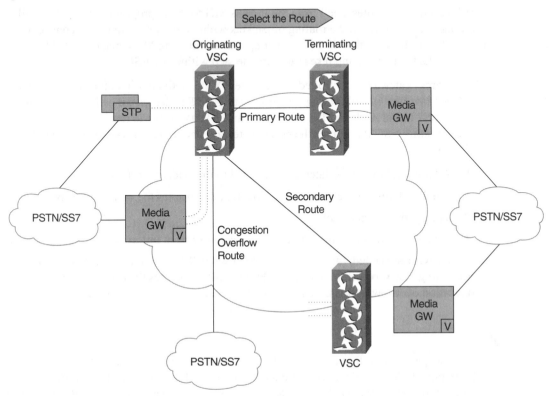

Reroute on Congestion

The VSC contains the status of trunks connected to the egress gateways (a busy/idle map) that the VSC controls. If an egress gateway cannot complete a call due to an internal resource error, an explicit indication is sent back to the VSC with an MGCP/SGCP negative acknowledge. The VSC can then choose another route to attempt the call. If two VSCs are involved, the terminating VSC informs the originating VSC using E-ISUP (Release [REL] with congestion) and a call reroute is attempted if alternate routes were provisioned.

Figure 13-6 *Egress Gateway Selection*

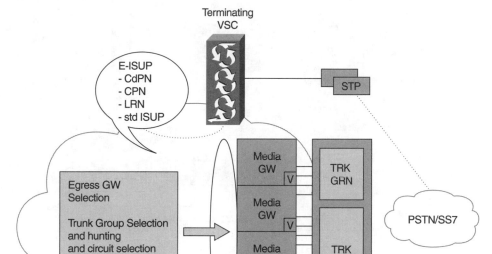

VSC Implementation

The VSC can provide a high level of availability equal to or better than a traditional switch. The system, as illustrated in Figure 13-7, is based on Sun fault-tolerant platforms consisting of an active and standby unit and a separate set of SLTs used to terminate SS7 traffic.

Call state information is copied from the active unit to the standby unit. This process also is called *check-pointing* and ensures that stable calls are not lost in the event of a switchover from active to standby VSC. The SLTs terminate the MTP L2 traffic and send the MTP L3 information to the active unit. Preliminary analysis indicates combined system availability of 0.9999985 or 0.782 minutes of downtime per year.

Figure 13-7 *VSC Implementation*

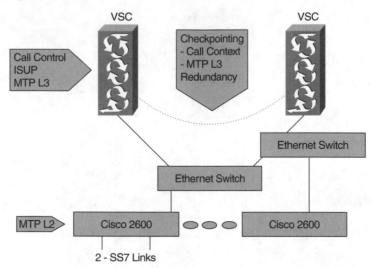

To maximize VSC fault tolerance, MTP L2 traffic is terminated on separate hardware platforms and MTP L3 traffic is transmitted across dual Ethernet switches. This level of redundancy enables the active and standby systems to share the SS7 links and local-area networks/wide-area networks (LANs/WANs).

The Cisco 2600 is the first router to support SLT functionality. You can remove, add, or service an SLT without disrupting the SS7 network. The Cisco 2600 SLT supports two SS7 link ports, whereby each port can handle an aggregate of two erlangs of traffic. (An *erlang* is the number of calls multiplied by the Average Hold Time [AHT] of the call divided by 3600.) SLTs are connected through standard Ethernet and deliver MTP L3 information to the VSC through RUDP across the LAN/WAN.

Application Check-Pointing

Check-pointing occurs between VSCs and ensures that in-progress calls are preserved in the event of a failover. The call-processing engine sends checkpoint events to the local checkpoint process during the call setup and call release phases.

During the call setup phase, the first checkpoint event is generated when the resource manager secures the physical circuit resource from the packet gateway. The event contains enough information to enable the remote resource manager to update the logical state of the assigned circuit. The second checkpoint event is generated when the call is answered. The event data stored in the remote resource manager contains only enough information for the remote call-processing engine to maintain the call until it is released. Therefore, in the event of a failover, calls are kept in service, however no service features are supported.

During the call release phase, a checkpoint is generated when the resource manager receives an acknowledgment from the packet gateway associated with the call release request.

Check-pointing also is applied to protocol supervisory messages in case logical state changes of bearer circuits occur between initial call setup and release. These messages include:

- Blocking and unblocking messages and commands
- Circuit reset messages and commands

Virtual Switch Manager

The Virtual Switch Manager (VSM) is a Telecommunication Management Network (TMN)-based solution for the end-to-end management of networks providing SS7-enabled services. VSM provides consolidated management of Cisco's network elements (NEs), thus enabling the virtual switch system to be treated as a single managed element. VSM responsibilities include the physical network elements that comprise the voice and signaling portions of the virtual switch, including:

- VSC
- Voice-encoding units
- Voice traffic within the virtual switch domain
- Intra-switch and inter-virtual switch signaling traffic
- Signaling traffic between the PSTN or PBX and the virtual switch network as seen by the VSC

VSM responsibilities exclude:

- External voice network elements (telephone switches)
- Data or TDM networks providing voice or signaling transmission to the virtual switch
- Signaling traffic to and from the PSTN and the virtual switch domain

The VSM's domain encompasses signaling and traffic voice elements and is illustrated in Figure 13-8.

Accounting

Every call the VSC handles produces call detail information. The amount of detail generated is comprehensive; each CDR contains the following information:

- Called and calling number
- Answer time, disconnect time, and call completion codes
- Route information, originating trunk group and member, and terminating trunk group and member
- ISUP information
- ISDN service information and extensions
- Account codes and pins

Along with this information, more than 80 additional elements are available for custom CDR configuration in flexible user-defined formats. If a data or usage element is not available, the TransPath Message Definition Language (MDL) can generate separate fields in a special array marked "custom" for future CDR requirements. These arrays are set to both ITU and American National Standards Institute (ANSI) standards.

Call detail records are written to a spool file which is automatically closed at customer-definable intervals, or when the file exceeds a specified size. You can retrieve closed files or send them to downstream processing systems, such as Automatic Messaging Accounting (AMA) formatting or billing mediation devices, as needed. Customers also can generate mid-call CDR information that logs data from up to eight event points in a call.

Summary

The OPT architecture enables you to separate application, call-control, and bearer planes. The call agent is a major component of this architecture, as it helps bridge applications to bearer planes. The VSC is Cisco's instantiation of a call agent. As this architecture implies, the VSC enables customers to use different vendors in each component of the architecture (application, call control, and bearers). This enables you to use Cisco MGs with other vendors' call agents as well as with the VSC.

Building a call agent for an SP customer requires paying attention to many details. Route selection, call control, and reliability are just a few of the issues covered when building this piece of the OPT architecture.

PART IV

Voice over IP Applied

Dial-Plan Problems

Administrators of private enterprise voice networks usually run into dial-plan problems when they launch a companywide dial plan that encompasses multiple remote sites.

In this topology, enterprise voice network administrators must decide on a usable number of digits in the dial plan and ensure that numbers do not overlap. For the network administrator, *feature transparency*— or the capability of using the same functions across multiple Private Branch eXchanges (PBXs) and throughout all locations—is one of the major requirement.

To illustrate this concept, assume that CompanyBlue has a headquarters location with a five-digit dial plan. CompanyBlue has 20 remote sales sites and wants to incorporate a dial plan that enables all its sites to have a cohesive look and feel.

CompanyBlue must proceed with the following steps to ensure that its dial plan is consistent:

1 CompanyBlue must analyze corporate and remote sites to ensure that no overlapping digits with a five-digit plan exist. If overlapping digits do exist, it must decide whether to move to a six- or seven-digit plan or to give each site its own two-digit code.

NOTE   For some large corporations with thousands of sites, the first three or four digits represent the store number and the remaining one or two digits represent each extension. Usually, large corporations with thousands of remote sites use only a few extensions. Referring back to Chapter 7, "IP Tutorial," this is somewhat akin to subnetting. You must decide what part of the phone number you should use for addressing the location (if necessary) and what part you should use for station identification.

---

2 CompanyBlue must transition the PBX dial plan to translate the new five- or six-digit extensions into valid E.164 addresses so that the call can still traverse the PSTN.

3 After this initial change is made and the users begin to use the new dial plan, CompanyBlue must transition to VoIP by simply modifying the Automatic Route Selection (ARS) table.

In some circumstances, enterprises with several remote branches must allocate a large number of digits to meet the needs of all possible users. Such enterprises simplify their dial plan by implementing a two-stage dialing procedure.

With *two-stage dialing,* the caller can dial an access code (similar to using a calling card) that routes him or her to a specific place in the network. The caller is then presented with a second dial tone, at which point he or she can dial the actual number to be called. Two-stage dialing offers two main advantages: the remote PBX's dial plan can be simple, and the network does not need to have a dial-plan outlining the entire network's dial plan. Instead, the network uses a group of access codes, which map to remote switching points.

The limitations of such an approach are that users must follow a two-step procedure, and they must wait for the network to properly prompt them for additional inputs. Despite these limitations, however, private enterprise networks implement two-stage dialing for three main reasons: if they experienced rapid growth, if they merged with another corporation, or if they acquired another corporation that uses another type of PBX technology.

Cisco's VoIP implementation enables both single- and two-stage dial plans. Using a single-stage dial plan (also known as a *translational* plan) generally requires that users not change their dialing habits. If a company did not have a dial-plan architecture in the past, imposing a VoIP architecture can introduce some challenges, such as number-overlapping and a lack of call-routing features.

These problems are not necessarily due to VoIP, but they are exacerbated by the fact that no one at CompanyBlue put together a cohesive dial plan in the past that would sustain the company if its branches and main offices were on one central dial plan.

VoIP supports two-stage dialing, but when you use this plan you must be careful for the following reasons:

- You can lose Dual-Tone Multi-Frequency (DTMF) tones as they traverse the Internet Protocol (IP) network if you use inappropriate encodings. Coding a voice stream—carried over a Real-Time Transport Protocol (RTP) and through alternative methods—within a signaling path (such as H.245) enables the transport of DTMF inputs on the network.

- Tandem encodings (dual compressions), which reduce call quality, can now occur due to poor network planning.

- Multiple digital-to-analog (D/A) conversions can occur, which also reduce call quality.

Packet loss is common when using an IP network. If the DTMF tone is carried in a User Datagram Protocol (UDP) stream, however, the packet or tone can be lost or improperly ordered, which causes the wrong sequence of digits to be dialed.

If the VoIP provider uses DTMF relay, which enables DTMF tones to be carried in the Transmission Control Protocol (TCP), the DTMF carriage is just as reliable as the PSTN. Cisco IOS system software supports this feature. The Cisco IOS command-line interface (CLI) is as follows:

```
dtmf-relay H245-signal
```

This command is configured on the VoIP *dial-peer* (which is defined later in this chapter).

If no single entity controls the voice and data network, however, it is possible in single- and two-stage dialing to have multiple compression cycles, which affect voice quality. You must take great care to make sure that tandem encodings do not occur, as you cannot improve such encodings.

Multiple D/A conversions also can affect voice quality. Where D/A conversions really rear their head, however, is when modems or some other data transmission over voice is handled. When using a 56-kbps modem, for example, you can have only one D/A conversion (at residential facilities).

Feature Transparency

Switching from time-division multiplexing (TDM) voice networks to packet-based voice solutions also requires that you move and support existing applications and functionality in a similar manner.

Often, many PBXs have proprietary signaling methods that currently have no way to move onto IP. This makes it difficult to have a cost-effective VoIP network that offers limited features. The reason this makes VoIP networks difficult is because of the proprietary nature of inter-PBX signaling protocols. Often, these proprietary signaling methods cannot be carried across a VoIP network.

In an attempt to provide some interoperability between PBXs and vendors using digital signaling, the ETSI Q.Sig standard was developed. This standard is based on the Q.931 signaling stack, but it contains extensions that enable additional signaling information to be passed between the PBXs.

Q.Sig is a standards-based protocol that enables different brands of PBXs, as well as different networks, to interoperate. Cisco makes Q.Sig available on its VoIP gateways and can complete Q.sig calls, as well as make a Q.Sig tunnel between multiple PBXs. This enables enterprise customers to do the following:

- Achieve a feature-rich, cohesive telephony network
- Integrate different vendors' PBXs throughout their network

Enterprise customers who are either unwilling to or cannot upgrade to Q.Sig can have a telephony network with only basic voice calls. Often, the cost savings and ability to use new IP-enabled applications are enough to encourage enterprise telephony customers to move to this new network.

PSTN Feature Transparency

Features in the PSTN are based mainly on Signaling System 7 (SS7) and the applications built on top of it. To transparently transport and tunnel features across multiple networks, SS7 must be supported as the mandatory baseline interface. Chapter 13, "Virtual Switch Controller" discusses ways in which these features can be carried through an IP network.

The H.323 protocol suite was developed assuming Q.931 (Integrated Services Digital Network [ISDN]) interfaces on the voice gateways. The protocol suite has no transparent mechanism to carry and tunnel SS7 messages, including Intelligent Network (IN)-based protocols.

Cisco, however, has an SS7 solution that uses H.323, but feature transparency is still not available.

Cisco's Dial-Plan Implementation

This section takes a look at the basics of setting up a Cisco VoIP gateway dial plan.

A fundamental VoIP network must have the following features:

- Local dial-peers to map phone numbers to a physical port
- Network dial-peers to map phone numbers to an IP address
- The ability to strip and add digits
- Number expansion

A *dial-peer* enables all these basic features. Both a concept and a command, a dial-peer exists in two forms: as local (PSTN) and as network (*VoIP*) dial-peers. A prefix command adds digits before the telephone number is sent out of a local dial-peer. To route a call more efficiently, network managers can add, replace, or reduce the number of dialed digits, a procedure called *number expansion*. This procedure also enables overlapping dial plans to coexist.

Local dial-peers strip all digits matching a specific substring noted in the destination-pattern command. The dial-peer in Figure 14-1 shows a possible configuration of a simple VoIP network.

Figure 14-1 *Cisco Dial-Plan Configuration*

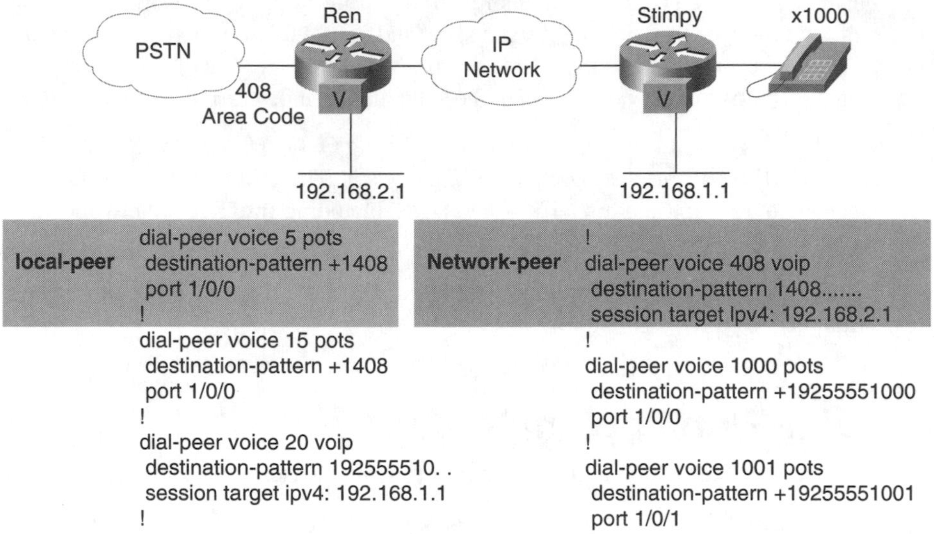
Ren
Stimpy
x1000
PSTN
IP Network
408 Area Code
V
V
192.168.2.1
192.168.1.1
local-peer
dial-peer voice 5 pots
destination-pattern +1408
port 1/0/0
!
dial-peer voice 15 pots
destination-pattern +1408
port 1/0/0
!
dial-peer voice 20 voip
destination-pattern 192555510. .
session target ipv4: 192.168.1.1
!
Network-peer
!
dial-peer voice 408 voip
destination-pattern 1408.......
session target lpv4: 192.168.2.1
!
dial-peer voice 1000 pots
destination-pattern +19255551000
port 1/0/0
!
dial-peer voice 1001 pots
destination-pattern +19255551001
port 1/0/1

Figure 14-1 shows that `dial-peer 5` is a local peer, denoted by the `pots` tag. Figure 14-1 also shows that port 1/0/0 on Router Ren is mapped to the phone number "1408."

Router Stimpy has a network peer, denoted by the `voip` tag, which maps the phone number "1408......." to an IP address. The periods act as wildcards; in this scenario, seven periods tell the phone to wait until 1408 plus seven more digits are received before attempting to complete the call.

Explained slightly differently, if the voice gateway receives 1408 plus seven digits, it matches that dial-peer statement and attempts to connect to the session target.

If a user at extension 1000 calls 14085551212, `dial-peer 408` on Stimpy places an H.323 call to Ren. Ren matches the incoming number to `dial-peer 5 pots`. Because all digits that match are stripped, only the digits 5551212 are sent to the PSTN. If, for some reason, 1408 needs to remain on the outbound call, you can use the `prefix` command to add 1408 back into the outbound digits.

Another possibility is to use two-stage dialing. Figure 14-2 shows the changes to the dial plan when two-stage dialing is implemented.

Figure 14-2 *Cisco's Two-Stage Dialing Configuration*

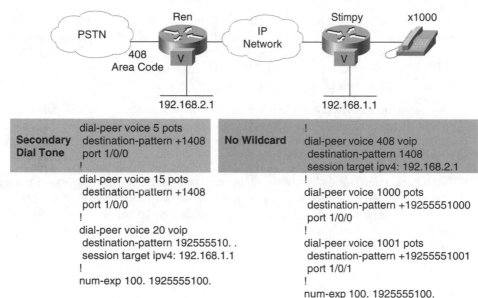

Figure 14-2 shows that wildcards are removed from the Stimpy router. Because the Ren router strips all the digits based on dial-peer voice 5 pots, only a secondary dial tone is offered back to the user at extension 1000 on router Stimpy. This enables the user at extension 1000 to dial any location because the dial plan on either router is no longer used.

The following features also are available on Cisco routers:

- Hunt groups—Enable the voice gateway to hunt through dial-peers to ensure delivery of a phone call to a valid IP gateway.

- Call failover—Enables an IP call to be routed to a different location if the first IP destination is unreachable.

- Busy out—Enables the gateway to set the physical voice-signaling port to "busy" when network congestion or network failure occurs.

- Trunking—Enables two VoIP gateways to act as a tie-line (both digital tie-lines and analog tie-lines are supported).

Summary

Although this chapter did not include all the information you need to configure a large-scale VoIP network, it did cover the basics of Cisco IOS configuration for VoIP. It also explained the various components a network administrator must consider before designing and deploying a VoIP network, including dial-plan considerations, such as single- and two-stage dialing, and their ramifications on voice dialing plans.

This chapter also covered ways in which single- and two-stage dialing affect users, and it provided details on feature transparency. With a move to VoIP, it is important to determine whether any of the features you rely upon today are transparently passed across this new VoIP network.

The chapter concluded with information on ways in which Cisco uses dial-peers to map IP addresses and physical interfaces to phone numbers. This technique provides a great deal of flexibility to network administrators, as it enables them to create whatever type of dial plan best fits their user base.

CHAPTER 15

Voice over IP Applications and Services

As enterprise businesses enter the 21st century, they are faced with constant demands to create more goods and services, improve the quality of their customer service, and reduce expenses in an effort to remain competitive. In addition, they are discovering that not only is their data network a mission-critical piece of their business, but if they use it properly, it can be a competitive advantage for obtaining and retaining customer loyalty.

For many years, businesses have been building networks based on Transmission Control Protocol/Internet Protocol (TCP/IP) to take advantage of the power of TCP/IP networking and the many services it can provide. These services include ubiquitous Internet access for remote users, easy-to-use Web browsers, internal corporate Intranets and Web servers, Java applications, and Extranets with trading partners and suppliers. All these services make it easier for enterprise businesses to build new business applications, enable Web-browser access to information databases, and provide new services to both internal and external customers.

Enterprise Applications and Benefits

When enterprise businesses begin thinking about consolidating their voice and data networks into a single multiservice network, the initial application they usually consider is *toll-bypass*. Toll-bypass enables businesses to send their intra-office voice and fax calls over their existing TCP/IP network. By moving this traffic off the Public Switched Telephone Network (PSTN), businesses can immediately save on long-distance charges by using extra bandwidth on their data network without losing existing functionality.

You can immediately quantify the savings you can glean with toll-bypass. In fact, some businesses with plenty of intra-office calling, both domestic and international, have seen a Return On Investment (ROI) in as little as three to six months.

As enterprise businesses become more comfortable with Voice over IP (VoIP) and toll-bypass, the next applications they usually consider are ones they can apply to customer service, interactive project groups, and distance-based training. Some examples of applications that you can apply to these areas include Netspeak's Click-2-Dial, Microsoft's Netmeeting, and Cisco IP phones and PC-based soft phones.

- Click-2-Dial enables businesses to put a link on their Web sites that automatically places a call from a customer to a customer service representative.

- Microsoft Netmeeting provides integration between traditional phone services with application-sharing and H.323-based video-conferencing. This integration of services enables employees in different locations to easily collaborate on projects as well as reduce expenses by consolidating equipment and data/voice networks.

- Cisco's IP phone provides the look and feel of a traditional handset, with the added functionality of IP connectivity. Instead of relying on an existing Private Branch eXchange (PBX) for functionality, such as dial tone, an IP phone works in conjunction with newer IP-based PBXs. These IP-PBXs not only provide the same functionality as traditional PBXs (dial tone, voice-mail, and conferencing), they also take advantage of all IP-based services available in the network to offer new features. Because it is an IP device, the IP phone can utilize not only VoIP services, but also any other IP-based multiservice application available on the network.

- Cisco's PC-based soft phone extends the handset functionality onto the PC with a graphical user interface that provides the same functionality as the handset and integrates with other multiservice applications such as Web browsing, Netmeeting, or directory services based on Lightweight Directory Access Protocol (LDAP). It also eliminates the need to have an additional device (the handset) on each desktop, as the soft phone utilizes headsets and speakers, which are commonplace on most standard PCs.

All the services discussed so far are considered first-generation, standards-based services. Just as TCP/IP data services rapidly evolved, second-generation VoIP and integrated data/ voice services based on TCP/IP will quickly evolve as well. These services will be driven by increased competition between businesses, open-standard Application Programming Interfaces (APIs), protocols such as H.323, Lightweight Directory Access Protocol (LDAP), Telephone Application Programming Interface (TAPI) and Java Telephony API (JTAPI), and the creativity of enterprise network managers and programmers.

Enterprise VoIP Case Study: B.A.N.C. Financing International

The following case study describes ways a fictional international financial institution can use VoIP to initially reduce expenses and eventually offer new internal and external services that provide greater flexibility to both its employees and customers.

The Background and Setup of B.A.N.C.

B.A.N.C. Financing International is a multinational financial institution headquarted on the East Coast of the United States. It provides mortgage lending, brokerage accounts, and other financial services, and it has offices throughout the United States, as well as in Europe and Asia.

Like many businesses within the financial industry, it is quickly moving into new markets through expansion and mergers with other financial institutions. It recently acquired two small banks in the United States and plans to add three or four financial services groups in Europe and Asia within the next 18 to 24 months.

B.A.N.C. currently provides loan and mortgage rate details to customers through its Web page, but it wants to offer additional services through the Web. It also wants to reduce its customer service costs.

B.A.N.C.'s existing data network comprises about 50 percent TCP/IP, 35 percent Systems Network Architecture (SNA), and 15 percent Internetwork Packet Exchange (IPX) traffic. Its data infrastructure is made up of Cisco routers and switches, and it is actively working to enable quality of service (QoS) on its campus local-area network (LAN) and wide-area network (WAN) backbone in anticipation of future multimedia applications. As it acquires new companies, it standardizes on Cisco routers and switches and removes any protocols other than IP, IPX, and SNA.

In the future, B.A.N.C. hopes to transition its IPX servers to TCP/IP so that it can consolidate on two protocols. The majority of its traffic consists of intraoffice communications between loan officers and the IP or SNA databases at headquarters. Its WAN is made up of an international Frame Relay backbone; most sites have 256 Kbps circuits with 128 Kbps committed information rate (CIR).

B.A.N.C.'s voice network was initially made up of a single PBX vendor with remote key-systems, but with its recent acquisitions it also acquired PBX technology from other vendors. Although it can still provide telephony services, B.A.N.C. cannot provide feature transparency between the different PBX vendors. All its remote sites use leased lines to interconnect the branch offices with the headquarters PBX and voice-mail system. Some of these remote connections are full T1 lines, and others are fractional T1 lines. A representative diagram of B.A.N.C.'s existing network is shown in Figure 15-1.

Figure 15-1 *Existing B.A.N.C. Data/Voice Network*

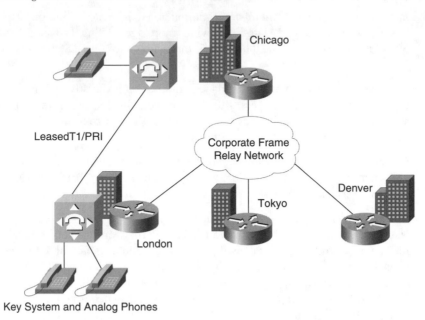

B.A.N.C.'s Plan of Expansion

As B.A.N.C. began to investigate ways to meet its goals of greater customer service and reduced costs, senior management challenged the Information Technology (IT) group to drive initiatives toward those goals. It wanted IT to provide systems that could not only meet the goals, but also provide the flexibility to handle 21st-century challenges.

As the IT group began to analyze the cost of maintaining both its voice and data networks, it realized that more than 50 percent of all IT expenses were associated with long-distance voice and fax calls between its remote and headquarters offices. In particular, international calls made up 65 percent of those long-distance charges. In addition to these charges, B.A.N.C. also determined that the expense of providing office space for the customer service group in the headquarters buildings was growing at a rate greater than the return on that portion of the business.

As its first initiative, it sought ways to reduce these two expenses while maintaining the existing services these functions provided.

When the B.A.N.C. IT group also began to analyze its data network, it further determined that on average its WAN was about 60 to 70 percent utilized during peak hours of the day. This means that on most of its 128 Kbps circuits, it was using only 77 to 90 Kbps.

Consolidating the Networks

After it collected this information, B.A.N.C. sought to find a way to consolidate its networks in an effort to reduce costs and maintain functionality. B.A.N.C. laid out the following guidelines for its discussions with multiservice network vendors:

- It wanted to work with one of its existing PBX or networking vendors to provide an end-to-end solution, if possible.

- It wanted to provide 21st-century technology to its internal and external customers, but it didn't want to be on the bleeding edge in terms of technology risk.

- It wanted to avoid *forklift-upgrades* to its existing infrastructure. A forklift-upgrade occurs when most or all of a company's existing network hardware and software needs to be replaced with newer hardware and software. This is not only expensive in terms of capital expenditure, but it also involves physical visits to each site and disruptions of the existing network functionality.

- It wanted its new multiservice network to be Internet-capable so that it could interact with new technologies in the future.

- It didn't want to have to retrain its employees to use the new multiservice network, nor did it want to eliminate the expertise it had in its existing IT groups for both voice and data.

- It wanted the new multiservice network to be cost-effective and expense-reducing.

After B.A.N.C. defined its objectives, it began discussions with its incumbent data and PBX vendors. As the discussions progressed and the vendors explained their existing solutions and future visions of multiservice networking, it became clear to B.A.N.C. that its data applications (both traditional and Web-based) were growing faster than its voice-related interactions with customers.

It also realized that its competitors, in fields such as online banking and brokerage services, were quickly surpassing B.A.N.C. because of their capability to offer new services at reduced costs using Internet-based technologies.

As the B.A.N.C. IT group evaluated the vendors' proposals, it determined that Cisco Systems' current multiservice offerings could provide an end-to-end solution that would meet all its stated needs. In addition to B.A.N.C.'s immediate needs, the Cisco Systems solution provided the capability to integrated B.A.N.C.'s voice and data network with future Web-based TCP/IP applications.

The highlights of the Cisco Systems solution include the following:

- Leveraged B.A.N.C.'s existing data network, which was made up of 2600 and 3600 series routers. Both the 2600 and 3600 series are modular routers/VoIP gateways. They provide more than 60 LAN and WAN interfaces, from async to optical carrier 3 (OC-3) ATM, as well as analog and digital voice interfaces such as T1/E1, Foreign Exchange Station (FXS), FXO, and recEive and transMit (E&M). Both routers share the same network modules, so stocking, sparing, and consistency across the family of products is maintained. The 2600 series offers up to two LAN interfaces and up to four WAN interfaces, plus the capability to add up to four analog or two digital voice interfaces. The 3600 series includes the 3620, 3640, and 3660. These routers can have up to 14 LAN interfaces, up to 96 WAN interfaces, up to 24 analog voice interfaces, or up to 12 digital voice interfaces.

- Based on open-standard, H.323 protocols.

- Provided an integration path that utilized B.A.N.C.'s existing data network and PBX equipment.

- Required neither extensive reconfiguration of existing data and voice equipment, nor a forklift-upgrade of any equipment.

- Enabled the B.A.N.C. IT group to continue utilizing the expertise of both its voice and data support staff.

- Interoperated with other multiservice technologies that Cisco Systems offers, including Cisco IP phones and IP PBXs, as well as H.323-based applications, such as Click-2-Dial and Netmeeting.

A representation of the proposed Cisco Systems solution is shown in Figure 15-2.

Figure 15-2 *Proposed Multiservice Network*

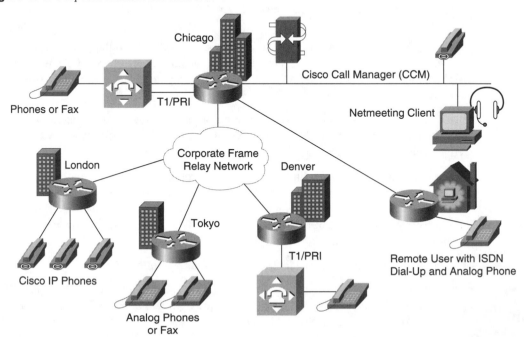

Highlights of the proposed solution include:

- Continued use of the 2600, 3620, and 3660 series routers that B.A.N.C. was using for its data networks. B.A.N.C. also can add analog and digital voice network modules where appropriate to its existing empty module slots.

- Immediate cost savings by moving B.A.N.C.'s intraoffice voice and fax calls onto its TCP/IP data network. B.A.N.C. eliminated the leased lines as well as reduced its long-distance charges associated with those calls.

- Future capability to replace small-office key-systems with Cisco IP phones and to reduce lease costs when the key-system leases expired.

- Capability to integrate both Cisco IP phones and existing voice equipment with multiservice applications such as Netmeeting or Intel ProShare video-conferencing using H.323.

In addition to moving intraoffice voice and fax calls onto its data network, the B.A.N.C. IT group also realized that, with the flexibility of VoIP, it could offer its customer service representatives the option of working from home without losing any functionality.

Using a Cisco Systems small office, home office (SOHO) router such as the 1750, B.A.N.C. could offer low-cost Integrated Services Digital Network (ISDN) dial-up access at an annual cost that was a fraction of the office-space charges it was currently paying.

Chicago Router Overview

The router configurations for the B.A.N.C. project are as follows (only relevant portions of the configuration files are shown):

```
hostname Chicago
!
voice-card 1
 codec complexity high
* This command defines which codecs can be used with the Voice Network Module.
High Complexity allows G.711, G.726, G.728, G.729, G.723.1 and Fax-Relay
!
ipx routing
!
dlsw local-peer peer-id 192.168.101.1 promiscuous
!
controller T1 1/0
description "1-8:Denver, 9-10:Tokyo"
framing esf
linecoding b8zs
clock source line
ds0-group 1 timeslots 1-8 type e&m-wink-start
ds0-group 2 timeslots 9 type fxo-loop-start
ds0-group 3 timeslots 10 type fxo-loop-start
* These commands define the clocking, framing, linecoding and signaling for each DS0
within the T1 controller card.
!
voice-port 1/0:1
*  A Voice-Port is created for each ds0-group that is created above.
!
```

```
voice-port 1/0:2
connection trunk 998
*  Connection trunk creates a permanent VoIP call between 2 VoIP gateways. It allows
features such as hookflash or stuttuer dialtone to be passed over the IP network to
the connected telephony devices. The digits with connection trunk as dialed
"internally" by the router and are not seen by the user. The digits are matched
against a VoIP dial-peer to complete the call.
!
voice-port 1/0:3
 connection trunk 999
!
dial-peer voice 1 voip
description "trunk/opx connections to Tokyo"
destination-pattern 99.
session target ipv4:192.168.102.2
!
dial-peer voice 2 voip
description "calls to Denver office"
destination-pattern 5....
session target ipv4:192.168.103.2
!
dial-peer voice 3 voip
description "calls to IP Phones..CallMgr."
codec g723r63
destination-pattern 4....
session target ipv4:192.168.101.100
!
dial-peer voice 4 pots
destination-pattern 6....
prefix 6
port 1/0:1
!
dial-peer voice 5 pots
destination-pattern 6....
prefix 6
port 1/0:2
!
dial-peer voice 6 pots
destination-pattern 6....
prefix 6
port 1/0:3
interface FastEthernet 1/0/0
ip address 192.168.100.1 255.255.255.0
ipx network 100
!
interface FastEthernet 1/0/1
ip address 192.168.101.1 255.255.255.0
ipx network 101
!
interface serial 2/0/0
encapsulation frame-relay
frame-relay traffic-shaping
!
interface serial 2/0/0.1
ip address 192.168.102.1 255.255.255.0
ipx network 102
frame-relay interface-dlci 102
frame-relay class voip_qos_128k
*This command maps the frame-relay traffic-shaping, FRF.12 and QoS features to this
PVC.
!
interface serial 2/0/0.2
ip address 192.168.103.1 255.255.255.0
frame-relay interface-dlci 103
```

```
frame-relay class voip_qos_128k
ipx network 103
!
interface serial 2/0/0.3
ip address 192.168.104.1 255.255.255.0
frame-relay interface-dlci 104
frame-relay class voip_qos_256k
ipx network 104
!
map-class frame-relay voip_qos_128k
no frame-relay adaptive-shaping becn
frame-relay ip rtp priority 16384 16383 48
frame-relay cir 128000
frame-relay bc 560
frame-relay fragment 160
frame-relay fair-queue
frame-relay ip rtp header compression
* These commands define the rules for Frame-Relay Traffic-Shaping, FRF.12 fragment
size and VoIP QoS using IP RTP Priority.
!
map-class frame-relay voip_qos_256k
no frame-relay adaptive-shaping becn
frame-relay ip rtp priority 16384 16383 48
frame-relay cir 256000
frame-relay bc 560
frame-relay fragment 320
frame-relay fair-queue
frame-relay ip rtp header compression
!
router rip
network 192.168.100.0
network 192.168.101.0
network 192.168.102.0
network 192.168.103.0
network 192.168.104.0
```

B.A.N.C has a five-digit dialing plan so that any employee can call another office by dialing five digits. The numbering is as follows:

```
Chicago Office: 6xxxx
IP Phones: 4xxxx
Denver: 5xxxx
Tokyo:  Uses 6xxxx Off-Premise Extensions from the PBX
```

The 3660 router in B.A.N.C.'s Chicago office has VoIP dial-peers that point to all the company's remote offices. The Tokyo office is a special case because it has *hookflash* functionality, which makes it appear to the PBX as though it is a directly connected station. Hookflash is a method of providing additional services, such as call waiting or conferencing between the PBX and the handset. Hookflash is activated when a user briefly presses the cradle button on his or her phone. Hookflash sends a momentary on-hook/off-hook signal to the PBX, notifying the PBX that the user is requesting additional services.

Hookflash requires a permanent VoIP call between two gateways. A *connection trunk* provides this capability. A permanent call is created when the IP connectivity between two gateways is established. This differs from a switched call, which is established when a user needs to place a call. Also, a permanent call provides the capability to emulate a "wire" between the two devices so that they appear to be directly connected, and it enables the passing of certain signaling such as hookflash or stutter dial tone. This is often useful when users want to maintain their dial plan on their connected PBXs, or when they want to maintain "directly connected to PBX" functionality for remote stations.

Each Chicago Frame Relay permanent virtual switch (PVC) is traffic-shaped to enable only data and voice traffic up to the guaranteed CIR. This is done to prevent packets from being dropped or excessively delayed (queued in the Frame Relay switch). Each PVC uses Frame Relay Forum 12 (FRF.12) to fragment the data packets at Layer 2, thereby preventing serialization delay. The PVCs also use IP RTP Priority to identify the VoIP packets and to give them highest priority for outbound queuing.

The 3660 in the Tokyo office is configured to use a connection trunk which provides a permanent VoIP call that can pass hookflash calls as well as keep the dial plan on the PBX for digital signal level 0 (DS-0) calls. The 3660 in this office also has a VoIP dial-peer that points to the IP address of the Cisco Call Manager for Cisco IP phones.

Cisco Call Manager is an IP-PBX system. It provides all PBX functionality to IP phones through Call Manager software that runs on a Windows NT server. All communication between CCM, the IP phones, and VoIP gateways is done through IP.

You also can integrate Cisco Call Manager with legacy PBXs or key-systems using VoIP gateways.

Cisco Call Manager can support only G.711 or G.723.1 codecs. In this case, G.723.1 is configured to conserve bandwidth, and all the other connections are made with the G.729 codec. The Frame Relay PVCs are traffic-shaped so that data or voice cannot burst above CIR. This guarantees that the voice packets are not dropped within the Frame Relay cloud or queued so that delay and jitter are created within the cloud. Also, the VoIP traffic is defined to receive the highest QoS on the WAN links.

London Router Overview

The London router configuration is as follows:

```
hostname London
!
ipx routing
!
dlsw local-peer peer-id 192.168.105.1
dlsw remote-peer 0 tcp 192.168.101.1
!
interface Ethernet 0
description "will pass DHCP and BootP requests to CCM"
ip address 192.168.105.1 255.255.255.0
ip helper-address 192.168.101.100
ipx network 200
!
interface serial 1/0
encapsulation frame-relay
frame-relay traffic-shaping
!
interface serial 1/0.1
ip address 192.168.102.2 255.255.255.0
```

```
frame-relay interface-dlci 102
frame-relay class voip_qos_128k
ipx network 102
!
map-class frame-relay voip_qos_128k
no frame-relay adaptive-shaping becn
frame-relay ip rtp priority 16384 16383 48
frame-relay cir 128000
frame-relay bc 560
frame-relay fragment 160
frame-relay fair-queue
frame-relay ip rtp header compression
!
router rip
network 192.168.102.0
network 192.168.105.0
```

The London site has Cisco IP phones. It has no defined VoIP or plain old telephone service (POTS) dial-peers. All the dial-plan information for its IP phones resides on its CCM. B.A.N.C. made the following changes to its London configuration:

- It traffic-shaped the Frame Relay PVC to the CIR. Traffic-shaping monitors and restricted the amount of traffic passed onto a WAN circuit. Frame Relay guarantees data within the CIR only. Therefore, the router traffic-shapes the data rate so that no traffic is sent above CIR, eliminating the possibility of dropped traffic. This is done because VoIP traffic does not tolerate dropped or lost packets that can reduce overall call quality.

- It added an `ip helper-address` to pass Dynamic Host Configuration Protocol (DHCP) and Bootstrap Protocol (BOOTP) requests from the Cisco IP phones.

- It configured the VoIP traffic to have higher QoS on the WAN link.

Tokyo Router Overview

The Tokyo router configuration is as follows:

```
hostname Tokyo
!
ipx routing
!
dlsw local-peer peer-id 192.168.106.1
dlsw remote-peer 0 tcp 192.168.101.1
!
dial-peer voice 1 voip
destination-pattern 77.
session target ipv4:192.168.103.1
!
dial-peer voice 2 pots
description "off-premise extension on DS0 #9 from Chicago"
destination-pattern 998
port 1/0/0
!
dial-peer voice 3 pots
description "off-premise extension on DS0 #10 from Chicago"
destination-pattern 999
port 1/0/1
!
```

```
voice-port 1/0/0
connection trunk 777
!
voice-port 1/0/1
connection trunk 778
!
interface Ethernet 0
ip address 192.168.106.1 255.255.255.0
ipx network 106
!
interface serial 1/0
encapsulation frame-relay
frame-relay traffic-shaping
!
interface serial 1/0.1
ip address 192.168.103.2 255.255.255.0
frame-relay interface-dlci 103
frame-relay class voip_qos_128k
ipx network 103
!
map-class frame-relay voip_qos_128k
no frame-relay adaptive-shaping becn
frame-relay ip rtp priority 16384 16383 48
frame-relay cir 128000
frame-relay bc 560
frame-relay fragment 160
frame-relay fair-queue
frame-relay ip rtp header compression
!
router rip
network 192.168.106.0
network 192.168.103.0
```

Because the Tokyo phones must have *hookflash* functionality, they are configured as a trunk connection back to the central PBX in Chicago.

This means they receive a dial tone from the Chicago PBX, and the PBX interprets any digits they dial. For this reason, the Tokyo router needs only one VoIP dial-peer. Like the other routers, the Tokyo Frame Relay PVC is traffic-shaped to CIR, and the VoIP traffic is given highest QoS.

Denver Router Overview

The Denver router configuration is as follows:

```
hostname Denver
!
voice-card 1
 codec complexity high
!
ipx routing
!
dlsw local-peer peer-id 192.168.107.1
dlsw remote-peer 0 tcp 192.168.101.1
!
controller T1 1/0
framing esf
linecoding b8zs
clock source line
```

```
ds0-group 1 timeslots 1-8 type e&m-wink-start
!
voice-port 1/0:1
!
dial-peer voice 1 pots
destination-pattern 5….
prefix 5
port 1/0:1
!
dial-peer voice 2 voip
destination-pattern 4….
codec g723r63
session-target ipv4:192.168.101.100
!
dial-peer voice 3 voip
destination-pattern 6….
session target ipv4:192.168.104.1
!
interface FastEthernet 1/0/0
ip address 192.168.107.1 255.255.255.0
ipx network 107
!
interface serial 2/0/0
encapsulation frame-relay
frame-relay traffic-shaping
!
interface serial 2/0/0.1
ip address 192.168.104.2 255.255.255.0
frame-relay interface-dlci 104
frame-relay class voip_qos_256k
ipx network 104
!
map-class frame-relay voip_qos_256k
no frame-relay adaptive-shaping becn
frame-relay ip rtp priority 16384 16383 48
frame-relay cir 256000
frame-relay bc 1000
frame-relay fragment 80
frame-relay fair-queue
frame-relay ip rtp header compression
!
router rip
network 192.168.107.0
network 192.168.104.0
```

The Denver office owns the 5xxxx extensions, so the Denver router has a POTS dial-peer for those extensions. It also has a VoIP dial-peer pointing to the 6xxxx extensions and the 4xxxx extensions on the CCM. Like the other routers, it has Frame Relay PVC traffic-shaped to CIR, and the VoIP traffic is given the highest QoS.

CCM Overview

The CCM manages all the dial plans for the IP phones. It appears to the Cisco VoIP gateways as another H.323 device and acts as a proxy for all the IP phones. The Cisco IP phones can use either the G.711 or G.723.1 codec. B.A.N.C. chose the G.723.1 codec to reduce the bandwidth used on the WAN links.

Service Provider Case Study: Prepaid Calling Card

The following case study discusses a service that enables service providers to handle prepaid and debit calling cards. With this new service, service providers can utilize their existing VoIP network, gateways, and gatekeepers. They also can differentiate themselves from other VoIP service providers by offering bundled services as well as realizing greater profits that they can use to fund network expansions or reduce toll-bypass costs.

BOWIE.net Multiservice Networks

BOWIE.net is a regional Internet service provider (ISP) with 60 points of presence (POPs) throughout the Southeast and along the East Coast of the United States. It has a Cisco-powered network and currently provides residential and business access to the Internet, managed network services, and Web hosting.

In early 1999, BOWIE.net began offering 10¢/minute long-distance VoIP services throughout its 60 POPs. It focused this service primarily to its existing business customers because it had a number of traveling salespeople and consultants who were incurring large long-distance charges from cellular phones.

As competition in the residential market space grew, BOWIE.net sought alternative ways to differentiate itself from its competitors. One initiative it explored was offering prepaid or debit card services with its VoIP network.

As BOWIE.net already used AS5300s for VoIP access, it was a natural fit to use the prepaid calling-card feature added in the Cisco 12.0(6)T IOS system software. The service would not only provide BOWIE.net with prepaid revenue, but it also could be offered at a premium price because of its flexibility.

BOWIE.net worked with Cisco Systems and its partners to implement the prepaid calling-card service. The partners provided the billing applications, and Cisco provided the VoIP infrastructure. Because of these partnerships, BOWIE.net was able to determine which partner could meet its technology and cost needs without concern that the solution would not interoperate.

BOWIE.net implemented the prepaid calling-card solution with minimal configuration changes and equipment additions. The biggest pieces it had to add were the servers that hosted the billing applications. BOWIE.net utilized its existing Remote Access Dial-In User Service (RADIUS) authentication servers and Trivial File Transfer Protocol (TFTP) servers for the implementation. It used the RADIUS servers for account-number and pin-number verification and the TFTP servers to store the prompts played to the subscribers when they enter the service. In addition, it used its existing AS5300s and 3640s for VoIP gateways and gatekeepers.

Figure 15-3 shows a simplified topology of BOWIE.net's network. The key points to notice are that the billing, TFTP, and RADIUS servers can reside anywhere in the IP network, and that the existing IP backbone and VoIP gateways are being utilized.

Figure 15-3 *BOWIE.net's H.323 Network Components*

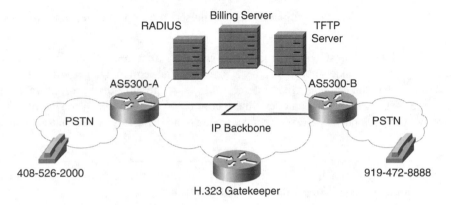

A typical prepaid calling-card call proceeds as follows:

1 A subscriber purchases a prepaid calling card from BOWIE.net in $10/20/50/100 increments. The card is activated and the account and pin numbers are defined in the RADIUS server and billing system.

2 When a subscriber wants to place a call, he or she dials into BOWIE.net's VoIP network through a 1-800 access number.

3 The AS5300 receives the call from the PSTN, and the subscriber is prompted with a greeting from BOWIE.net. The subscriber is asked to choose whether he or she wants the remaining prompts played in English or another language, such as Spanish or Mandarin Chinese.

4 The subscriber is then asked to enter the account and pin numbers from his or her calling card. At this point, the RADIUS/billing server authenticates the subscriber information. After the subscriber is authenticated, he or she is asked to enter the destination phone number. Based on the called-party number, the billing server determines the billing rate, and the subscriber is prompted with his or her remaining time and currency balance for that account.

5 After the subscriber enters the called number, the billing server starts the Call Detail Record (CDR) for both originating and terminating gateways.

6 When the subscriber's account balance reaches a low-water threshold, he or she is prompted that the balance is about to terminate. If the subscriber continues to talk past the allowed account balance, the call automatically is terminated. At this point, the subscriber has the option to extend the balance on this calling card or purchase a new card from BOWIE.net.

7 After the call is terminated, the billing server completes the CDRs for that specific call.

The TFTP server stores the prompts (in .au format) that the AS5300 VoIP gateways play for greetings, balance status, currency status, and time remaining. These files require more space than the AS5300's Flash memory allows, so the subscriber must download them from the TFTP server. You can obtain these prompts from the Cisco Web site (http://www.cisco.com), or BOWIE.net can create them using any .au-format-capable tool.

NOTE This configuration highlights the prepaid calling-card features, but you can add additional configurations utilizing gatekeeper or other features.

The configurations of the two AS5300 gateways are as follows:

```
hostname AS5300-A
!
aaa new-model
aaa authentication login h323 group radius
aaa authentication exec h323 group radius
aaa accounting connection h323 start-stop group radius
*These commands define the AAA interaction between the gateway and Billing Server.
!
isdn switch-type primary-5ess
!
gw-accounting h323 vsa
*This command tells the gateway to use VSAs (Vendor Specific Attributes) when
creating billing records.
!
call application voice bowie.net tftp://tftp.bowie.net/tcl/prepaid.tcl
* This command tells the router where the Prepaid Calling-Card application scripts
reside.
!
call application voice bowie.net uid-len 10
call application voice bowie.net pin-len 4
call application voice bowie.net language 1 en
call application voice bowie.net language 2 ch
call application voice bowie.net set-location en 0 tftp://tftp.bowie.net/prepaid-
prompts/
call application voice bowie.net set-location ch 0 tftp://tftp.bowie.net/prepaid-
prompts/
* These commands tell the router the parameters to consider when interacting with
the Billing server…parameters such as User ID# length, PIN# length, Preferred
Language, and so on.
!
radius-server host 168.150.100.10 auth-port 1645 acct-port 1646
radius-server key bowie.net
```

```
radius-server vsa send accounting
radius-server vsa send authentication
* These commands define the RADIUS specific details the gateway should use when
interacting with the billing server.
!
ntp clock-period 17179993
ntp master 1
ntp server 168.150.100.20
* These commands tell the gateway how to use NTP (Network Time Protocol) so that all
CDR and Billing records are synchronized for timing and timestamps.
!
controller T1 1/0
pri-group 1 timeslots 1-24
clock source line primary
framing esf
linecoding b8zs
!
voice-port 0:D
!
dial-peer voice 1 pots
application bowie.net
destination-pattern 1408…….
prefix 1408
port 0:D
* The Application command tells the gateway to use the "bowie.net" application when
this voice-port is engaged. The bowie.net application is defined above in the "call
application" section.
!
dial-peer voice 2 voip
destination-pattern 1919…….
session target ipv4:192.168.120.1
!
interface FastEthernet 0
ip address 168.150.100.1 255.255.255.0
```

AS5300—A Router Overview

The "call application voice" section of this configuration differs from basic VoIP services. It defines how many digits should be collected for the account and pin numbers, the digits to signify English or other language prompts, and the location of the .au prompts for each language. Also, the "application bowie.net" section is defined on the POTS dial-peer associated with the T1 Primary Rate Interface (PRI) connected to the PSTN.

Summary

This chapter covered two different VoIP customers. The enterprise customer (B.A.N.C.) used VoIP to not only consolidate its voice and data network, but also to take advantage of this convergence to consolidate its voice and data support mechanisms. Although this chapter covered configuration details for B.A.N.C.'s various sites, it is important to note that this is just the beginning of configuration. Network design opens a whole new set of questions that must be answered. These questions include the performance of the gateway itself, carrier reliability, and many other concerns.

The second customer, BOWIE.net, is a service provider that is using VoIP to add value and differentiate itself from the competition. Also, BOWIE.net can extract more revenue per customer by offering additional value-added services.

The BOWIE.net configurations discussed in this chapter detailed many new commands in the Cisco IOS system software. You can find more information on these commands at http://www.cisco.com, in the command reference section. This chapter discussed only the basic configuration necessary; therefore, service providers must take caution when designing, planning, and implementing a network to ensure consistent quality and stability.

ISUP Messages/ Types Formats

Table A-1   *ISUP Messages and Message Types*

ISUP Signaling Message	Message Type Value
Initial Address Message (IAM)	00000001
Address Complete Message (ACM)	00000110
Answer Message (ANM)	00001001
Release Message (REL)	00001100
Release Complete Message (RLC)	00010000
Continuity Message (COT)	00000101
Call Progress Message (CPG)	00101100
Suspend Message (SUS)	00001101
Resume Message (RES)	00001110
Forward Transfer Message (FOT)	00001000
Information Request Message (INR)	00000011
Information Message (INF)	00000100

Source: ITU-T Q.763 (9/97)

Table A-2   *Initial Address Message (IAM)*

Signaling Parameter	Type	Length (Octets)
Message Type	M	1
Nature of Connection Indicators	M	1
Forward Call Indicators	M	2

continues

Table A-2 *Initial Address Message (IAM) (Continued)*

Signaling Parameter	Type	Length (Octets)
Calling Party's Category	M	1
Transmission Medium Requirement	M	1
Called Party Number	M	Variable
Transmit Network Selection	O	Variable
Call Reference	O	7
Calling Party Number	O	Variable
Optional Forward Call Indicators	O	3
Redirecting Number	O	Variable
Redirection Information	O	3-4
Closed User Group Interlock Code	O	6
Connection Request	O	7-9
Original Called Number	O	Variable
User-to-user Information	O	3-131
Access Transport	O	Variable
User Service Information	O	4-13
User-to-user Indicators	O	3
Generic Number Parameter	O	Variable
Propagation Delay Number	O	4
User Service Information Prime	O	4-13
Network Specific Facility	O	Variable
Generic Digit	O	Variable
Origination ISC Point Code	O	4
User Teleservice Information	O	4-5
Remote Operations	O	Variable
Parameter Compatibility Information	O	Variable

Table A-2   *Initial Address Message (IAM) (Continued)*

Signaling Parameter	Type	Length (Octets)
Generic Notification Identifier	O	3
Service Activation	O	Variable
Generic Reference	O	Variable
MLPP precedence	O	8
Transmission Medium Requirement Prime	O	3
Location Number	O	Variable
Forward GVNS	O	5-26
CCSS	O	Variable
Network Management Controls	O	Variable
Circuit Assignment Map	O	6-7
Correlation ID	O	Variable
Call Diversion Treatment Indicators	O	Variable
Called IN Number	O	Variable
Call Offering Treatment Indicators	O	Variable
Conference Treatment Indicators	O	Variable
SCF ID	O	Variable
UID Capability Indicators	O	Variable
Echo Control Information	O	3
Hop Counter	O	3
Collect Call Request	O	3
End of Optional Parameters	O	1

Source: ITU-T Q.763 (9/97)

Table A-3 *Address Complete Message (ACM)*

Signaling Parameter	Type	Length (Octets)
Message Type	M	1
Backward Call Indicators	O	2
Optional Backward Call Indicators	O	3
Call Reference	O	7
Cause Indicators	O	Variable
User-to-user Indicators	O	3
User-to-user Information	O	3-131
Access Transport	O	Variable
Generic Notification Indicator	O	3
Transmission Medium Used	O	3
Echo Control Information	O	3
Access Delivery Information	O	3
Redirection Number	O	Variable
Parameter Compatibility Information	O	Variable
Call Diversion Information	O	3
Network Specific Facility	O	Variable
Remote Operations	O	Variable
Service Activation	O	Variable
Redirection Number Restriction Indicator	O	3
Conference Treatment Indicators	O	Variable
UID Action Indicators	O	Variable
End of Optional Parameters	O	1

Source: ITU-T Q.763 (9/97)

Table A-4   *Address Message (ANM)*

Signaling Parameter	Type	Length (Octets)
Message Type	M	1
Backward Call Indicators	O	2
Optional Backward Call Indicators	O	3
Call Reference	O	7
User-to-user Indicators	O	3
User-to-user Information	O	3-131
Connected Number	O	Variable
Access Transport	O	Variable
Access Delivery Information	O	3
Generic Notification Indicator	O	3
Parameter Capability Information	O	Variable
Backward GVNS	O	Variable
Call History Information	O	4
Generic Number	O	Variable
Transmission Medium Used	O	3
Network Specific Facility	O	Variable
Remote Operations	O	Variable
Redirection Number	O	Variable
Service Activation	O	Variable
Echo Control Information	O	3
Redirection Number Restriction Indicator	O	3
Display Information	O	Variable
End of Optional Parameters	O	1

Source: ITU-T Q.763 (9/97)

Table A-5 *Release Message (REL)*

Signaling Parameter	Type	Length (Octets)
Message Type	M	1
Cause Indicators	M	Variable
Redirection Information	O	3-4
Redirection Number	O	Variable
Access Transport	O	Variable
Signaling Point Code	O	4
User-to-user Information	O	3-131
Automatic Congestion Control	O	3
Network Specific Facility	O	Variable
Access Delivery Information	O	3
Parameter Capability Information	O	Variable
User-to-user Indicators	O	3
Display Information	O	Variable
Remote Operations	O	Variable
End of Optional Parameters	O	1

Source: ITU-T Q.763 (9/97)

Table A-6 *Release Complete Message (RLC)*

Signaling Parameter	Type	Length (Octets)
Message Type	M	1
Cause Indicators	O	5-6
End of Optional Parameters	O	1

Source: ITU-T Q.763 (9/97)

Table A-7   *Continuity Message (COT)*

Signaling Parameter	Type	Length (Octets)
Message Type	M	1
Continuity Indicators	M	1

Source: ITU-T Q.763 (9/97)

Table A-8   *Call Progress Message (CPG)*

Signaling Parameter	Type	Length (Octets)
Message Type	M	1
Event Information	M	1
Cause Indicators	O	Variable
Call Reference	O	7
Backward Call Indicators	O	4
Optional Backward Call Indicators	O	3
Access Transport	O	Variable
User-to-user Indicators	O	3
Redirection Number	O	Variable
User-to-user information	O	3-131
Generic Notification Indicator	O	3
Network Specific Facility	O	Variable
Remote Operations	O	Variable
Transmission Medium Used	O	3
Access Delivery Information	O	3
Parameter Capability Information	O	Variable
Call Diversion Information	O	3
Service Activation	O	Variable
Redirection Number Restriction Indicator	O	3
Call Transfer Number	O	Variable

continues

Table A-8   *Call Progress Message (CPG) (Continued)*

Signaling Parameter	Type	Length (Octets)
Echo Control Information	O	3
Connected Number	O	Variable
Backward GVNS	O	Variable
Generic Number	O	Variable
Call History Information	O	4
Conference Treatment Indicators	O	Variable
UID Action Indicators	O	Variable
End of Optional Parameters	O	1

Source: ITU-T Q.763 (9/97)

Table A-9   *Suspend Message (SUS) and Resume Message (RES)*

Signaling Parameter	Type	Length (Octets)
Message Type	M	1
Suspend/Resume Indicators	M	1
Call Reference	O	7
End of Optional Parameters	O	1

Source: ITU-T Q.763 (9/97)

Table A-10   *Forward Transfer Message (FOT)*

Signaling Parameter	Type	Length (Octets)
Message Type	M	1
Call Reference	O	7
End of Optional Parameters	O	1

Source: ITU-T Q.763 (9/97)I

Table A-11 *Information Request Message (INR)*

Signaling Parameter	Type	Length (Octets)
Message Type	M	1
Information Request Indicators	M	2
Call Reference	O	7
Network Specific Facility	O	Variable
Parameter Compatibility Information	O	Variable
End of Optional Parameters	O	1

Source: ITU-T Q.763 (9/97)

Table A-12 *Information Message (INF)*

Signaling Parameter	Type	Length (Octets)
Message Type	M	1
Information Indicators	M	2
Signaling Parameter	Type	Length (Octets)
Calling Party's Category	O	3
Calling Party Number	O	Variable
Call Reference	O	7
Connection Request	O	7-9
Parameter Compatibility Information	O	Variable
Network Specific Facility	O	Variable
End of Optional Parameters	O	1

Source: ITU-T Q.763 (9/97)

J-K

L

N

T

CCIE Professional Development

Cisco LAN Switching
Kennedy Clark, CCIE; Kevin Hamilton, CCIE
1-57870-094-9 • AVAILABLE NOW

This volume provides an in-depth analysis of Cisco LAN switching technologies, architectures, and deployments, including unique coverage of Catalyst network design essentials. Network designs and configuration examples are incorporated throughout to demonstrate the principles and enable easy translation of the material into practice in production networks.

Advanced IP Network Design
Alvaro Retana, CCIE; Don Slice, CCIE; and Russ White, CCIE
1-57870-097-3 • AVAILABLE NOW

Network engineers and managers can use these case studies, which highlight various network design goals, to explore issues including protocol choice, network stability, and growth. This book also includes theoretical discussion on advanced design topics.

Large-Scale IP Network Solutions
Khalid Raza, CCIE; and Mark Turner
1-57870-084-1 • AVAILABLE NOW

Network engineers can find solutions as their IP networks grow in size and complexity. Examine all the major IP protocols in-depth and learn about scalability, migration planning, network management, and security for large-scale networks.

Routing TCP/IP, Volume I
Jeff Doyle, CCIE
1-57870-041-8 • AVAILABLE NOW

This book takes the reader from a basic understanding of routers and routing protocols through a detailed examination of each of the IP interior routing protocols. Learn techniques for designing networks that maximize the efficiency of the protocol being used. Exercises and review questions provide core study for the CCIE Routing and Switching exam.

www.ciscopress.com

Cisco Career Certifications

Cisco CCNA Exam #640-507 Certification Guide
Wendell Odom, CCIE

0-7357-0971-8 • AVAILABLE IN APRIL

Although it's only the first step in Cisco Career Certification, the Cisco Certified Network Associate (CCNA) exam is a difficult test. Your first attempt at becoming Cisco certified requires a lot of study and confidence in your networking knowledge. When you're ready to test your skills, complete your knowledge of the exam topics, and prepare for exam day, you need the preparation tools found in *Cisco CCNA Exam #640-507 Certification Guide* from Cisco Press.

CCDA Exam Certification Guide
Anthony Bruno, CCIE & Jacqueline Kim

0-7357-0074-5 • AVAILABLE NOW

CCDA Exam Certification Guide is a comprehensive study tool for DCN Exam #640-441. Written by a CCIE and a CCDA, and reviewed by Cisco technical experts, *CCDA Exam Certification Guide* will help you understand and master the exam objectives. In this solid review on the design areas of the DCN exam, you'll learn to design a network that meets a customer's requirements for performance, security, capacity, and scalability.

Interconnecting Cisco Network Devices
Edited by Steve McQuerry

1-57870-111-2 • AVAILABLE NOW

Based on the Cisco course taught worldwide, *Interconnecting Cisco Network Devices* teaches you how to configure Cisco switches and routers in multi-protocol internetworks. ICND is the primary course recommended by Cisco Systems for CCNA #640-507 preparation. If you are pursuing CCNA certification, this book is an excellent starting point for your study.

Designing Cisco Networks
Edited by Diane Teare

1-57870-105-8 • AVAILABLE NOW

Based on the Cisco Systems instructor-led and self-study course available worldwide, *Designing Cisco Networks* will help you understand how to analyze and solve existing network problems while building a framework that supports the functionality, performance, and scalability required from any given environment. Self-assessment through exercises and chapter-ending tests starts you down the path for attaining your CCDA certification.

www.ciscopress.com

Cisco Press Solutions

Enhanced IP Services for Cisco Networks
Donald C. Lee, CCIE

1-57870-106-6 • AVAILABLE NOW

This is a guide to improving your network's capabilities by understanding the new enabling and advanced Cisco IOS services that build more scalable, intelligent, and secure networks. Learn the technical details necessary to deploy Quality of Service, VPN technologies, IPsec, the IOS firewall and IOS Intrusion Detection. These services will allow you to extend the network to new frontiers securely, protect your network from attacks, and increase the sophistication of network services.

Developing IP Multicast Networks, Volume I
Beau Williamson, CCIE

1-57870-077-9 • AVAILABLE NOW

This book provides a solid foundation of IP multicast concepts and explains how to design and deploy the networks that will support appplications such as audio and video conferencing, distance-learning, and data replication. Includes an in-depth discussion of the PIM protocol used in Cisco routers and detailed coverage of the rules that control the creation and maintenance of Cisco mroute state entries.

Designing Network Security
Merike Kaeo

1-57870-043-4 • AVAILABLE NOW

Designing Network Security is a practical guide designed to help you understand the fundamentals of securing your corporate infrastructure. This book takes a comprehensive look at underlying security technologies, the process of creating a security policy, and the practical requirements necessary to implement a corporate security policy.

Cisco Press Solutions

EIGRP Network Design Solutions
Ivan Pepelnjak, CCIE
1-57870-165-1 • AVAILABLE NOW

EIGRP Network Design Solutions uses case studies and real-world configuration examples to help you gain an in-depth understanding of the issues involved in designing, deploying, and managing EIGRP-based networks. This book details proper designs that can be used to build large and scalable EIGRP-based networks and documents possible ways each EIGRP feature can be used in network design, implmentation, troubleshooting, and monitoring.

Top-Down Network Design
Priscilla Oppenheimer
1-57870-069-8 • AVAILABLE NOW

Building reliable, secure, and manageable networks is every network professional's goal. This practical guide teaches you a systematic method for network design that can be applied to campus LANs, remote-access networks, WAN links, and large-scale internetworks. Learn how to analyze business and technical requirements, examine traffic flow and Quality of Service requirements, and select protocols and technologies based on performance goals.

Cisco IOS Releases: The Complete Reference
Mack M. Coulibaly
1-57870-179-1 • AVAILABLE NOW

Cisco IOS Releases: The Complete Reference is the first comprehensive guide to the more than three dozen types of Cisco IOS releases being used today on enterprise and service provider networks. It details the release process and its numbering and naming conventions, as well as when, where, and how to use the various releases. A complete map of Cisco IOS software releases and their relationships to one another, in addition to insights into decoding information contained within the software, make this book an indispensable resource for any network professional.

Cisco Press Solutions

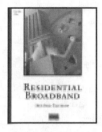

Residential Broadband, Second Edition

George Abe

1-57870-177-5 • AVAILABLE NOW

This book will answer basic questions of residential broadband networks such as: Why do we need high speed networks at home? How will high speed residential services be delivered to the home? How do regulatory or commercial factors affect this technology? Explore such networking topics as xDSL, cable, and wireless.

Internetworking Technologies Handbook, Second Edition

Kevin Downes, CCIE, Merilee Ford, H. Kim Lew, Steve Spanier, Tim Stevenson

1-57870-102-3 • AVAILABLE NOW

This comprehensive reference provides a foundation for understanding and implementing contemporary internetworking technologies, providing you with the necessary information needed to make rational networking decisions. Master terms, concepts, technologies, and devices that are used in the internetworking industry today. You also learn how to incorporate networking technologies into a LAN/WAN environment, as well as how to apply the OSI reference model to categorize protocols, technologies, and devices.

OpenCable Architecture

Michael Adams

1-57870-135-X • AVAILABLE NOW

Whether you're a television, data communications, or telecommunications professional, or simply an interested business person, this book will help you understand the technical and business issues surrounding interactive television services. It will also provide you with an inside look at the combined efforts of the cable, data, and consumer electronics industries' efforts to develop those new services.

Cisco Press Fundamentals

IP Routing Primer
Robert Wright, CCIE

1-57870-108-2 • AVAILABLE NOW

Learn how IP routing behaves in a Cisco router environment. In addition to teaching the core fundamentals, this book enhances your ability to troubleshoot IP routing problems yourself, often eliminating the need to call for additional technical support. The information is presented in an approachable, workbook-type format with dozens of detailed illustrations and real-life scenarios integrated throughout.

Cisco Router Configuration
Allan Leinwand, Bruce Pinsky, Mark Culpepper

1-57870-022-1 • AVAILABLE NOW

An example-oriented and chronological approach helps you implement and administer your internetworking devices. Starting with the configuration devices "out of the box;" this book moves to configuring Cisco IOS for the three most popular networking protocols today: TCP/IP, AppleTalk, and Novell Interwork Packet Exchange (IPX). You also learn basic administrative and management configuration, including access control with TACACS+ and RADIUS, network management with SNMP, logging of messages, and time control with NTP.

IP Routing Fundamentals
Mark A. Sportack

1-57870-071-x • AVAILABLE NOW

This comprehensive guide provides essential background information on routing in IP networks for network professionals who are deploying and maintaining LANs and WANs daily. Explore the mechanics of routers, routing protocols, network interfaces, and operating systems.

Cisco Press Fundamentals

Internetworking Routing Architectures
Bassam Halabi

1-56205-652-2 • AVAILABLE NOW

Explore the ins and outs of interdomain routing network designs. Learn to integrate your network into the global Internet, become an expert in data routing manipulation, build large-scale autonomous systems, and configure the required policies using the Cisco IOS language.

For the latest on Cisco Press resources and Certification and

Training guides, or for information on publishing opportunities, visit

www.ciscopress.com

Cisco Press

Staying Connected to Networkers

We want to hear from **you**! Help Cisco Press **stay connected** to the issues and challenges you face on a daily basis by registering your book and filling out our brief survey.

Complete and mail this form, or better yet, jump to **www.ciscopress.com** and do it online. Each complete entry will be eligible for our monthly drawing to **win a FREE book** from the Cisco Press Library.

Thank you for choosing Cisco Press to help you work the network.

Name _____

Address _____

City _____ State/Province _____

Country _____ Zip/Post code _____

E-mail address _____

May we contact you via e-mail for product updates and customer benefits?
❏ Yes   ❏ No

Where did you buy this product?
❏ Bookstore   ❏ Computer store   ❏ Electronics store
❏ Online retailer   ❏ Office supply store   ❏ Discount store
❏ Mail order   ❏ Class/Seminar
❏ Other _____

When did you buy this product? _____ Month _____ Year

What price did you pay for this product?
❏ Full retail price   ❏ Discounted price   ❏ Gift

How did you learn about this product?
❏ Friend   ❏ Store personnel   ❏ In-store ad
❏ Catalog   ❏ Postcard in the mail   ❏ Saw it on the shelf
❏ Magazine ad   ❏ Article or review   ❏ Used other products
❏ School   ❏ Professional Organization
❏ Other _____

What will this product be used for?
❏ Business use   ❏ Personal use   ❏ School/Education
❏ Other _____

How many years have you been employed in a computer-related industry?
❏ 2 years or less   ❏ 3-5 years   ❏ 5+ years

CISCO SYSTEMS

CISCO PRESS

www.ciscopress.com

CISCO SYSTEMS
CISCO PRESS®

www.ciscopress.com

Which best describes your job function?

❏ Corporate Management   ❏ Systems Engineering   ❏ IS Management
❏ Network Design   ❏ Network Support   ❏ Webmaster
❏ Marketing/Sales   ❏ Consultant   ❏ Student
❏ Professor/Teacher

❏ Other _____

What is your formal education background?

❏ High school   ❏ Vocational/Technical degree   ❏ Some college
❏ College degree   ❏ Masters degree   ❏ Professional or Doctoral degree

Have you purchased a Cisco Press product before?

❏ Yes   ❏ No

On what topics would you like to see more coverage?

_____

_____

Do you have any additional comments or suggestions?

_____

_____

Voice over IP Fundamentals (1-57870-168-6)

Cisco Press

201 West 103rd Street
Indianapolis, IN 46290

www.ciscopress.com

Place
Stamp
Here

Cisco Press
Customer Registration
P.O. Box 189014
Battle Creek, MI 49018-9947